Looking Up

An account of the COBUILD Project

COLLINS
PUBLISHERS

THE UNIVERSITY
OF BIRMINGHAM

COBUILD
is the Collins Birmingham University
International Language Database

Looking Up

An account of the COBUILD Project in lexical
computing and the development of the Collins
COBUILD English Language Dictionary

Edited by J M Sinclair

Collins ELT
London and Glasgow

Collins ELT
8 Grafton Street
LONDON W1X 3LA

COBUILD is a trademark of William Collins Sons & Co Ltd
© William Collins Sons & Co Ltd 1987
First Published 1987

10 9 8 7 6 5 4 3 2 1

ISBN 0 00 370256 1

Typeset by Katerprint Typesetting Services, Oxford
Printed in Great Britain by Scotprint Ltd, Musselburgh

Contents

Introduction

This book is for the most part a record of the project in lexical computing which has led to the publication of a new kind of English Dictionary – the *Collins Cobuild English Language Dictionary*. It was undertaken by a research team in the English Department of the University of Birmingham and is an example of co-operation between academic and industrial expertise. It has been in financial terms the University's largest single research project, and it has required co-ordination of resources within the University going well beyond normal practice.

Work started in 1980 on a feasibility study, swiftly followed by the appointment of a small core team. The starting point was in research dating back to 1961 and the earliest academic computing. The plan was to gather a large and representative selection of contemporary English – spoken and written – and put it into machine-readable form. The original corpus thus formed was over seven million words in length (called the Main Corpus).

The computer sorts the words in various ways, and delivers information on each word to a team of editors and compilers. They study the words and build up an elaborate profile of their meanings and uses in a database, back inside the computer. The database is then the primary source of a family of books which will span many years of editorial work.

What is new about the project, apart from the technology, is the ability to get for the first time a view of a language which is both broad and comprehensive. Many thousands of the observations are about the commonest patterns in the language. For example, we think of verbs like *see, give, keep*, as having each a basic meaning; we would probably expect those meanings to be the commonest. However, the database tells us that *see* is commonest in uses like *I see, you see, give* in uses like *give a talk* and *keep* in uses like *keep warm*.

The power of meanings made by phrases and near-phrases like the above is gradually being understood, and the database holds copious examples for future work. The following chapters give plentiful examples of the kind of information we have recorded.

Cobuild has created the first wholly new dictionary for many years, and the first which is based on a thorough study of the way words are used. So it was felt appropriate to overhaul the usual way in which dictionaries are written and presented. Many users have difficulty understanding the conventions of dictionaries – brackets, abbreviations, special symbols and different type faces. The new dictionary is aimed at the whole world of English users, who need a simple and practical presentation.

The text corpus of general English now stands at around 20 million words in daily use, backed up by a range of more specialised texts coming to a total of about another 20 million. The project is already the stimulus for some exciting and up-to-date research, and is attracting attention from all corners of the world.

This volume is written by several members of the Cobuild project team, each one taking an area of their expertise and writing about the way in which the project was developed in that area. The papers, though composed individually, were all written specially for this occasion. The result is a fairly comprehensive account of the design, progress and achievement of the project.

We begin with an account of the work done in Birmingham on the collection of texts in machine-readable form. This constitutes the basic evidence on which everything else depends, and the paper here brings the story right up to date. It is written by Antoinette Renouf, who was the Project Co-ordinator from 1980–83. Under her guidance was built up the very large and distinctive set of corpora that we now use, and although she moved from the Dictionary to other work, mentioned below, she has retained overall responsibility for corpus development.

Having created a corpus for a computer, it is necessary to process it in various ways. As Chapter 2 shows, the principles of basic text processing – word lists, concordances, etc. – were well known and various packages could handle short texts, but the millions of words that our project had accumulated were quite unmanageable. The account of how such problems were resolved is by Jeremy Clear, the Senior Computer Officer, who tackled them and went on to solve ever more difficult problems throughout the life of the project. He describes the construction of the database in some detail, and the ways in which the computer helped in editing.

The database is the intellectual centre of the project. It is created by the conjunction of human and machine effort, and from it can be retrieved an account of the language from many different points of view, of which the published dictionary is but the first. In Chapter 3 there is a description of how the database was compiled. It is written by Ramesh Krishnamurthy, a Senior Compiler who has taken a particular interest in the integrity of the database.

The business of compiling the database was the largest single component of the work, and it constantly raised problems of the organisation of meaning. Rosamund Moon, an Editor with experience on previous dictionaries, has made this a personal research interest and in Chapter 4 she raises some of the issues which all lexicographers have to face, but which are sharpened by the need in the Cobuild project to account for the whole of the language of a large collection of texts.

In Chapter 5 I discuss the attitude which the project developed towards grammars in a dictionary. The twofold problem of what to say and how to say it was a major preoccupation for some members of the team, and both the policy line chosen and the way in which we present the grammar are novel.

The next chapter deals with the way in which the main text of the Dictionary is composed – a fairly sharp break with traditional lexicography. In this we were led by Patrick Hanks, the Project Manager since 1983, a very experienced dictionary maker. He gives in Chapter 6 an account of the Cobuild style set against the traditions of the past. The target was to make the Dictionary read like English, and we look forward to the opinion of users on that point.

Another point of possible controversy is discussed in Chapter 7. Here we are not so much innovating as returning to the hallowed tradition of citing actual recorded examples. But since our method of collecting examples is quite new, there are a number of important issues to attend to. Gwyneth Fox, who is an Editor with a strong background in language teaching, explains how Cobuild examples are selected to do a unique job.

In Chapter 8 I try to illustrate the way in which our observations relate to the evidence by going through a very small area of the description of a word, both counting up and pointing to new descriptions of the future.

Chapter 9 is written by a colleague in the University English Department, David Brazil. Dr Brazil's work on intonation is well known, and he was asked to advise us on how the words might be transcribed in order to show their likely actual pronunciation. He responded with an elegant use of the International Phonetic Alphabet incorporating variability in some vowels, dropping of consonants and a treatment of stress which locates it firmly within discourse.

That chapter ends the account of the Dictionary but it does not end the account of Cobuild activities. In Chapter 10 Antoinette Renouf takes up the story from where she moved from the dictionary project in 1983, to lead a team in a new enterprise which was designed to run in parallel with the evolving dictionary. This new project was to design an English Course for adult false beginners, featuring the insights that were becoming available in the compilation.

The work continues, and the team has largely kept together. A new company, jointly owned by Collins and Birmingham University, has taken over the pursuit of further objectives based on the unique database and expertise which has accumulated. We hope that any others who wish to harness computers to the study of language will find things to think about in this account.

John Sinclair
Editor-in-Chief, Cobuild

Acknowledgement

I am most grateful for the help given in the later stages of editing by Deborah Kirby.

CHAPTER 1: **Corpus Development**

Antoinette Renouf

Introduction

The purpose of this paper is to outline the development of corpora at the University of Birmingham, with special reference to the Cobuild Project. The term 'corpus' will be used to refer to a collection of texts, of the written or spoken word, which is stored and processed on computer for the purposes of linguistic research.

Work on corpora has been going on at Birmingham University for over 20 years, since 135,000 running words of informal conversation were transcribed and computerised to form the data resource for the OSTI project in lexical collocation (Sinclair, Jones and Daley 1969).

In the 1970s, the creation and study of text corpora became a regular feature of work at Birmingham. Corpora include 35,000 words of classroom discourse (Sinclair and Coulthard 1975); one million words of applied science text (Roe 1977; Phillips 1983; and Yang 1986); three quarters of a million words of economic text (Tadros 1981); and an assortment of texts known as the NATLAN collection.

At each point, it became clear just how much could be learnt, and how much there was to learn, from examining instances of natural language. It was also clear that, for many purposes, the larger the amount of data available, the more reliable would be the statements which could be made about language.

Against this background of ideas and experience, the Cobuild project was conceived and set up as a joint venture between the University of Birmingham and Collins publishers in 1980. The reason for this was the realisation that the two parties shared an interest in developing a new, thorough-going, description of the English language, and one which was not based on the introspections of its authors, but which recorded their observations of linguistic behaviour as revealed in naturally-occurring text. The analysis should have a lexical focus. The parties were further in agreement that the findings should be disseminated in a series of publications, reference and pedagogical works, the first major one of which was to be a dictionary of current English for advanced learners of the language.

Central to the enterprise was the availability of sufficient and relevant textual evidence. To this end, a corpus was to be assembled on computer and processed in such a way that the data could conveniently be referred to by the lexicographic team that were to be appointed. The corpus work which had been carried out at Birmingham University, and elsewhere, indicated that a corpus of around one million words, whilst being adequate for some types of analysis, notably syntactic, could not support the lexical and semantic study which we had in mind. Accordingly, it was decided in the first instance to build a corpus of six million words, a size which we estimated would probably meet our needs, and which fitted into the project time-scale.

There was also a plan to build a technical corpus of 26 million words, covering 26 technical disciplines, which would serve as a basis for the production of booklets which would supplement the information given in the dictionary in dealing with the specialised lexis in the chosen fields. For the time being, this project was held at the design stage, so that all efforts could be concentrated on the primary task.

In late 1980, the process of corpus creation began. Details of the selection, acquisition and digitising of data which took place in the early stages of the project have been communicated in a previous paper (Renouf 1984), but the major events will again be included here, in order to provide a comprehensive account.

The 'Main' Corpus

Corpus Design

When constructing a text corpus, one seeks to make a selection of data which is in some sense representative, providing an authoritative body of linguistic evidence which can support generalisations and against which hypotheses can be tested.

The first step towards achieving this aim is to define the whole of which the corpus is to be a sample. The simplest case will be where the whole is known and finite, as with Shakespeare's works or the Bible. In many cases, it is not so easily identifiable; yet some means of identification must be devised.

This problem faced us at Cobuild, as it has faced other colleagues in the field of corpus linguistics. One possible strategy, and that which was adopted by Yang (1985) at Shanghai, is to take a library as a microcosm of the (written) language. Or one can rely on the comprehensiveness of established bibliographical sources, as did the creators of the LOB Corpus (Hofland and Johansson 1982).

For our purposes at Cobuild, however, no source of documentary evidence existed. Our aim was to identify those aspects of the English language which were relevant to the needs of the international user. We therefore defined these for ourselves as follows:

- written and spoken modes
- broadly general, rather than technical, language
- current usage, from 1960, and preferably very recent
- 'naturally occurring' text, not drama
- prose, including fiction and excluding poetry
- adult language, 16 years or over
- 'standard' English, no regional dialects
- predominantly British English, with some American and other varieties.

We also identified circumstances of the production of language which it seemed wise to monitor; in particular, some characteristics of authorship, such as age and sex. And we made inventories of what we judged to be major text types and central topics in the language, to ensure that the range was covered. Within our accepted parameters, we wished to gather as broad a spread of language use as possible.

There were decisions to make in relation to the balance between certain corpus components. For different reasons, the following proportions were agreed upon:

book authorship	–	75% male: 25% female
English language variety	–	70% British: 20% American: 5% Other
language mode	–	75% writing: 25% speech

Since the operations of text selection, clearance and acquisition would be running in parallel, it was felt that balance in all other respects could be monitored and maintained as the Corpus accumulated. Statistics relating to the composition of the Main Corpus upon completion can be found in Appendices 1, 2 and 3.

The effect of planning a corpus on the above lines was the creation of a resource that is relevant to the needs of learners, teachers and other users, while also being of value to researchers in contemporary English language.

Identification and Acquisition of Texts

Written Texts

In November 1980, we tackled the next question, which was how to identify a range of writing which fitted our selectional criteria. For books and journals, one way of achieving this would have been to make a random selection from one or other bibliographical source, as is commonly done. However, this did not seem appropriate in our case. We did not want to make a random choice, but to select works which met our particular requirements. Moreover, traditional methods of classification can often obscure the lexical profile of a text, and it was this which interested us.

In addition to the linguistic criteria listed above, we wished to restrict the choice to works which enjoyed a wide readership, since it could be argued that they exerted an influence, to varying degrees, on the linguistic choices readers make. So our selection was made with reference to three main sources of information.

The first line of enquiry was to investigate what we, our colleagues and visiting scholars regarded as the texts most typically being read in Britain and abroad. School reading lists were, in addition, investigated. The British list comprised both current best sellers and established works, of fiction and non-fiction; a wide range of titles was thereby elicited. The works thought to be read abroad proved to be a more homogeneous group, and consisted largely of fictional works, often in translation.

To balance this view, a second approach was made. British Council Libraries around the world were asked to identify titles which were proving continuingly popular with indigenous library users. Interestingly, it was reference material which featured most prominently in their analysis, but a fairly consistent range of lending works were also in demand.

We further consulted the best seller lists published weekly in major newspapers, and the various book reviews that appear periodically. The latter included annual nominations of books which were considered especially worthy and likely to endure.

Catalogues from the leading publishing houses were also very valuable as a final aide-memoire. With these and all the information which we had gathered, we were able in December 1981 to draw up and agree on a preliminary list of books, newspapers and journals for the Corpus.

Permissions

It was -then necessary to apply to the relevant rights holders to secure permission to use the texts. This took the form of a letter which sought to explain our short- and long-term aspirations. We had to make clear to the lay person that, on the one hand, we wanted to process the whole of a work onto computer, whilst, on the other, not intending to make it available to anyone in its original format. We then wanted to transform it into a series of one-line extracts, or 'concordance lines', which would be printed out on fiches or paper for our researchers to consult, but this would not amount to 'reproduction' in the copyright sense, which came into play only in the case of a few one- or two-line quotations for publications which were expected to emerge from the analysis. We also had to explain that, though the text was of interest to us for its particular linguistic character, we intended to dissect it and render it all but unrecognisable.

It was not always clear whether the copyright holders were the authors or the publishers but, in the first instance, we decided to address the latter. The response was positive, if not always prompt, and we were soon able to begin obtaining actual copies of the texts. Many were purchased; those that were out of print had to be borrowed from libraries.

Spoken Texts

In the case of spoken material, a different strategy for selection and acquisition was necessary. We were aware that we had insufficient time to make our own recordings, and that we would have to rely on those we already possessed and on the material which other sources were kind enough to provide. In effect, then, the identification and acquisition of texts would be the same operation, and permission for use would generally also be acquired at this stage.

Requests were made to various bodies in Britain who we felt might have suitable data, on tape or in transcription. We approached likely departments of all the universities, and received a reasonable crop of replies. There were some particularly generous offers of help from individuals. As we expected, a lot of spoken material was available which had been recorded for different research purposes, and we were offered quite a range. However, relatively little of it was the current, mainstream, adult language which we were looking for.

Nevertheless, the search yielded some useful data. A major find was the collection of radio interviews made at the University of Sussex, in which staff members explained the relevance of their own specialisms to the community at large. These recordings were rich in lexis which was marginal to our repertoire and intuitions as lay people, without being so technical that it fell outside the scope of our research.

We also approached the BBC, who were very co-operative in agreeing to supply us with batches of transcribed data on a regular basis. The material consisted of radio broadcasts of reports, interviews and discussion. The particular programmes were: 'Any Questions', 'Kaleidoscope', and 'Money Box'. So again we had material which was rich in specific areas of lexis, namely current affairs, the arts and domestic finance, but suitably slanted towards a non-specialist audience. This material was fairly structured, in that each programme had an established format, but it was unscripted and up-to-date. It was very beguiling to be offered unlimited amounts of such material, but we had to ration ourselves in the interests of corpus balance.

The British Council was similarly responsive to our enquiry, and produced a useful series of transcripts of unscripted and informal conversation.

Meanwhile, we collected within the department transcripts of lectures and classes which had been made as an integral part of the inter-disciplinary teaching programme of our non-native-speaking students. We searched through past research theses of the University for relevant data. We also transcribed more of the conversation tapes referred to in the first section, and this material formed a substantial part of the final Spoken Corpus.

Processing the Text onto Computer

Material was processed into digital form in two ways: by being keyboarded; or by means of an optical character reader, which in our case was a KDEM, or 'Kurzweil Data Entry Machine'.

Keyboarding

We keyboarded almost all the spoken data, except for the better printed BBC transcripts. We also keyed most of the newspapers and some journals. Newspaper material was initially sent to a commercial agency for reasons of speed, but the expense involved led us to undertake later work in-house. The cost factor, combined with the time penalty involved in keyboarding material, made the KDEM our preferred alternative, wherever the material was suitable.

KDEMing

The KDEM is superior to the conventional optical character reader in being able to recognise any set of letters, provided that they are printed separately.

This machine can be conceptualised as a photocopier that, instead of producing paper copy, converts print into computer code. The book, or other text, is placed face-down on a glass plate, and a suspended scanning device moves to and fro beneath it, shining a light onto the page and recording the images. Each letter is viewed through a matrix as a pattern of black and absence of black, and this pattern is compared with an alphabet that the machine stores, which has been modified during its training phase on the text.

The resultant interpretation of the text is viewed on an accompanying screen by an operator, whose job it is to confirm or correct the textual representation offered. Once this is done, the text is converted by the processor to digital form and stored on magnetic tape.

KDEM machines have, by all accounts, improved over the years. Our model was an early one, which nevertheless worked on average at least twice as fast as any keyboarder could, and sometimes much faster, depending on the quality of the text. We had hoped to be able to KDEM all of our material, but we discovered very soon that there were certain constraints. The KDEM functioned best with paper and print of high quality. Blurred print and differing intensity in the ink from one page to another sometimes slowed the process down to the point where keying would be quicker. In the case of books, it was typically paperbacks which caused problems of this kind, but not solely, since some of the hardback books nowadays can be of rather poor print quality.

Newspapers and journals posed additional problems. Both have columnar layout, which current KDEM models cater for, but which at that time meant that the pages had to be folded, cut or masked to delimit the scanning area for the machine. The text also does not run sequentially, but to retain the integrity of articles was prohibitive in terms of operator time. Ephemeral publications often have the added disadvantage of being printed on transparent paper, and the KDEM will diligently incorporate, albeit nonsensically, images which are visible through the page.

During our learning phase, the KDEMing process was very slow. Even taking the above physical factors into account, it was inexplicably so. We made some investigations, and discovered that the reason was a combination of wrong practice, such as overtraining of the KDEM, and the misleadingly optimistic throughput figures with which we had been supplied. We made the appropriate adjustments.

In March 1981, we again took stock of progress. Throughput figures remained low. Several newspapers and magazines were immediately consigned for keyboarding, and we hired a second terminal, so that two operators could work simultaneously. By dint of staffing and running the machine round the clock, we quickly made up lost ground, and in fact surpassed our expectations. By December 1981, we had KDEMed and keyboarded sufficient material to allow us some choice in putting together six million words for concordancing.

The digitised material was then processed in various ways, which are described in detail in Chapter 2, with the purpose of producing concordances and word-frequency lists for our lexicographic work. The concordanced material was fully available on micro-fiches in early 1982.

Enlarging the Main Corpus

As lexicographers began to work on the concordances, they were able to form a view of the usefulness of the data. In this context, usefulness was defined in terms of the extent to which the data both confirmed and extended their intuitions about the characteristics of a word. It was felt that the Corpus would be enhanced by the addition of certain categories of material, namely journalistic and spoken, which would broaden and balance the view of language already available.

By late spring of 1982, further material of these kinds had become available, having been in the process of digitisation earlier. It was therefore decided to concordance a further batch of written material, consisting largely of newspapers and journals, and to augment and re-concordance the existing batch of spoken material. The result was that we had, by August 1982, a corpus of approximately 7.3 million words, held on fiches in the form of six batches of concordances.

Merging the Main Corpus Concordance Batches

With the arrival of the new University mainframe computer in summer 1983, it was possible to merge the batches. However, it was still a mammoth task, and certain measures, including the omission of data on the fifty commonest words, had to be taken to make it more manageable. Details of our strategy are provided in Chapter 2. Thereafter the operation ran relatively smoothly, and the new Merged Corpus was fiched and ready for use by November 1983.

As time went on, we felt that it was necessary to provide access to concordances on paper as well as fiches. The physical results of this undertaking were considerable, and a small room was accordingly designated 'Hard-Copy Library', and devoted to the storage of the printout.

The System of Concordance Coding

A sample extract of the concordances which were produced can be found in Appendix 4. At the left-hand side of each concordance line can be seen a series of letters and numbers. This is intended to convey information about its origin. Running from left to right, the coding is interpretable as follows:

1. Text Source:	G/T	= General/Technical Corpus
	W/S	= Written/Spoken material
	000n	= Text reference number
2. Author's Cultural Identity:	BR	= British
	AM	= American, from USA/Canada
	AU	= Australian
	AA	= Anglo-American
	AG	= Anglo-German
	OT	= Other (e.g. S. African)
3. Country of Publication:	BR	= British
	AM	= American, from USA
4. Page Reference:	nnn	

Accordingly to this system, then, the book *The Fire Next Time*, by James Baldwin, is coded: GW 0008 AM BR (027, etc.).

Our purpose in identifying the country in which a text was published, as in 3 above, was to alert users of the Corpus to cases where an American writer's work was published by a British publishing house, and might have been rendered hybrid in the process of being edited for the British market. In the case of spoken material, since none had been published, and all was British, this distinction was not relevant.

The coding system above was the one used during the first concordancing operation, in 1981. On subsequent occasions, modifications took place, as can be seen in the concordances for *veritable*, in Appendix 1 to Chapter 3. In the 1984 concordances, the page reference was omitted, in order to allow more context per line. In 1985, in response to local request, the page reference was reinstated, and the information about author and publishing house removed. Ideally, one would retain all such information, but this must be weighed against the importance of maximising the amount of context provided in each line.

Corpus Correction

The material which was destined for the Main Corpus was heterogeneous when it came to us. The books and newspapers varied in print quality; the spoken data had been transcribed according to a range of conventions.

The heterogeneity grew during the process of digitisation, but we made a decision not to tackle it at the time, since we did not have the resources and because we felt that the Corpus in its uncorrected state was quite adequate for our purposes. In the concordancing process, the erroneous elements would be sifted out and grouped separately, and could simply be ignored.

At the start of the academic year in 1984, the situation changed. Our staffing situation was improved by the addition of two visiting students, from the Maastricht School of Translation, and a visiting lecturer in computing, from Malaysia, who all came to help us for an extended period. An appropriate task for this team seemed to be to commence the task of correcting the Main Corpus. With them, we devised a system of correction that combined automatic and manual procedures, and this was subsequently programmed by the computing specialist and implemented by the students. In 1985–86, we were similarly fortunate in having student help, so that the work could be continued. In 1986–87, work continued, but on other corpora.

Error Types

There were four kinds of error to deal with. The first were fairly standard typing errors, introduced at the keyboarding stage, in the copying of text. Then, in the transcription of spoken data, homophonic confusions, such as between 'their' and 'they're', and various mis-spellings occurred. A third and major category of error were those occurring in the KDEMing process.

KDEM errors are caused where an image on the page is misinterpreted because it is imperfectly printed or paler than the KDEM has been trained to accept. Typical misreadings include:

'I' for 'l'	as in 'usuaIly'
'i' for 'l'	as in 'smali'
'ni' for 'm'	as in 'nian'
'c' for 'e'	as in 'thc'

Smaller elements, such as punctuation marks, might disappear altogether.

As can be seen, these are different from human typing errors, but still easy for the human editor to overlook, and it is the undetected ones which make their way into the computer. They also differ from human typing errors in the regularity with which they can occur. In the Cobuild Main Corpus concordances, the commonest of them was 'thc', of which there were over 500 instances, although most occurred fewer than 30 times.

There were also human errors introduced at the KDEMing stage, such as the incomplete insertion of bracketing around chapter headings and other material to be omitted in the concordancing, and the occasional duplicate scanning of a page.

A fourth cause of error lay in the computing software, so that, for example, an end-of-line hyphen was treated as a bona fide letter in the concordancing. In this case, the result would be that instances of *man-age* were grouped under *age*; *re-fuses* under *fuses*.

Automatic Correction Procedure

Global changes were made automatically as far as possible. They included:

- insertion of spaces after punctuation marks
- reduction of double dashes and hyphens
- changing of single quotation marks to double, to distinguish them from apostrophes. Where there was possible confusion, as with S', the machine searched for specified clues in the text, such as a previous opening quotation mark.
- joining of hyphenated words at line end
- removal of hyphens
- correction of known KDEM errors

The automatic correction programme having been run on the text, it was then passed for manual correction.

Manual Correction Procedure

In order to minimise the task of manual correction, it was necessary to ensure that as few non-errors as possible were scrutinised. Accordingly, a list of bona fide words was compiled, with which the Corpus texts could be automatically compared in order to isolate a residue of items for manual checking. The 'dictionary' of correct items was modified at various stages, and finally consisted of approximately 50,000 items, combining the dictionary of 9,000 word forms internal to our software, the 22,000 priority items in the Cobuild Dictionary Headword List, and another list of 18,000 or so common word forms. From the combined list, all word forms containing apostrophes and proper nouns were then subtracted.

The list of correct items was run against each text, leaving a series of potential errors for checking. These were presented to the human editor, who examined each instance, using a line editor. By these methods, the book component of the Main Corpus, comprising approximately five million words, has been corrected, and work has also been done on two specialised corpora which will be described later.

Reserve Corpus

Creating the Reserve Corpus

In 1982, when the Main Corpus was complete, the general aim of building large corpora remained. With a wide range of research purposes in mind, the University English Department continued to amass data via the optical scanner, and this became known as the 'Reserve Corpus', which currently stands at around 13 million running words in size. We had no visible resources available to us in this undertaking, and so we relied on library loan, and monitoring in spare moments.

An analysis of its contents can be found in Appendices 1 and 2, and some accompanying comments on the process of selection are offered here.

The first texts to be processed were the remainders of books which had contributed their first 70,000 words to the Main Corpus. It was felt important to store these, because permission had been obtained to do so, and so that complete texts might be available for concordancing for use by text linguists. There are 28 texts in this category, as can be seen in the analysis referred to above. There were also a number of books for which we had obtained publishers' clearance, but which we had not yet processed onto computer, usually because we had been unable to trace a hardback or other copy of good quality.

A further selection was then made, from topic areas which had been thinly represented in the Main Corpus. This was sometimes due to the heterogeneity of the topic, which had prevented us from finding a book which was representative of the area as a whole. We now added books on animals: for example, *Friends of the Forest*, by Joy Adamson. Books on sports were also introduced, such as *Play Golf with Peter Alliss*; likewise on activities, such as *Collins Encyclopaedia of Fishing in the British Isles*.

Sometimes the topic area was one which had grown in importance since we began the original process of selection. By 1984, ecology and conservation were areas from which emanated important topical issues and corresponding language, so we concentrated on them, and selected recent texts, of 1984 and 1985 vintage, such as *Solar Prospects*, by Michael Flood; and *The Death of Trees*, by Nigel Dudley. Other topics became fashionable and were included, such as the animal rights campaign, represented by *Voiceless Victims*, by Rebecca Hall; prison reform, touched on in *A Woman in Custody*, by Audrey Peckham; specialised diets, as in *Diet for Life*, by Mary Laver and Margaret Smith, and so on.

The decision to select non-fictional material was a deliberate choice, since one of our observations in using the Main Corpus was that it was in non-fictional text that mainstream usage was concentrated. However, at a late stage, we decided to try to include in the Reserve Corpus the various fictional texts which individual research students had put onto computer for their own use. This entailed our returning to publishers for authorisation separate from that which the students already had. It yielded, for example, a small crop of thrillers which had been processed for the purpose of studying the word *get* as used in colloquial text. The group included *Fire Fox*, by Craig Thomas, and *The Berlin Memorandum*, by Adam Hall.

In addition to books, the Reserve Corpus contains eleven journals, as shown in the analysis. It also contains a number of brochures and leaflets – including holiday brochures, which again contribute to the topic category of 'Activities', which we felt was lacking before: see, for example, *NAT Holidays, Caravans and Tents in the Sun (Summer 1983)*. There is no newspaper or spoken material in the Reserve Corpus.

It will be clear that topic choice in itself brings no guarantee either of the lexis or of the type of discourse which will be found in a text. Choice of lexis will vary according to socio-linguistic factors such as the assumed knowledge of the reader, even if the topic is apparently held constant. There is no reason to believe that the language used to describe *How to Service a Bicycle* will be closely related to that used to describe *My Best Race*.

The Reserve Corpus was not built with attention to the parameters of register and discourse. What was aimed for was variety, not balance, since it was conceived to be an on-going accumulation of data. A reasonable variety of topic and discourse type can be found in it as it currently stands, due in part to its size and to the modest monitoring which has taken place.

The Role of the Reserve Corpus in the Cobuild Project

At two points in the creation of the dictionary database, we had created a static corpus in order to form a stable databank for our reference purposes. In the first case, we decided on a corpus of six million running words, a round figure, which we felt would be an adequate source of data for many of the words in which we were interested. First-hand experience with the Corpus concordances then made us realise that newspaper language and spoken data made particularly valuable contributions, and our system was sufficiently flexible to allow us to augment the Corpus appropriately, so that it reached 7.3 million running words.

As the compilation progressed, and lexicographers moved from the middle range of words towards the outer extremities of corpus frequency, it was clear that, whilst there was more than enough corpus data available for the very common words, there was rather too little for many of the less common ones. Furthermore, the evidence that we did have for rarer words was in some cases revealing unexpectedly important linguistic facts about their use. Clearly, still more corpus evidence was required.

Again, we had the resources and flexibility to provide it, this time owing to the existence of the Reserve Corpus. At Collins' request, this collection of 13 million words was concordanced, in December 1985. In the interests of speed, a total concordance was not produced, and instead, only the evidence relating to word forms which occurred with a frequency of 50 or less in the Main Corpus was taken from it. However, this accounted for about 90 per cent of the word types in the Main Corpus, so it was considerable.

The concordances from the Reserve Corpus were collated with those of the Main Corpus and printed out on fiches, with the latter data preceding the former data for each word form. An illustration of the layout and content of the combined information is provided in Appendix 1 of Chapter 3.

Analysis of Contents for the Main and Reserve Corpora

Main and Reserve Corpora—Written Component

As explained at previous points in this paper, a statistical analysis of the written components of the Main and Reserve Corpora is offered in Appendices 1 and 2. The analysis assigns texts to a number of categories. Without claiming precision, we sought to categorise texts according to their primary discourse function. It is in the nature of text, of course, that a primary function is accompanied by secondary ones, so that a narrative text will, for example, contain description; every text will also contain authorial evaluation at some level. This should be borne in mind in relation to the following generalisations:

Non-fiction

A split has been made between fictional and non-fictional works, although this distinction is not always clear-cut in linguistic terms. Some texts deal with imagined phenomena as though they were fact, as is particularly the case with a prophetic novel like *The Third World War*, by General Sir John Hackett. Here, a seemingly documentary account is given of events which have not yet occurred in the real world. Such texts have been grouped under the 'fictional' banner, in the 'Future Worlds/Fantasy' category. Other texts present facts in the manner of a fictional account, or embellish some established facts with hypothetical detail in order to present a readable case, as in *The Boston Strangler*, by Gerold Frank. Such texts are largely narrative, and have been placed in the 'non-fiction' section, under 'Narrative – Other'.

Survey

This term is used of texts which, by a process of description and comment, seek to inform the reader about an area of life. An example is *The Language of Clothes*, by Alison Lurie. The text is not putting forward a case, but surveying a particular field.

Procedure

Procedural texts give advice on how to proceed in a given area, if the reader has given aims. They do not exhort the reader to do a particular thing, but only provide relevant facts, and suggest what is intended to be an appropriate course of action, should the desire be there. An example is *Learning to Read*, by Margaret Meek, which is a handbook. A travel guide can also be procedural, as in the case of *The Companion Guide to London*, by David Piper.

There is a grey area between 'procedural' and 'hortatory' discourse, however, and some texts are assigned one way or the other on balance. For example, in *Superwoman*, Shirley Conran is implicitly addressing women, and explicitly stating that women should not waste more time than necessary on household work. But the bulk of the text is given over to a series of accounts of relevant procedures, so the book has been designated 'procedural'.

Argument–Positional/Hortatory

In a 'positional' text, the author puts forward his or her case in relation to a particular topic or issue. He or she will also provide relevant information, in terms of a descriptive and/or narrative account, which will be intended to support his or her position. An example is *Seeing Green*, by Jonathon Porritt.

'Hortatory' texts are particular in that in them the reader tends to be addressed more directly, and exhorted to do or become something which the author argues is desirable. However, they have not been treated as a separate category, since where positional texts are arguing for a change which would be within the scope of the reader, it is often difficult to differentiate them from hortatory texts. One such example is *Can You Avoid Cancer?*, by Peter Goodwin.

Argument–Balanced

In these texts, some background information about a particular issue is given, and various points of view which are held in relation to it are presented. The author may or may not hold one of them, but the presentation of arguments is balanced. An example of this type of discussion is *The Pendulum Years*, by Bernard Levin.

Narrative

This is a general term to refer to texts which present a sequence of events for one purpose or other. The communicative intention might be to entertain or edify, to gain sympathy, exorcise guilt, and so on. The sequence is traditionally chronological, but this is sometimes varied for stylistic effect. There is invariably an element of description in such texts, and sometimes an underlying position held by the author towards the subject.

Narrative–Travelogue

Travelogues are narrative accounts of journeys made and experiences had en route; in our Corpora, they are always autobiographical. An example is *Tracks*, by Robyn Davidson.

Narrative–Biography

This is a fairly traditional category of texts, in which a narrative account is given of an individual whom the author thinks is sufficiently interesting to draw to the reader's attention. The author's personal estimation of the subject is therefore likely to be evident. An example is *Tony Benn: A Political Biography*, by Robert Jenkins. As in this case, the account will not generally be exhaustive, but will focus on salient areas of the subject's life. Exceptionally, the biography will be of a group of people, as in *Portrait of a Marriage*, by Nigel Nicolson.

Narrative–Autobiography

Again, this is a traditional category, in which the author recounts aspects of his or her own life, generally chronologically, for a range of purposes which have been discussed earlier. The focus is placed in varying measure on the personal experiences of the narrator and on formative events in the outside world. An example is *Asking for Trouble*, by Donald Woods.

Narrative–Other

This category contains a miscellaneous group of texts which are narrative in style, but which do not fit into the sub-categories above. They include *The Bermuda Triangle*, by Charles Berlitz, and *Breaking the Mould? The Birth and Prospects of the SDP*, by Ian Bradley.

Humour

This is a category reserved for texts in which the main communicative purpose seems to be to amuse the reader, and which do not fit neatly into one of the other categories. The two assignments to this category are *How to be an Alien*, by George Mikes, and *It's an Odd Thing, but . . .*, by Paul Jennings. There are several humorous texts in the Corpora which have been assigned elsewhere, because they seem to have other primary features. The humorous element in such texts is indicated parenthetically in the analysis. An example of this type is *Let Sleeping Vets Lie*, by James Herriot.

Fiction–General

This category contains works which deal primarily with human relations, but with a variety of different foci and settings, e.g. *The Godfather*, by Mario

Puzo; and *The Pearl*, by John Steinbeck. Narratives with an unexpected ending, such as those in *Kiss, Kiss*, by Roald Dahl, are included.

Fiction–Historical

'Historical' texts differ from 'general' ones chiefly in their setting, and in the preoccupations of the characters. In some cases, the language is dated (although this renders it only relatively less natural than modern fictionalised dialogue). An example of an historical novel is *Far Pavilions*, by M. M. Kaye.

Fiction–Thriller

This category subsumes also the 'detective' novel. One of the various thrillers in the corpora is *Jaws*, by Peter Benchley.

Fiction–Academic

An alternative term for this category is the 'campus' novel. An example is *Changing Places*, by David Lodge.

Fiction–Future Worlds/Fantasy

This category contains a variety of texts which have in common a setting and a set of events which have no basis in historical fact, but which are sufficiently conceivable in historical, scientific, psychological or other terms to be of interest to the reader. They are based in future worlds, fantasy worlds, or a world almost like our own.

Most of the Corpus texts in this category have a social message. Examples are *Lord of the Flies*, by William Golding; and *Benefits*, by Zoe Fairbairn.

The Newspaper Component

This category is fairly uncontroversial. The British newspapers involved are *The Guardian* and *The Times*; the American newspaper is *The Herald Tribune*.

The Magazine/Journal Component

We adopted a narrow definition of 'newspaper'. So some publications would call themselves 'newspapers' which are included here.

The British weekly journals referred to are *The Sunday Times Colour Supplement, Now!, Punch* and *The Economist*. The American weekly journal is *Newsweek*. The British monthly journals are *Cosmopolitan, Homes and Gardens*, and *The Illustrated London News*; whilst the monthly American journal is *The National Geographic*.

Brochures and Leaflets

This is a small, fairly mixed group of publications, providing information of various kinds. All texts are procedural in nature, except for the University of Birmingham prospectuses, which are descriptive.

Letters

This is a small collection of personal letters, communicating informally between family and friends. It was our intention to augment the data, with a range of private and business letters.

Main Corpus—Spoken Component

Some statistics on the 167 texts in the spoken component of the Main Corpus are offered in Appendix 3. They are fairly self-explanatory, although a few comments can be made on the major categories:

Face to Face Informal Conversation

This material is largely taken from the Edinburgh data. There are not so many texts, but each is long and varied, drifting from one topic into another.

Radio Discussion

The radio discussion programmes are mainly those contributed by the BBC, namely the *Any Questions, Kaleidoscope* and *Money Box* broadcasts.

Radio Interview

These programmes were contributed by Dr Brian Smith, of Sussex University, who made them for broadcasting on Radio Sussex in 1979. They cover many topics which are subsumed under the general headings provided.

   As said earlier, the Reserve Corpus contains no spoken material.

Specialised Corpora

Subsequent to the creation of the main data resources and the meeting of lexicographers' immediate needs, attention was turned to relevant new ventures in the field. Between 1982 and 1985, with various purposes in mind, we produced a series of smaller corpora, of which the first was known as the 'TEFL Side Corpus', or 'TEFL Corpus'.

The TEFL Corpus

The Main Corpus reflected 'the world' of the native speaker. Early in 1982, it was felt that another, smaller, corpus, composed of EFL course materials, which would reflect the known world of the learner in several ways, should be created to complement it.

Design and Selection

We reasoned that the texts which would be most representative of the learner's known lexis would be those which had been and were still being used with the majority of English language learners in formal education. To identify these seemed to be a feasible objective, and we set about achieving it by approaching the British Council Language Officers with a questionnaire about textbook use in their host countries. We were interested in courses devised for the international rather than the internal market, since this would make the choice more homogeneous and easier to evaluate.

It would have been interesting to carry out a more detailed study, and to investigate the differing known worlds of the different nationalities of learner. But the anticipated complexity of the task placed it outside the scope and time-scale of our project.

The replies to our questionnaire brought few surprises, and the 20 or so texts which were clear favourites, together with one or two newer titles which we ourselves selected on the strength of their incipient popularity, suggested a corpus size of around one million words. The final choice can be found in Appendix 5.

The questionnaire completed, the publishers concerned were approached for permission to use their books. They were all most co-operative, and in some cases supplied us with copies.

Preparing and Processing the Data

The preparation which was involved in the case of these books was more complicated than for the texts in the Main and Reserve Corpora. It was a matter of devising and applying a system of codification which would be of maximal informational value to users of the new corpus. In addition to interlinear coding, which would identify the source of each concordance line, we felt it was important to introduce an intralinear coding which would distinguish between the different language types which occurred in the text. So each concordance line would not only begin with a left-hand reference to source, such as 'e002', but it would contain at points within it markers of a change in language. We decided to make the following distinctions:

Code	Language Type
0	metalanguage, including rubric and page heading
1	constructed spoken text
2	authentic speech in transcription
3	constructed written text
4	authentic written text

In order that these codings were understood by the keyboarders, it was necessary to prepare the texts for processing. This involved colour-coding the text, which took several months. The texts were concordanced on our local

PDP mini-computer and the concordance was fiched by the end of January 1983. Sample printout is provided in Appendix 6.

Uses of the TEFL Corpus

The TEFL Corpus is unique in the type and amount of information which it offers. It reveals hitherto inaccessible facts about the language which occurs in the major course books, both as a whole and individually. It shows, for instance, at which point in a book, and at which level in a course, new items are introduced.

Statistics on the number of times a particular phenomenon occurs can also be provided, thereby giving an indication of what in pedagogical terms is known as the degree of 're-inforcement' of the item. Whereas previous studies of the language used in course books have focused exclusively on such statistical information, however, the TEFL Corpus has been concordanced, thereby providing for analysis a record of the contextual constraints placed on each item. Finally, the coding of the text for language type allows an inspection, statistical and contextualised, of the different linguistic planes in the course book.

The TEFL Corpus served a number of important purposes in the course of dictionary database production. In the formative stages of the compilation process, concordances from this Corpus gave guidance on the sort of linguistic choices which would be familiar to many users of the dictionary, and therefore suitable for use in definition. In lexical terms, for example, this could inform the choice between the phrases 'so as to' and 'in order to', or between 'animal' and 'creature'.

It was also helpful to the lexicographers to be reminded of the categories of meaning and use which were likely to be less familiar to the learner. This was indicated by the relative infrequency with which a feature occurred in the Corpus, or by the fact of its restriction to Volume 3 of a particular course. Special care could then be taken in dealing with that part of a dictionary entry.

The concordances from the TEFL Corpus also served generally to sensitise lexicographers to those features of natural language which they had perhaps hitherto not been conscious of, by presenting them with instances of non-natural contextualisation.

In early 1984, as part of the preparation for the later Collins Cobuild English Course, the TEFL Corpus was analysed in detail in order to identify the linguistic structures and speech functions which were common to most of its books at the lower levels. This analysis could be said to mirror the 'received' or 'concensus' syllabus for the teaching of English as a foreign language which operates currently in those areas. As an explicit statement of accepted practice, it served as a point of departure for the design of the new Cobuild Course.

Outside the Cobuild project, the TEFL Corpus has become a popular research resource, both in the department and beyond. Applied linguists are becoming increasingly concerned to evaluate the linguistic content of teaching materials, particularly the hitherto neglected aspects of lexis and meta-language, and the TEFL Corpus offers an objective means of doing so.

The Sub-Corpus

The single lines of context offered in a KWIC concordance were sufficient to support an analysis of the majority of items in the Cobuild Headword List, but there were certain classes of, generally commoner, words which were better observed in larger stretches of context. These included conjunctions, pronouns, determiners, and 'sub-technical' nouns, such as *case* or *factor*, all of which had an influence in the larger discourse. The lexicographers felt a need to examine such data to discover the extent and nature of the influence which these words had, and to this end it was agreed to create a 'sub-corpus', of texts drawn from the Main Corpus, which could yield the required information.

On the basis of their daily experience of the texts in the Main Corpus, the lexicographers chose a number for the Sub-Corpus. Their selection was felt to retain some of the variety of the larger Corpus, whilst contributing more everyday, mainstream language use than some other texts would. Written and spoken language were both to be included, in an approximate ratio of 2:1. There were nevertheless to be a larger number of spoken transcriptions in the Sub-Corpus than written ones, since the former are typically much shorter. The contents of the Sub-Corpus are listed in Appendix 7.

Books were, where available, to be included in their entirety. This provision was intended to ensure that no large-scale discourse features could possibly be missed. We had in fact processed only the first 70,000 words of each book for the Main Corpus, but for two of the titles now chosen, whole texts were able to be supplied. The journals were in any case complete, as were the majority of spoken events.

For ease of access to the new Sub-Corpus, it was decided to aim at around one million words of text. This would mean that the data could be held in one place and accessed immediately, rather than being stored on a number of tapes which had to be loaded separately by operators at the Computer Centre. In the event, the team's final selection amounted to around 870,000 words, consisting of about 300,000 words of speech and 570,000 words of writing.

The Sub-Corpus was moved to the local mini-computer, which was capable of allowing several users to have interactive access to data simultaneously. The lexicographers, who were all within easy reach of a computer terminal, were able to submit a request for data relating to a particular word, which was retrieved from the storage disk and displayed on screen.

Choices had to be made about the number of concordance lines which were required, from a single instance to the total number available for the word in question. It was also necessary to specify the amount of context which was required, and whether concordances should be sorted alphabetically to the right or the left of the node-word. An example of the data offered by this facility can be found in Appendix 8.

Lexicographers soon came to the conclusion that a paper printout of the screen display would be desirable, for the purposes of annotation, and this option was soon built in.

The Corpus of Spoken Interaction

For the Main Corpus, we managed to collect about 1.3 million running words of speech. This consisted of fairly structured discussion on the one hand, and of informal conversation on the other. We had not recorded any data ourselves within the Cobuild project, since there was insufficient time, but some of us had had previous experience of the process.

Within the English Department, as in most English departments which carry out text-based study, there was a general desire for access to natural spoken data. This was coupled with the knowledge that we had the expertise to process it once it had been acquired, and that colleagues world-wide would appreciate our taking the initiative. However, there were problems which were preventing us from going ahead. Firstly, there was the question of cost. Secondly, there was the fact that natural speech normally occurs in adverse recording conditions and is correspondingly tortuous to transcribe. Next was the fact that natural speech is often poor in lexis and linguistic variety. Finally, the recording of speech without the knowledge of the speaker was prohibited by the University authorities.

Within the Cobuild project, we began in early 1983 to discuss the development of a new English Course, and, given the innovatory features which we had in mind, there was a realisation that some spoken data would be required for the purposes of contextualisation.

The two interests again came together, and we came up with the idea of eliciting rather than waiting for spoken data, by setting up a series of task-based recordings. From the point of view of the proposed Course, it was hoped that the assignment of short interactive tasks would concentrate and highlight the interactive structuring of the discourse. Speakers would be given a set of instructions that were minimally worded, in the hope that they would produce language which was economical but reasonably natural. The openings and closings of each interaction would probably suffer, since these were externally controlled, but the substance of the dialogue would approximate to the natural behaviour of the participants.

The processes of elicitation which subsequently took place at Birmingham are outlined in some detail in another paper (Renouf 1986).

The first set of recordings were to be experimental. They were made in a University recording studio in March 1984, and were planned and organised jointly by the authors of the Course (Willis and Willis, forthcoming), editorial staff from Collins, and myself. Students were given a variety of tasks, outlined on card, to carry out. Some tasks required information exchange, some required co-operative talk and action, others the sharing of personal experience, and so on.

The material proved interesting, and usable for research purposes. It amounted to 70,000 words. Meanwhile, plans were made for a second batch of recordings, and these took place in July 1984. This time, adult non-students were used, and the tasks were somewhat more circumscribed. Again the data proved useful, both for research purposes and for inclusion in the English Course. This time, it amounted in total to around 40,000 words.

Both sets of data were transcribed at, or immediately after, the time of utterance, which was an ideal arrangement. The first batch has since been concordanced.

On the basis of our experiences, it was possible for a further set of recordings to be made in a commercial, sound-proofed, recording studio in London, with the aim of capturing the same economy and simplicity of language, but with optimal sound quality. On this third occasion, in early 1985, another 50,000 or so words were recorded. As the studio proved satisfactory, additional recordings have since been made there for the Course, both of the semi-authentic and the scripted variety.

In July 1985, a separate recording experiment was carried out at Birmingham, by a research student (Warren 1985) who was interested in discovering the effects of minimising the unnatural elements in studio recording. A further 10,000 words were recorded.

The Future

The main thrust of corpus development at Birmingham University is towards larger text corpora. We already have considerable experience of text processing and in the creation of finite corpora, and our sights are now set on the development of a 'monitor' corpus. This will be a dynamic rather than a static phenomenon, consisting of very large amounts of electronically-held text which will pass through the computer. A certain proportion of the data will be stored at any one time, but the bulk will necessarily be discarded after processing. The object will be to 'monitor' such data, from various points of view, in order to record facts about the changing nature of the language.

In the short term, we are continuing to create other, more specialised corpora, such as the following:

The Shape Corpus

We in the English Department are very fortunate in being able to build up a million-word corpus of writing and speech from the Language Centre of NATO. This will comprise 750,000 words of written correspondence, in the form of reports, newsletters, handbooks, and so on, and 250,000 words of telephone conversation, radio bulletins and interviews. It is language which is largely informal in register, exhibiting the corresponding features in the lay treatment of technical topics.

The Sizewell Corpus

After several years of friendly negotiation with the Central Electricity Generating Board, we have been fortunate in managing to acquire a complete copy of the proceedings of the recent Public Enquiry.

The Sizewell Corpus amounts to some 13 million words of spoken text, covering a range of text types, topics and lexis. It is largely polemical in nature. The overall topic is clear, but there are a number of sub-topics relating to it, including the legal and scientific matters which are discussed by experts, and the issues of conservation, pollution, and so on, that affect and are discussed by the lay public.

Such a large corpus is sufficient as a testing ground for various processing techniques, such as the automatic categorisation of provenance, discourse type and topic through the characteristic patterning of lexis in text, and so on. As such, it is also a stepping-stone on the road to the 'monitor' corpus.

For linguistic research purposes, it also offers us a wealth of the very spoken material which is so hard to come by.

References

Hofland, K. and **S. Johansson** 1982. *Word Frequencies in British and American English*. The Norwegian Computing Centre for the Humanities, Bergen.

Phillips, M. (1983). *Lexical Macrostructure in Science Text*. PhD Thesis, Dept. of English, University of Birmingham.

Renouf, A. J. (1984). 'Corpus Development at Birmingham University' in *Corpus Linguistics: Recent Developments in the Use of Computer Corpora in English Language Research*, J. Aarts and W. Meijs (eds.). Rodopi, Amsterdam.

Renouf, A. J. (1986). 'The Elicitation of Spoken English' in *English in Speech and Writing: A Symposium*, G. Tottie and I. Backlund (eds.). Studia Anglistica Upsaliensia 60, University of Uppsala.

Renouf, A. J. (1987). 'Lexical Resolution' in *Corpus Linguistics and Beyond; Proceedings of the 7th International Conference on English Language Research on Computerized Corpora*, W. Meijs (ed.). Rodopi, Amsterdam.

Roe, P. (1977). *The Notion of Difficulty in Science Text*, unpublished PhD Thesis, Dept. of English, University of Birmingham.

Sinclair, J. M., S. Jones and **R. Daley** (1969). *English Lexical Studies*, Univesity of Birmingham for the Office for Scientific and Technical Information.

Sinclair, J. M. and **R. M. Coulthard** (1975). *Towards an Analysis of Discourse: The English Used by Teachers and Pupils*, Oxford University Press.

Tadros, A. A. (1981). *Linguistic Prediction in Economics Text*, unpublished PhD Thesis, Dept. of English, University of Birmingham.

Tadros, A. A. (1985). 'Prediction in Text', *Discourse Analysis Monograph no. 10*, English Language Research, University of Birmingham.

Warren, M. J. (1985). *Discourse Analysis and English Language Teaching*. MA Thesis, Dept. of English, University of Birmingham.

Willis, J. and D. (forthcoming). *The Collins Cobuild English Course*, Collins, London.

Yang, H. J. (1985). 'The Use of Computers in English Teaching and Research in China' in *English in the World*, R. Quirk and H. G. Widdowson (eds.). Cambridge University Press.

Yang, H. J. (1986). 'A New Technique for Identifying Scientific/Technical Terms and Describing Science Texts' in *Literary and Linguistic Computing*. Oxford University Press.

APPENDIX 1: An Analysis of the Written Data in the Birmingham Main and Reserve Corpora (Main C and RC)

1. The Book Component

Number of books

	Main C	RC (+ Remainders)	Total
number of texts	66	148 (+28)	214
single authorship	63	125 (+28)	188
joint authorship	1	19	20
anthologies	2	4	6
non-fictional texts	43	94 (+20)	137
fictional texts	23	54 (+8)	77

Text Size

Main Corpus:	an average of 70,000 words or fewer
Reserve Corpus:	a) remainders from the Main Corpus
	b) total texts

Contents

1.1 Non-Fiction

Text Types	Topics	No. Books in Main C	(Remainders in RC)	No. Books in RC	Total
Survey					
– extended texts					
	– American Indians	—	—	1	1
	– anthropology	1	(1)	1	2
	– art, modern	1	(1)	—	1
	– child care	1	—	—	1
	– civilization	—	—	2	2
	– clothes	—	—	1	1
	– economics, Third World	1	(1)	—	1
	– history, social	1	—	—	1
	– history, social, architecture	—	—	1	1
	– history, world	—	—	1	1
	– myths and cults	—	—	1	1
	– natural history	1	—	—	1

Text Types	Topics	No. Books in Main C	(Remainders in RC)	No. Books in RC	Total
	– old age	1	—	—	1
	– politics	1	(1)	—	1
	– psychology	1	(1)	—	1
	– psychology, social	—	—	1	1
	– technology, computing	1	(1)	—	1
	– witchcraft	—	—	1	1
		10	(6)	10 (+6)	20
– collections of articles					
	– anecdotes, humorous	—	—	1	1
	– anecdotes, sporting	—	—	2	2
	– reference, fishing	—	—	1	1
	– society, American	1	—	—	1
		1	—	4	5

Procedure

– handbooks

	– British institutions	1	—	—	1
	– career advancement	1	—	—	1
	– child care	1	(1)	—	1
	– cookery, general	—	—	1	1
	– cookery, arthritic	—	—	1	1
	– dramaturgy	—	—	1	1
	– examinations	—	—	1	1
	– food, free	—	—	1	1
	– health, reference book	—	—	1	1
	– health and exercise	—	—	2	2
	– household management	1	—	—	1
	– literacy	—	—	1	1
	– mental efficiency	—	—	1	1
	– self-sufficiency	—	—	1	1
	– social advancement, (satirical)	—	—	1	1
	– sport, badminton	—	—	1	1
	– sport, golf	—	—	1	1

Text Types	Topics	No. Books in Main C	(Remainders in RC)	No. Books in RC	Total
	– sport, rugby	—	—	1	1
	– sport, running	—	—	1	1
	– sport, show-jumping	—	—	1	1
	– technology, modern	—	—	1	1
		4	(1)	18 (+1)	22
– guidebooks					
	– London	1	(1)	— (+1)	1

Argument—Positional/Hortatory

– extended texts

Text Types	Topics	No. Books in Main C	(Remainders in RC)	No. Books in RC	Total
	– animal rights	—	—	1	1
	– cancer cure	—	—	1	1
	– conservation, general	—	—	1	1
	– conservation, rural	—	—	1	1
	– conservation, trees	—	—	1	1
	– design, human ecology	—	—	1	1
	– ecology, policy	—	—	1	1
	– ecology, politics	—	—	1	1
	– ecology, pollution	—	—	1	1
	– ecology, farming	—	—	1	1
	– economics, micro	1	(1)	—	1
	– education, alternative	—	—	1	1
	– education, progressive	1	(1)	—	1
	– energy, nuclear	—	—	1	1
	– energy, solar	—	—	1	1
	– housing	—	—	1	1
	– industrial health	—	—	1	1
	– industrial relations	—	—	1	1
	– literacy, adult	1	—	—	1
	– media, power of	—	—	1	1
	– nuclear weapons	1	—	—	1
	– nutrition	—	—	1	1
	– politics, parliament	—	—	1	1
	– politics, socialism	—	—	1	1

Text Types	Topics/ Settings	No. Books in Main C	(Remainders in RC)	No. Books in RC	Total
	– politics, Soviet Union	—	—	1	1
	– politics, Third World	1	(1)	—	1
	– politics, world	—	—	1	1
	– psychology, behavioural	1	—	—	1
	– psychology, criminal	—	—	1	1
	– socio-economics, poverty	—	—	1	1
		6	(3)	24 (+3)	30
– collections of articles					
	– anthology, feminist	—	—	1	1
	– letters, black America	1	—	—	1
	– scripted broadcasts, religion	—	—	1	1
		1	—	2	3
Argument—Balanced					
– extended texts					
	– astronomy	—	—	1	1
	– business, future	—	—	1	1
	– education	—	—	1	1
	– education, post-school	—	—	1	1
	– history, social	1	(1)	—	1
	– paranormal	—	—	1	1
	– philosophy, love	1	—	—	1
	– politics, economics	—	—	1	1
	– religion, society	1	—	—	1
	– religious relics	—	—	1	1
	– social mobility	—	—	1	1
	– society, contemporary	1	—	—	1
	– society, future	1	(1)	—	1
	– society, National Front	—	—	1	1
	– urban planning	—	—	1	1
		5	(2)	10 (+2)	15

Text Types	Topics/ Settings	No. Books in Main C	(Remainders in RC)	No. Books in RC	Total
Narrative					
– *Travelogue*					
	– cycling through USA	—	—	1	1
	– camels and desert	1	(1)	—	1
	– mountaineering	1	—	—	1
		2	(1)	1 (+1)	3
– *Biography* *extended texts*					
	– politician, British	1	(1)	—	1
	– Bloomsbury set	1	—	—	1
		2	(1)	— (+1)	2
collections					
	– press barons	1	(1)	—	1
	– espionage	—	—	1	1
		1	(1)	1 (+1)	2
– *Autobiography* *extended texts*					
	– acting, films	2	—	1	3
	– acting, theatre	1	—	—	1
	– London, homo-sexuality	—	—	1	1
	– journalism, South Africa	1	(1)	—	1
	– journalism, Vietnam	1	(1)	—	1
	– man and modern technology	1	(1)	—	1
	– mother and daughter	—	—	1	1
	– nature, otters	—	—	1	1
	– philosophy	—	—	1	1
	– politics, black	1	(1)	—	1
	– prison experiences	—	—	1	1
	– rural life	—	—	2	2
	– veterinary medicine, (humorous)	—	—	1	1
		7	(4)	9	16

Text Types	Topics/ Settings	No. Books in Main C	(Remainders in RC)	No. Books in RC	Total
collections					
	– anecdotes, (humorous)	—	—	1	1
	– nature, monkeys	—	—	1	1
	– reminiscences, music	—	—	1	1
		—	—	3	3
– Other extended texts					
	– Bermuda Triangle	—	—	1	1
	– cricketing	—	—	1	1
	– criminal	—	—	1	1
	– espionage	—	—	1	1
	– murder	—	—	1	1
	– politics, SDP	—	—	1	1
	– politics, Watergate	—	—	1	1
		—	—	7	7
– Humour					
– collections					
	– British society	1	—	—	1
	– various	1	—	—	1
		2	—	—	2
Mixed					
– collections					
	– *Bedside Guardian*	1	—	2	3
	– *Good News Bible*	—	—	1	1
	– society, American	—	—	1	1
	– society, Sri Lankan	—	—	1	1
		1	—	5	6
Total No. Non-fictional texts		43	20	94 (+20)	137

1.2 Fiction

Text Types	Topics/ Settings	No. Books Main C	(Remainders in RC)	No. Books RC	Total
General					
-- novels					
	– Africa	—	—	1	1
	– human relations	6	(1)	8	14
	– religion, the army	—	—	1	1
	– middle class life	—	—	3	3
	– mid-life crisis	—	—	1	1
	– human relations, sex	1	—	4	5
	– human relations, sex, humorous	—	—	1	1
	– American mafia	—	—	1	1
	– local politics	—	—	1	1
	– medicine, humorous	—	—	1	1
	– human values, parable	—	—	1	1
	– India, post-Raj	1	—	—	1
	– Israel	—	—	1	1
	– New York Jewish life	—	—	2	2
	– American slavery	1	—	—	1
	– South Africa, boyhood	—	—	1	1
		9	(1)	27 (+1)	36
– short stories					
	– Australian/ Jewish	—	—	1	1
	– human relations	—	—	1	1
	– human weaknesses, humorous	1	—	—	1
	– various, humorous	1	—	—	1
		2	—	2	4
Historical					
– novels					
	– family life, Victorian	—	—	1	1
	– human relations, (humorous)	—	—	1	1
	– society, politics	—	—	1	1

Text Types	Topics/ Settings	No. Books in Main C	(Remainders in RC)	No. Books in RC	Total
	– India, Raj	—	—	2	2
	– Italy, love, politics	—	—	1	1
		—	—	6	6

Thriller

– novels

	– air disaster	—	—	1	1
	– America, sharks	1	(1)	—	1
	– assassination	1	(1)	—	1
	– espionage	1	(1)	3	4
	– James Bond	—	—	1	1
	– murder	1	—	—	1
	– murder at sea	1	(1)	—	1
	– political	—	—	1	1
	– psychological, popular	—	—	1	1
	– treasure hunt	—	—	2	2
	– war	—	—	1	1
	– war time, France	—	—	1	1
		5	4	11 (+4)	16

Academic

– novels

	– campus, America	—	—	1	1
	– campus, Britain, 50s humorous	—	—	1	1
	– life-swap humorous	1	(1)	—	1
	– provincial univ., 60s	1	—	—	1
	– Oxford University, 50s	1	—	—	1
		3	(1)	2 (+1)	5

Future Worlds/Fantasy

– novels

	– future society, fable	—	—	1	1
	– future society, feminism	1	(1)	—	1

Text Types	Topics/ Settings	No. Books in Main C	(Remainders in RC)	No. Books in RC	Total
	– future society, children	1	(1)	—	1
	– Nazism, cloning	1	—	—	1
	– prophecy, finance, intrigue	—	—	1	1
	– prophecy, 3rd World War	1	—	—	1
	– space travel, evolution	—	—	1	1
	– supernatural children	—	—	1	1
	– totalitarian society	—	—	2	2
		4	(2)	6 (+2)	10
Total No. Fictional Texts		23	8	54 (+8)	77

2. The Newspaper Component

Circulation	Frequency	English Lang. Variety	No. in Main C	No. in RC	No. in Total
national	daily	British	4	—	4
international	daily	American	1	—	1
			5	—	5

3. The Magazine and Journal Component

Circulation	Freq.	Eng. Lang. Variety	Topics	No. in Main C	No. in RC	No. in Total
national	wkly	British	current affairs	4	5	9
national	wkly	British	economics	1	1	2
internat.	wkly	American	current affairs	2	1	3
national	mthly	British	modern woman	2	—	2
national	mthly	British	home and garden	1	—	1

Circulation	Freq.	Eng. Lang. Variety	Topics	No. in Main C	No. in RC	No. in Total
national	mthly	British	current affairs	1	2	3
internat.	mthly	American	world cultures	1	2	3
				12	11	23

4. Brochures and Leaflets

Type	No. in Main C	No. in RC	No. in Total
Dept. of Health and Social Security Leaflets	5	—	5
Bank Leaflets	—	16	16
Holiday Brochures	—	4	4
British Council Leaflet: Info. for Foreign Students	—	1	1
BICOSA Leaflet for Students in Birmingham	—	1	1
University of Birmingham Prospectuses	—	9	9
	5	31	36

5. Correspondence

Type	No. in Main C	No. in RC	No. in Total
Personal Letters	6	—	6

APPENDIX 2: Statistics Relating to the Authorship of the Book Component of the Main and Reserve Corpora

(NB Books common to both corpora are only accounted for once, in the figures for the Main Corpus)

Date of Publication

	Main Corpus	Reserve Corpus	Total
1980–81	10	51	61
1975–79	29	43	72
1970–74	13	20	33
1960–69	10	22	32
1950–59	3	6	9
pre-1950	1	6	7
	66	148	214

Sex of Author

male	49	115	164
female	15	25	40
unknown/various	2	8	10
	66	148	214

Language Variety of Author

British English	45	112	157
American English	16	29	45
Other varieties			
—Australian English	1	1	2
—S. African English	1	—	1
—Anglo-Indian	—	1	1
—Anglo-Russian	1	1	2
—Anglo-Austrian	—	1	1
unknown/various	2	3	5
	66	148	214

APPENDIX 3: An Analysis of the Text Types and Topics in the Spoken Component of the Main Corpus

Text Type	General Topic Area	No. of Texts
face to face, informal conversation	– various, domestic – current affairs	13 2
		15
telephone conversation	– service encounters	6
face to face discussion	– education	3
lesson discussion	– accountancy – physics – geography	2 1 1
		4
radio discussion	– current affairs – the arts – education – finance – energy issues – technology – law	8 24 3 3 4 1 1
		44
TV discussion	– politics	6
face to face interview	– interview for teaching appointment – domestic matters – personal preference	1 1 1
		3
radio interview	– government and law – politics – economics – the arts – religion – education – society and sociology – language – history – biology – technology	3 3 2 9 4 6 10 1 1 4 6

Text Type	General Topic Area	No. of Texts
	– physics	5
	– other sciences	5
	– maths	1
		60
video interview	– interview for undergraduate admission to university course	1
personal narration	– content of dream	2
talk given to class	– British Education system	1
oral class demonstration	– maths	1
radio talk	– physics	2
university lecture	– perception	9
	– artificial intelligence	1
	– instrumentation	1
	– biology	1
	– technology	3
	– various	4
		19

APPENDIX 4: Concordance Extract from the Main Corpus for 'mind'

```
GW0034 BR BR  ay inhibit the formation of an original idea in a  mind  capable of original ideas. It may be better t
GW0086 BR BR  the first chance!" But Mr. Evans in his tormented  mind  cared nothing whether John liked the tower or
GW0033 BR BR  er bother with more? Why even mention love, never  mind  carry on about how love itself must evolve to
GW0086 BR BR  e the little urchin again." And then Tom Barter's  mind  ceased suddenly to think in definite words. br
GW0086 BR BR  as if they were perfectly meaningless sounds, his  mind  ceased to be. He felt the pressure of her. br
GW0052 BR BR  JACWA, in developing their plans, had to bear in   mind  certain considerations arising from the new c
GW0052 BR BR  ?' "I suppose he left it in the safe." "Would you  mind  checking up?" "I'll ask his secretary—oh, I'
GW0071 AM BR  who are impelled by their own inner needs, often   mind  children when the job is really beyond their
GW0012 BR BR  lasses and she paid for her own meals. She didn't  mind  cigarette smoke any more. She had no lovers.
GW0075 BR BR  all museums for the curious Londoner, making the   mind  clang with astonishment – consid? er the neol
GW0075 BR BR  ffering from anaemia. When this was rectified her  mind  cleared and she was able to return to normal
GW0078 OT BR  public readings; and the worry in the back of his  mind  clouds the understanding he is fighting for a
GW0078 BR BR  irt and scanties? Did I have something special in  mind?  coaxing voices asked me. Swimming suits? We
GW0086 BR BR  s, however improbable such a creature may be. The  mind  comprehends facts and is at ease with fiction
GW0072 AM BR  nded on from generation to generation. The modern  mind,  conditioned as it is to the devouring needs
GW0032 AM BR  . Geard; but I'm a black sheep, you know. I don't  mind  confessing to all you kind people "—here he
GW0032 AM BR  just live with this and not fight it mentally ..   mind  control.. I should talk now about Phaedrus,
GW0032 AM BR  is idea that the entire world is within one's own  mind  could be dismissed as absurd if Hume had just
GW0034 BR BR  go I became interested in finding out whether the  mind  could experience a visual hallucination which
GW0055 AM BR  thetic mysticism, but an inquiry into whether the  mind  could hold vividly in consciousness an experi
GW0034 BR BR  been burned by the hot iron. He found that his     mind  could focus better now on the only choice tha
GW0072 AM BR  t her mouth to my ear -- but for quite a while my  mind  could not separate into words the hot thunder
GW0072 AM BR  stion that what may be partly in the questioner's  mind  could be answered by reference to language p
GS0022 OT BR  f organization seemed trivial and easy, and one's  mind  could jubilantly soar on the wings of that su
GW0117 OT BR  ."" Occur where?" enquired Mr. Dekker. "In the     mind!" cried the Welshman, raising his hand to his
GW0086 BR BR  eth. I got away from the gate for a second and my  mind  crystallized. I raced for some ropes, a wood
GW0019 AU BR  elf, with his chin against his clasped knees, his  mind  darts back when you Mine is a weatherbeaten,
GW0058 AM AM  ace t0 which; for no explicable reason your adult  mind  dazed and reeling with all that he had seen a
GW0055 AM BR  ics. She had tried to educate herself gently, her  mind  dazed by even the simplest terms, and had in
GW0068 BR BR  d of that rocky day; and hear her saying, "Never   mind, dear, you can't win 'em all.' And he says, "
GW0001 AA BR  which had disintegrated. Moreover, some habits of  mind  decay to make way for the new. The same might
GW0031 AM BR  ed circle of celebrithood, and old images in the   mind  derived from it, notably traditional habitua t
GW0073 BR BR  ut. Man, being dexterous of hand and inventive of  mind  did neither. He hunted the furred animals,
GW0004 AM BR  andle!" thought Mr. Evans. The Welshman's triadic  mind  dived like a plummet, then, to the sea- botto
GW0034 BR BR  ore difficult to change the parts themselves. The  mind  divides the continuity of the world around us
GW0086 BR BR  s waiting for the blow to fall; <p 24> "You don't  mind, do you, Sarah asked, "if it's a cold meal t
GW0052 BR BR  urely? (B) I don't mind ((C)) Would Nick really    mind, do you think? (B) Erm. No, I shouldn't thi
GS0127 BR BR  But I just feel so happy in this house. You don't  mind, do you?" "I'm not sure it's a wildly good id
GW0119 BR BR  ng the right rituals at the right times. I don't   mind  doing those things, I thing the trouble is t
GS0039 BR BR  s Howard, "we'd better rush." "Howard, would you   mind  doing up my top button again ?' says Henry, a
GW0119 BR BR  ng no excuse for the anxieties which drag a man's  mind  down to the exigencies of survival, he is fre
GW0119 OT BR  left the children and the village behind, Kunta's  mind  drifted off Lamin to other things. He thought
GW0055 AM BR  octors always do, don't they ? <P 163> "I don't   mind  drinking alone.' "He said if I didn't pull up
GW0052 BR BR  p and stopped. I asked them if they <P 146> would  mind  driving a little way along and seeing if they
GW0019 AU BR  interesting type," he said. "Rick nearly blew his  mind  drugs, drink, everything. He hates universit
GW0143 AM BR  constantly and obsessively planted in my conscious mind  during my daymares and insomnias More prec
GW0072 AM BR  fficially George's idea, doubtless planted in his  mind  during pillow-talk; his preoccupation with th
GW0080 BR BR  ma? de between what a man is given in the way of    mind  emotional make-up and body on the one hand a
GW0078 OT BR  and rejection of the partial images through which  mind  emotion and senses maintain their hold on re
GW0078 OT BR  eresting. I can remember things when I can get my  mind  engaged with them, I can see a sort of intell

GS0098 AM BR  s trying to study. If I was trying to improve my   mind  er, I just couldn't do it. I can't do it. I
GS0157 BR BR  t's the extent of your world and also bearing in   mind, er George Bernard Shaw, the English have no
GW0131 AM BR  ich this pessimis- tic prophecy grips the popular  mind, especially among young people. Hammered into
GW0026 BR BR  r any of the questions that had half-formed in my  mind  even as I had left the Strykers' cabin. If sh
GW0072 AM BR  ntation? than they present themselves with to my   mind  even now when I Know what to seek in the past
```

APPENDIX 5: **The Contents of the TEFL Corpus**

Code	Title	Author	Publisher
E001	*Encounters*	J. Garton-Sprenger et al.	Heinemann Educational Books
E002	*Kernel One*	R. O'Neill	Longman
E003	*Kernel Lessons Intermediate*	R. O'Neill et al.	Longman
E004	*Kernel Lessons Plus*	R. O'Neill	Longman
E005	*Access to English Starting Out*	M. Coles B. Lord	Oxford University Press
E006	*Access to English Getting On*	M. Coles B. Lord	OUP
E007	*Access to English Turning Point*	M. Coles B. Lord	OUP
E008	*Access to English Open Road*	M. Coles B. Lord	OUP
E009	*Streamline English Departures*	B. Hartley P. Viney	OUP
E010	*Streamline English Connections*	B. Hartley P. Viney	OUP
E011	*Streamline English Destinations*	B. Hartley P. Viney	OUP
E012	*Contact English 1*	C. Granger A. Hicks	Heinemann
E013	*Contact English 2*	C. Granger A. Hicks	Heinemann
E014	*Starting Strategies*	B. Abbs I. Freebairn	Longman
E015	*Building Strategies*	B. Abbs I. Freebairn	Longman
E016	*Developing Strategies*	B. Abbs I. Freebairn	Longman
E017	*Studying Strategies*	B. Abbs I. Freebairn	Longman
E018	*Follow Me 1*	L. G. Alexander R. Kingsbury	Longman
E019	*Follow Me 2*	L. G. Alexander R. Kingsbury	Longman
E020	*English Alive 1*	S. Nicholls et al.	Edward Arnold
E021	*English Alive 2*	S. Nicholls et al.	Edward Arnold
E022	*English Alive 3*	S. Nicholls C. Wrangham	Edward Arnold
E023	*First Things First*	L. G. Alexander	Longman
E024	*Practice and Progress*	L. G. Alexander	Longman
E025	*Developing Skills*	L. G. Alexander	Longman
E026	*Main Course English Exchanges (Pt A & B)*	P. Prowse et al.	Heinemann

APPENDIX 6: Concordance Extract from TEFL Corpus for 'today'

paper? it hasn't been ordered yet. +3 things to do +3	today	date 22 november urgent done post the letters, or	e029
+1 (pause) +1 oh, all right. woman: +1 how are you	today?	daughter: you're looking well. woman: mr ridley	e019
+1 do you know-mr smithers had a very nasty experience	today	didn't +1 you, mr smithers? yes, indeed! well, 9	e006
has to +1 x+0 picture two+3 what is terry going to do	today?	do you think +3 he wants to take the exam today?	e006
xplain it's really quite easy. +1 i'm feeling much better	today.	+1 doctor. +0 intonation and stress. respond to	e029
ay as in the example.+3 mary is working in the library	today.	+3 does mary work in the library everyday? +0 tw	e005
ct. we'll show you a film about +1 our factories later	today.	does that answer your question? <p 064> +0 unit set r	e029
he +1 back there? do you think you could feed the cat	today?	don't you? +1 make a sound! +1 thank you	e016
ey never know if it's doris or doreen who's +3 working	today?	doris? don't you? +1hm, perhaps i had. +3 gordon gives	e022
+3 injections together. i think you'd better start	today.	doris and doreen who's +3 working	e001
's wearing +3 a sweater today. bruce is going to work	today.	dr and mrs newton +3 are eating breakfast today.	e029
? your name. your job your telephone +3 number the date	today.	-0 drill example +3 address.address name +3 tele	e001
britain. schools a hundred years ago, a typical school	today.	+3 education in fifty year's time. anne page car	e029
the are good teams, they +3 usually play well. but	today	england are playing very well. +3 and scotland ar	e009
sh evolved from the mingling of the +3 three tongues.	today	+3 every british policeman carries a two-way radi	e011
i saw harry i have seen harry +3 two weeks ago already	today	every day this week every day last week +3 alread	e007
george is lonely and unhappy. his friends +3 are busy	today	+3 everyday conversation +1 would like to come	e008
+3 rude to mr james on the phone. billy had a bad day	today.	everyone +3 told him to do things. what did the	e013
the men mend the gas stove. i wonder if they'd mend it	today	+0 examples+3 mrs harrison was paid 5 pounds. 9	e006
oprtex national championships starting +3 blackpool	today	+0 car production rises by 5 pc car production in	e008
ulu. tell all the +3 players what the weather is like	today	feels +3 embarrassed about something. my place i	e015
y york to windermere we travel +3 across the pennines	today	(1y direct to tokyo.+3 you visit the pyramids i	e018
+p you done? +0 dialogue. describe: +3 how life is different	today	following one of yorkshire's famous +0 dales-wen	e029
ple in your country. describe +3 how life is different	today.	francis? i've typed a lot of letters. boss: i wan	e011
t's wrong with you and why you must see +0 the doctor	today.	from a hundred years ago what people +3 do now th	e011
+3 by king croesus of lydia in the sixth century bc.	today	give +p an appointment. ask what b's name is. rep	e012
ad other countries +3 travel news summer sun sale here	today.	gold +3 still play +an important part in the int	e012
(2) on the beach. +3 he (3) a newspaper. it's very hot	today.	gone tomorrow. +3 tourists coming to britain so	e018
1 twenty letters today. i haven't typed twenty letters	today.	harry (4.) +a hat and +3 sunglasses. harry and liz	e029
+3 homes. murderers should be executed. young people	today?	have you +1 typed twenty letters today? what hav	e029
st +0 ask each other +1 what are the main news stories	today?	have too +3 much freedom. +0 debate: choose one o	e029
main news stories today? +1 have you read a newspaper	today?	+1 have you read a newspaper today? have you lis	e006
getting on these days? x arthur newton's +3 wedding	today?	have you listened to the news +1 today? +3 stud	e008
pay +1 you back today. what! can't you pay me back	today?	he x mary stephens. the ceremony x st. mark's +3	e008
ford prison.+1 i'm afraid you can't see the manager +1	today.	he x to a conference in birmingham. do you know	e008
who has worked many years for you and is +0 retiring	today.	he is now in your office and you wish to thank.	e012
> +0 new language (th,ity) +3 robert. he's got a headache	today.	he had +3 a headache yesterday, too. you he had	e002
a job because he was in prison. frank is very unhappy	today.	+3 he was unhappy yesterday, too. <p 078> +0 the	e020
pearly this morning, he has +3 to take an examination	today.	he has to go to the university. +3 but he is thi	e002
drives a bus. mike wilson +3 usually drives a bus but	today	he is driving a car. +0 write +0 more sentences	e022
is job to train any new recruits that are +3 taken on.	today	he is with a trainee bus driver called david. who	e023
are. he usually +3 shaves at 7 o'clock every day. but	today.	he. she usually drinks tea +3 in the morning. but	e003
cise look at this: +3 he usually shaves at 7.0. +3 but	today	he at 8.0. he usually shaves at 7.0 but today.	e003
+3 but today. he at 8.0. he usually shaves at 7.0 but	today.	he is +3 shaving at 8.0. +0 do these in the same	e003
got tinned milk +3 frank wanted to leave work early	today.	he wanted to see a football +3 match. the boss	e009
ook +0 at this sentence: +1 i'm not going to see him	today.	+0 here +0 some more i the expressions that we u	e001
no,he isn't +3 the working today? no,he isn't working	today?	he's in the kitchen. +1 what's he doing? he's c	e013
we stop looking ahead! why don't we start +3 enjoying	today?	he's not sure what he's been to the sea	e018
ht lose. he lost: <p 063> +3 it's sam's free afternoon	today.	he's not going +3 to do. +0 writ	e021
for? mr james he did. he isn't +1 james in	today?	he's in a terrible mood. he told me to get out.	e023
erday? yes he did. he didn't. what's alan do+0 ing	today?	he's +1 hav-0 ing a rest. oh why? he didn't fee	—
also they +3 played with the radio in his police car.	today.	he's playing very badly. where's francis? he's	—
like doctors. <p 063> +0 lesson +1 doctor: how's jimmy	today?	he's at the airport +3 with a hundred other poli	—
o i wasn't. +1 i was at the greengrocer's. how's jimmy	today?	he's very well. thank +1 you. was he absent from	—

APPENDIX 7: **The Contents of the Sub-Corpus**

Written Texts

GW001	A. Cooke	*The Americans*
GW003	S. Conran	*Superwoman*
GW023		*The Economist* (May 1981)
GW030	M. Shanks	*What's Wrong with the Modern World*
GW039	D. Lodge	*Changing Places*
GW021		*Cosmopolitan* (May 1981)
GW071	I. Shaw	*Rich Man Poor Man*

Spoken Texts

GS002	Conversation
GS005	Lecture
GS006	Lecture
GS010	Conversation
GS011	Interview
GS016	Interview/talk
GS018	Interview/talk
GS021	Interview/talk
GS022	Interview/talk
GS029	Lecture
GS030	Lecture
GS036	Monologue
GS037	Interview/talk
GS046	Discussion/interview
GS054	Discussion
GS059	Debate
GS069	Discussion
GS072	Discussion
GS074	Discussion
GS095	Discussion
GS096	Lecture
GS097	Lecture
GS099	Conversation
GS102	Lecture
GS115	Conversation
GS120	Lecture
GS125	Discussion
GS126	Discussion
GS128	Discussion
GS144	Discussion
GS145	Discussion
GS148	Discussion
GS153	Discussion
GS154	Discussion
GS166	Discussion
GS168	Discussion

APPENDIX 8: Concordance Sample from the Sub Corpus for 'factor'

CONCORDANCE SAMPLE FROM THE SUB-CORPUS FOR 'FACTOR'

2, an oil for minimum protection (for skin that tans easily), to factor 6, a lotion for high
protection (for skin that usually bur

seen as a long-term investment in economic development, was one factor. Another was the
belief, which governments shared with the

nt after the first skills have been mastered may well be a major factor, because teachers
are teachers, and I don't think much has

the rewards for car theft will be falling off markedly. Another factor ensuring a reduction
in road-based crime will be a substan

ing world polarisation between rich and poor countries. One such factor has been the impact
of western technology, which has great

or seven years of learning in a school that discounts play as a factor in life. "But I always
have to add, "That is - if he ever

its origins much further back in time, it is undeniably a major factor in determining design
and marketing procedures for consume

n "a larger coalition", his CED members have become an important factor in California's
Democratic party. At the January state

vailable jobs to a much greater extent than ever before.A third factor is that young labour is
no longer, as in the past, cheap l

mors of change have already shaken contemporary society. A major factor is undoubtedly the
collapse of the traditional values of t

t because the question that was brought up the most important factor is that life now
can be prolonged and be dealt with

tices; for wages and salaries are the price at which the crucial factor of labour is
bought and sold. Wages and salaries may be ex

True altruism is a long time in coming, and it never loses its factor of selfishness.
Small children have quite a different atti

can be simple curiosity to see what's inside an object. The main factor that should concern
us is not the actual destruction of th

endly, pleasant, eager, but something is lacking - the emotional factor, the power to
subordinate thinking to feeling.

sation is to survive?" The radical alternatives share one common factor. They require a
general willingness on the part of the peo

transfer mechanisms and social investment of the State? A third factor was the way in which
the growing public sector has come to

programmes and the never programmes. (Um) for example, the first factor we can look at
would be that of purpose. On the whole the

rences in intelligence between animals. It is sure to be a major factor when we come to
making intellectual comparisons with compu

ogram. The development of the stored program is the major single factor which allowed computers
to advance way beyond the power of

CHAPTER 2: **Computing**

Jeremy Clear

Overview of the Role of Computing in Cobuild

From its inception, the Cobuild project placed great emphasis on the use of computers to assist with the compilation of a dictionary database. The computer was not only to be used for the very basic storage, alphabetical sorting and typesetting of the dictionary, but it was to make a significant contribution to the nature of the lexicography and the analysis of the English language. The sheer size of a corpus adequate to form the basis of a single volume learners' dictionary entailed the use of computational techniques for storing and manipulating the real text evidence. Computer processing of natural language texts was not new, and had been going on at Birmingham and around the world for many years, but the Cobuild project planned to make a comprehensive study of a larger corpus of general English than any which existed at the time.

It was clear to us that there was no possibility of extracting the linguistic information required for the dictionary from the corpus automatically. Of course, some linguistic information can be discovered easily – the relative frequencies of word types, for example – but most of the familiar analysis found in a dictionary (definition, grammatical information, semantic field labels, synonyms, etc.) has to be produced manually, based on the evidence furnished by the computer.

The value of the information which the computer can supply should not be underestimated, however. Simply the presentation of keywords in a KWIC format concordance brings out patterns in the text data which are then immediately obvious to the lexicographer but which would otherwise easily pass unnoticed.

So the computer was to analyse the data in ways which would make clearer the structure of English, the lexicographic team would use the computer output to supplement the traditional lexicographical tools and the results of the lexicographers' work would be fed straight back into the computer in the form of a structured database. Ideally the information about the language which is represented in the database is fully consistent with the corpus data, since it is derived directly from it. Any inconsistency will have arisen through the lexicographers' analysis and interpretation of the facts of the corpus. Moreover, the database itself becomes a further source of linguistic information. For example, word types are classified into syntactic categories by the lexicographers (and the classification is firmly rooted in the evidence of the corpus) and the database can supply a list of all word types currently stored which share some syntactic features. This enables the lexicographer to check for consistency in classification or to refine the analysis of a particular word under consideration through comparison and contrast. This information cannot be extracted easily from the raw corpus text, nor would it be available without extremely tedious searching of dictionary files which were not implemented as a database.

In order to reinforce the relationship between the real language data and the description of the language embodied in the database, text was copied verbatim, or with minor modifications, from the corpus into the database in the form of example sentences and phrases. These are, of course, widely recognised to be of value to the foreign learner in a dictionary entry. The database was compiled such that each observation about semantics, syntax or lexis should be adequately exemplified with text drawn from the corpus. This resulted in a large database which contained rather discursive definitions and copious exemplification. It could not be easily manipulated with the restrictive, fixed-format data fields which are assumed to be appropriate for most commercial database applications.

Corpus Processing

The computational aspects of processing the corpus were mainly determined by the sheer bulk of the data to be handled. It was important that the sample of natural English text be as large as we could compile and manage, for it was apparent that existing general English corpora of one million running words or less were quite inadequate as a basis for the analysis of lexis and semantics. The construction of the Cobuild corpus is fully described in Chapter One and I will make only summary points about the specifically computational facets of the text processing.

Since the principal concern was to supplement the existing collection of computer-held text at Birmingham to create a very large balanced sample of English, attention was given to acquiring text in machine-readable form, digitising printed text or keying speech transcriptions. The corpus is by design heterogeneous and consequently the data coming onto the computer did not conform to any rigorous standard form. It would have been desirable, of course, if all texts included in the corpus were fully proof-read and stored in a normalised form. The Brown (Kucera and Francis, 1967) and LOB (Johansson, 1980) corpora have been fully edited to smooth out difficulties concerned with representing the visual, typographical form of text in a restricted computer character set. Every text presents some problems of this kind; for example, the treatment of capitalisation (sentence initial, titles, proper names) pagination, paragraphing, columnar layouts, diagrams, end matter, foreign words and phrases, direct quotation, etc. The choice is to spend a great deal of time and money in manual editing of the machine-readable text before processing and to create a normalised text, or to take account of the poorly structured input data during processing. We inevitably took the latter approach, reasoning that since time and funds were not limitless, the disadvantages of having, say, the concordance for AM including a certain number of 'ante meridien' abbreviations were outweighed by the advantage of gathering more text in the time available. Since actual text examples were attached to every instance, most of these points could be attended to in later editing.

Resources

From October 1980 until April 1983, the period when the corpus building and processing was the main task, the equipment and personnel resources available to the project were as follows. I was responsible for all aspects of the computing work and was a full-time member of the project team. We employed a keyboarder and a data clerk and we had assistance from the Service Division of the University's Computer Centre. The University's ICL 1906A mainframe was to be the main workhorse for the corpus processing, and the project acquired several Zenith Z89 microcomputers with floppy disk drives for handling corpus texts (especially transcription of speech) and for data capture. In 1982, in anticipation of the replacement of the 1906A mainframe, the faculty acquired a DEC PDP 11/34 running the Unix operating system. This machine was equipped with an industry-standard magnetic tape unit and a 134 Mbyte Winchester disk and was intended to handle corpus processing and initial storage of the database during the period between the decommissioning of the ICL mainframe and the completed installation of its replacement, a Honeywell/Multics system. The Computer Centre's second mainframe, a DEC2050, was also available to the project for software development and other tasks for which a fully interactive environment is desirable. The DEC20 was not suited to large-scale corpus processing work.

Concordancing: Early Stages

The primary requirements for the lexicography were word frequency listings and full KWIC concordances to the corpus, which stood at six million running words by the end of 1981. There were many programs to do processing of this kind in existence at the time, the most generalised and widely available being COCOA (Berry-Rogghe, 1973), CLOC (Reed and Schonfelder, 1979) and OCP (Hockey and Marriott, 1979, 1980), an enhanced replacement for COCOA. These three packages were running on the ICL mainframe and each was tested on large subsections of the corpus data. What became apparent immediately was that none of these standard packages was designed to handle input texts of six million running words, and that each package in its ICL 1906A implementation failed to produce correct output for such a huge text file. Of course, we attempted to break down the whole task by using the facilities of the packages to produce output only for specified subsets of the complete vocabulary of the corpus. In each case the sheer length of the text made an initial pass through the input file impossible within the limitations imposed by the operating system and/or the package.

The corpus was therefore split into five batches of approximately 1.2 million words each, and each batch was processed repeatedly by the COCOA package to produce alphabetical files of concordance output. It was intended that the six, discrete concordances would be merged, using the ICL Sort/Merge package, to produce the desired single concordance to six million words.

The processing of each batch was very costly in CPU time and in disk storage space. Enough temporary scratch storage was required to hold the output files until they could be dumped onto magnetic tape, with backup copies for security. The COCOA runs were carried out during the weekend period, when the whole ICL 1906A computer was free for this task.

Although COCOA was a rather primitive package, and the oldest of the three available concordance generators, it was used because in its 1906A implementation it was significantly more efficient than CLOC or OCP. Additional macros were written for the GEORGE4 operating system so that in the event of a system break a long concordancing job could be restarted from the point in the processing at which the interruption occurred. Without this facility, several long jobs ran for many hours of real time, were terminated before completion by some system break, and had to be cleaned up and restarted from the beginning.

During 1982 when the concordancing work was being carried out, the PDP11 was installed and within a few weeks I had prepared a simple 'C' program on Unix which was designed specifically for the Cobuild task and which would produce a KWIC concordance for every type of a text file up to a maximum size of 1.5 million words. The advantages of having a dedicated system for large-scale concordancing were considerable. The fifth corpus batch of 1.2 million words was processed on the PDP11 more quickly and with less manual intervention than on the 1906A.

The ICL Sort/Merge package was tested on samples from the five enormous output files, but the data was found to contain a large number of inconsistencies in format which continually caused the merging process to fail. In particular, an obscure disk error in a few of the concordance runs had caused physical blocks of uninitialized storage to be included in the output files, which appeared as long stretches of seemingly random characters.

At this stage, the corpus content was reviewed and it was decided that a sixth batch of data should be added which would contain additional written material to improve the balance of text types making up the sample. This sixth batch brought the corpus size to approximately 7.3 million words. The lexicographers were able then to work with the microfiche of the six batches, and microfiche readers and a reader-printer were purchased. It was the job of the data clerk to make paper copies of the concordance output for headwords (along with their derived forms and inflections) to be handed out to the lexicographers.

Concordancing: Later Stages

The handling of the corpus was completely revised when the 1906A was replaced by the Honeywell/Multics system. The merging operation was still not complete by the summer of 1983 when the Honeywell came into operation, and it became clear that the Multics machine would be far better able to process the corpus than the 1906A. I asked the Computer Centre to assist by recoding my Unix 'C' concordance program in PL/1 to run on Multics. This streamlined program was able, with sufficient allocation of scratch filestore, to concordance 7.3 million words in three simple steps:

    a) creation of an index to the location of every token in the text
    b) complete alphabetical sorting of the index file
    c) generation of concordance lines for each token in the index.

These three steps can be discrete and the whole process can be broken down such that each step can be run within a reasonable amount of CPU time. The corpus was completely reconcordanced over the off-shift weekend period on the Honeywell, and the output files (one per letter of the alphabet) were dumped to tape.

Wordlists

By this time the question of arriving at a suitable headword list for the dictionary was under consideration. We had carried out a collation of six wordlists to produce a basic list of headword forms. Of the six lists, three were the headword lists from other dictionaries, two were vocabularies intended as target lists for foreign learners of English and one was a list drawn from a small corpus of TEFL examination papers. The collated headword list had a code attached to each word indicating its membership of the six lists. Obviously, THE was included in all six lists and, say, VALETUDINARIAN might only be included in one of the dictionary lists. This coded list was then compared with the word frequency list of the total corpus, and two products resulted. On the one hand, the headword list was run against the corpus frequency list, frequencies were attached to each headword and a group code was determined, partly automatically, for each headword. The final list was in this form:

A63	a	247132
G5	aardvark	0
F2	ab-	212
XO	abi	8

In the example, the word A was present in all six of the source lists (the numerical code is a six bit binary number, one bit per list – hence 63 indicates six 'yes' bits) and its frequency in the corpus was 247132. The word was assigned to the A group of headwords based on three factors:

a) its inclusion in the six lists
b) its corpus frequency
c) the proportion of printed text assigned to this headword in the *Longman Dictionary of Contemporary English*.

A simple computer algorithm assigned a group code to each headword. The main purpose of this coding was for day-to-day management of the database compilation, which is described more fully below. AARDVARK, which did not occur in the corpus, is assigned to group G; the prefix AB-, which occurred 212 times, went to group F, etc. The headword/concordance index is mentioned here because it was used in preparing a hard-copy of the concordances to the corpus. A program was run to add the text references to each keyword in the concordance files, and to delete from the concordance output files the citations for keywords occurring only once in the corpus and having no entry in the dictionary headword list. (The corpus contains a very large number of strings with a frequency of 1: the majority of these are strings which need not be considered as headwords or lexical items, and typically are typographical errors, formulae, initials, roman numerals, proper names, KDEM errors, etc. The bulk of concordance files was reduced by approximately 20 per cent by this means.) The program also used the headword list to determine how to paginate the concordance output, allowing 'sets' of concordance keywords to be printed continuously, thereby making further significant reductions in the bulk of paper produced in the laser print run of concordances.

It may seem incongruous that a dictionary project which makes use of such advanced electronic technology should produce concordance output on paper and file it on a large wall-mounted racking system, but it was clear that no on-line retrieval system for concordances would allow lexicographers as much freedom as a paper copy. It would not have been possible to set up an electronic system which would allow researchers to work at home, on the train or at their desks, and to annotate the concordances as they studied them. Microfiche copies were also provided as a backup for lost paper copies, and as a means of viewing concordances for headwords which were out of the library being compiled.

Database Development

The lexical database as it exists now is the result of a series of experiments and modifications. Throughout the project we adhered to a number of general design principles for the database.

a) The database should be a true lexical database, rather than a machine-readable version of a printed dictionary. It should be a comprehensive analysis of the central vocabulary of general English from which particular reference works could be extracted mainly automatically. The database should contain more information than any of the particular reference works which would be taken from it, and the format of the information in the database might be quite different from the format appropriate to a printed book.

b) Balancing point a), we should adopt a basic dictionary-style structure for the database, since dictionaries were to be its primary product. The transition from electronic database to printable dictionary should not be tortuous. Moreover the underlying structure of entries in British and American dictionaries has been developed over the centuries as an appropriate representation of the lexicon: the printed dictionary has many shortcomings but there was no reason to reject its format outright.

c) The database should be flexible. This was an informal principle, and in practice it meant that many detailed design decisions were revised as compilation of the database proceeded. The principle was established in order to ensure that linguistic and lexicographical concerns prevail over computational ones. The coding and storage of data should be sufficiently general to allow for the possibility of subsequent restructuring. This rather loose notion of flexibility will become clearer when I come to discuss in detail the development of the system.

d) The lexicographic team would have to work off-line. This principle, like the decision to access concordances on paper, was established for reasons of convenience and economy. Even microcomputer workstations networked into the central mainframe would constrain lexicographers' working routine in a way that compilation with pen and paper would not. And, of course, pen and paper is significantly cheaper.

e) The database should provide 'feedback' to the lexicographers during the compilation process. One of the disadvantages with traditional dictionary compilation is that, given the normal reasonable constraints of time and manpower, compilers work on particular headwords in isolation. Our database system was designed so that for each headword assigned for compilation the computer produced a printout of existing entries which were relevant to the new headword to be compiled. This was intended to ensure that subtle differences in meaning between near-synonyms were noted and accounted for; that compounds, idioms, phrases and other multi-word entries were consistently dealt with at each of the possible keywords; that the style of definitions for groups of related lexical items was consistent, and so on.

The following detailed description of the set-up and operation of the database will illustrate the extent to which these principles guided the computing work.

Dictionary 'Slips'

It was clearly not possible for the database compilation to be done electronically. At the beginning of 1987 as I write this, it is still the case that the technology of microcomputers and network communications is unable to offer an economically competitive system which will allow a large team of lexicographers to compile dictionary entries without using pen and paper. So a basic proforma was designed on which the dictionary entries would be recorded for subsequent keyboarding. There were two types of paper form; one printed on pink paper, and one on white; hence pink and white slips. The slips were based on the traditional structure of a printed dictionary entry. Broadly, a pink slip was completed for each sense of a dictionary headword, and would contain a definition and primary syntactic, lexical and semantic information. Each pink slip may be followed by a sequence of white slips each of which recorded an example sentence or citation drawn from the corpus, and detailed syntactic, lexical and semantic information relating to the carefully selected example.

The slips correspond closely to the concept of logical computer records in a data-processing sense. The whole database then could be stored as a sequential file of records of two types: pink slips introducing each sense, exemplified by one or more white slips. This is, of course, a slight distortion of the usual way in which a dictionary is structured: normally a dictionary is considered as a sequence of headwords each having one or more senses; in our system it is not the headword which is the primary unit of structure but the sense category. No theoretical statement was intended by this arrangement, since in practice the logical structure of the database is independent of the physical storage and organisation of data on the computer.

The pink and white slips constitute in effect the database model as it was in 1981. At that time we needed to begin preliminary compilation, but it was not decided how the database should be physically implemented. What was important at that stage was that there should be a method of data capture and some means of retrieval. We wrote our own program in BASIC for customized data entry on our Zenith Z89 microcomputers. The paper slips and the screen layout were matched to make the keyboarding efficient. The fields or 'boxes' on the slip, were drawn on the screen and the keyboarder used a set of function keys to display a blank pink or white slip, correct miskeyed fields, erase whole slips, etc. The program required double-keying of the critical headword (which would be the primary key for retrieval and must be correctly entered) and validated each field in a simple way by checking that each contained appropriate characters. Data was written to floppy disk, each file having header and trailer record added, to record the number of slips in that file along with the date code. A slip-editor program was written in assembly language so that the keyboarder could check and correct files of keyed slips. The editor displayed a slip on the screen and allowed full cursor movement, insertion, deletion, forward and backward searching, and it too checked the contents of data fields.

The slip files on floppy disk could then be transferred to any of three machines – the PDP11/34 minicomputer, the ICL 1906A mainframe or the DEC20 mainframe. In the early days, the slips went to all three.

Data Capture

The data files were stored on floppy disk as fairly simple files of sequential records. Each record consisted of a two character code, a blank and up to 77

HEADWORD sky	CATEGORY NO 1·1	SLIP NO 120
DEFINITION *the space around the earth which you can see when you stand outside and look upwards, and where you can see the sun, the moon, and the stars. [the plural form means the same as the note form but see note slips]*		
INFLECTED FORMS y → ies		
SYNTAX {-THE} ↑ {//DET-S + QUAL·BRD} : XP		

FIELD	STYLE	=	↑
space appearance height natural phenomena	MASSCONC	firmament heavens	
	+ natural phenomena blue-C cloud-C celestial-R	≠	PRAGMATICS

FIGURE 1a

data characters. The two character code indicates in which field the following data characters belong. Figure 1a shows a pink slip layout with the fields completed in typical fashion. Figure 1b shows the slip data as it is stored in sequential format.

```
  1     sky
 @@     1.1
 ~~     120
 00     the space around the earth which you can see when you stand outside
 00     and look upwards, and where you can see the sun, the moon, and the
 00     stars. [the plural form means the same as the sing form but see note slips.]
 11     y → ies
 22     N {-THE} ↑ {// DET-S + QUAL-BRD} : XP
 33     MASSCONC
 44     firmament
 44     heavens
 66     space
 66     appearance
 66     height
 66     natural phenomena
 88     natural
 88     phenomena
 88     blue - c
 88     cloud - c
 88     celestial - r
```

FIGURE 1b

The headword is coded '#1', the hash indicating that a new slip begins with this record: the 1 signifying a type 1 or pink slip. There follow all other fields, just as they are keyboarded, preceded by some two character code. The first three lines are the headword, category number and slip number. These three together uniquely identify this slip and form the primary key for retrieval in a database system. The category numbers may contain a period to allow two levels of categorization. No definite decision had been made about category numbers when the slip system was set up and we had to allow for the possibility that a three level system might be required. This detail exemplifies the need for caution in preparing a computerised database system – it would be tempting to store the category number as a numerical code in the database, but this would first preclude the possibility of having a category 3.1.2 and second would cause category 3.12 to be placed before category 3.2 in sorted sequence.

The slip number is an example of what we might refer to as housekeeping data: this information is not intended to appear as part of the dictionary entry (unlike the category number) but assists with behind-the-scenes organisation of the data. It will be seen later that careful design is required to ensure that there is enough housekeeping information to manage the dictionary data but not so much that the lexical information is buried in a mass of added computer codes. One undesirable result of housekeeping fields is that the data becomes unreadable to the non-computer personnel.

The definition (code 00) is often very brief (ten words or so) but may be very lengthy. This kind of variation in the data makes standard approaches to data capture less attractive. For example, the widely-used and revered dBase II and III packages allow the micro user to define data fields and to set up a screen display for data entry. However any serious user of micro database packages will know that if one defines a definition field of say, 512 bytes, then the package will allocate 512 bytes for every record even though the average number of data characters may only be, say, 36. The result is that the data fields cannot be squeezed onto the screen display, and the data consumes floppy disk space in a grossly inefficient manner. Ready-made, general-purpose database software for microcomputers we found to be ill-suited for our purposes. Our simple data capture program stores the definition field one line at a time, and the lines are variable length text. On screen, the lines automatically 'wrap over' words which run to the right hand edge of the data field.

The 'inflected forms' field (code 11) in the example contains text enclosed in square brackets. This illustrates how lexicographic demands were met by adopting expedient solutions in the computer handling. The earliest designs gave no opportunity for lexicographers to add informal notes to their entries, but in due course it was agreed that this facility was desirable. The computing options were:

a) to rewrite or modify the existing software to add a new NOTES field *or*
b) to allow notes to be added as square-bracketed text in the unused space of the inflected forms, example or definition fields.

Solution a) would result in the screen display becoming overcrowded, and a major redesign of the data entry program would have been needed. Solution b) though inelegant, could be implemented almost immediately and made fullest use of the 80 column by 24 line standard screen display. The use of square brackets must of course be restricted by the new convention.

The syntax field (code 22) is rather dense and is filled with syntactic expressions constructed from a set of basic symbols. An uneasy compromise had to be struck here between a rigorous formal language and free-format text. No adequate formalism could be designed *a priori*, since the facts of English syntax were yet to be fully uncovered. On the other hand a full description of the syntax of a particular instance of a headword might become very long and verbose if no grammatical terminology or codes were permitted. The resulting code uses a set of uncontroversial labels for noun, verb, count, uncount, adverb, adjective, etc. These may be combined using character symbols for 'followed by', 'preceded by', 'realised as the lexical item x', 'not', etc. The lexicographers are free to combine the codes according to simple combination rules. If further informal comment is needed, then square-bracket notes are permitted as part of the syntax field. The codes can be parsed automatically and thereby permit complex searches to be carried out across the database.

The other data fields may contain lists of words and phrases. This again is a structure of which standard database software takes little account. Lexicographers may wish to list 12 synonyms for a particular slip, each of which might need to be identifiable separately for cross-referencing or searching. These we call 'repeating fields' and they were a continual source of aggravation in the implementation of the database system. At the data entry stage they were easily recorded as lines of text – one entry per line, each line prefaced by the appropriate two character code. Once again, needs arose which were not foreseen at the time of the original design – this much we had expected. So the COLLOCATIONS field (code 88) contains some words with an -r or a -c following them. It became necessary to distinguish three types of lexical relation:

a) collocates – words which *co-occur* significantly with the headwords
b) 'related' words – to which the user of the database is directed, but which are not covered by any of the classical lexical or semantic relations of synonymy, hyponymy, autonymy, etc. *and*
c) other keywords in phrases – to direct the user to another entry to aid look-up.

The bulk of words entered here were of type c, so the -r and -c suffixes were added to the related words (b) and the collocates (a) respectively to distinguish the three types of entry for later processing.

The codes were selected from the standard set of characters for representing text (called *ascii*) so that the file could be treated as a stream format text file on almost any computer. This is unconventional according to received opinion about data processing: conventionally, structured data is handled by the computer operating system in a different way from text data. We chose not to adhere to the usual data processing techniques (fixed length fields, data type and character count fields, record length counts, header records, etc.) since these are often specific to a particular operating system. For example, it is not usually possible to use a standard text editor to view and edit a file containing binary data. Record sequential files often exploit hardware dependent features of the computer, such that 'padding' of data fields may be carried out by the system. On the other hand, a file containing simply a sequence of ascii bytes, although inefficient as a representation of a highly structured record, can be transferred to virtually any machine and processed with a wide range of computer languages. This is the kind of flexibility which was important for this type of work, carried out in the University environment.

The system is characterised by its simplicity: this is partly due to our uncertainty at the time about the final form in which the data would be stored, but it did have the convenient advantage that processing of these files could be quite easily carried out using any of several programming languages having some string handling features: BASIC, ALGOL68R or SNOBOL. One disadvantage with storing our slip data as ascii text is that any program which needs to process the data must 'parse' the input to retrieve the inherent structure. This means simply that, for example, a program reading the slip shown in Figure 1b can only determine the number of synonyms for this record by reading and counting the number of lines which begin with '44'. This is much slower for the computer than if it were reading, say, a structured PL/1 record from a sequential record file managed by the operating system. It also allows more scope for error, since we can imagine that if the lines '44 heavens' and '66 space' become transposed, then a program which reads lines beginning '44' until a line not beginning '44' in order to locate the synonyms will fail in this case.

With the installation of the PDP-based Unix system, the stream format we chose for the storage of keyed slip files proved to be very appropriate. One of the most useful features of the Unix operating system is that it includes a large number of general text handling tools: line editors, stream editors, pattern matching programs, text formatters, sorting and indexing commands, and so on. Once our files were transferred to Unix, they could be checked and manipulated automatically with the absolute minimum of program development. In many cases single commands or small command scripts could be used on the ascii files to sort, retrieve, and modify the data files.

Choosing the Database Management System

In 1983 the project saw the installation of Honeywell/Multics, the appointment of a second computer officer to Cobuild, and the assignment of a Computer Officer from CeCCS to assist with Cobuild computing.

Ian Sedwell joined the Cobuild team after research into Artificial Intelligence at the Open University, and Kumar Tambyraja gave us advice and programming help with the establishment of a database on the Multics system.

The new four-processor Honeywell was vastly more powerful than the 1906A it replaced, and it came with a very large amount of fast disk backing store, 6250 bpi tape units, and a very sophisticated virtual-memory operating system. Unix and Multics share many design concepts and features and since we were already using Unix very successfully the choice of Multics as the mainframe operating system was an excellent one from the Cobuild point of view.

We had already decided that it would not be economical or practical to attempt to write our own database management software. In collaboration with CeCCS we evaluated the two database systems which the Honeywell offered: the Multics Relational Database System (MRDS) and IDS-II. The former is a set of PL/1 routines which form the basis of a relational database package. It has an associated package, Logical Inquiry and Update System (LINUS), which provides a command level interface to MRDS for non-programmers. IDS-II is a CODASYL network database system which was designed for use within Honeywell's GCOS environment. It, too, is a set of programming tools intended to be managed from programs in a host language – COBOL or FORTRAN 77.

We decided to adopt MRDS and LINUS for the lexical database. The arguments for and against were briefly as follows:

For MRDS:
a) a relational database could be designed, defined and set up very easily and quickly, whereas a CODASYL system requires very detailed consideration of physical as well as logical data structure.
b) the structure of a relational database is easily perceived and understood, whereas CODASYL databases can become very complex.
c) MRDS consists of a set of PL/1 routines which are fully compatible with the operating system (which is also coded in PL/1).
d) PL/1 is a programming language more suitable for a wide variety of text processing tasks than COBOL or FORTRAN. The Multics PL/1 compiler includes some enhancements to the standard language, produces efficient code and there are excellent ancilliary software development tools for break-point debugging, execution profiling, library maintenance, etc.
e) data can be moved from one relational database system to another without much difficulty, so that the database is not locked in to the Multics/Honey-well system.
f) MRDS offers a useful command level package for inquiry, update and management of a database, which IDS does not have. This meant that many database operations could be carried out without the cost and effort of providing applications software to handle all the anticipated operations on the data.

For IDS-II:
a) a network database would be able to model more closely the logical structure of a dictionary. Cross-referencing could be achieved by using pointers between data items, for example.
b) the more sophisticated relationship between logical and physical structure of a network database would result in faster response for retrieval and update.
c) COBOL and FORTRAN 77 are available on almost every type of computer system. Both languages are widely used in data processing.
d) IDS offers comprehensive backup and roll-forward routines and transaction logging to assist in maintaining data security.

After careful consideration we adopted the MRDS system. In retrospect, I am convinced that this was a good decision. As with the concordancing problems, we found that a simple programming approach yielded best results. We did not have a team of computer professionals and programmers dedicated to setting up and maintaining the system – in this respect the Cobuild project is typical of University research in arts and humanities which makes use of computational methods – and so we always gave priority to minimising manual effort.

The decision was nevertheless something of a gamble at the time, since the Multics system was new to Birmingham and no ôther university could give us hard information about the relative performance or reliability of MRDS and IDS-II. At that time it was received opinion on relational database systems that they were suitable for small, simple applications but that the perform-ance would deteriorate badly if the database grew large and if the data became too fragmented. We reworked the slip records to minimize the fragmentation of the data, but the database grew to over 120 Mbytes. The speed of MRDS levelled off to an acceptable rate after the first 20 Mbytes. We wrote applications software only for those operations which were going to be regularly required (data entry, basic retrieval, on-screen updating) and relied on LINUS to handle all other demands for access to the data. LINUS is a general-purpose package, designed to be of use to the average user, and it is not particularly fast or efficient. When speed and efficiency became important we found that PL/1 programs could be developed very quickly, thanks to the simple data structures used in a relational system, the excellent PL/1 pro-grammer's tools, and the ease with which the operating system itself could be called to handle many low-level tasks: sorting, process control, interuser communications, etc.

Database Structure

The established slip system was already tending towards a list structure, so the basic design of the database suggested itself immediately. There are three basic tables expressing essential relations in the database: Categories, Examples and Cross-refs. The Cross-refs relation was added to handle retrievals keyed not on the headword but on the contents of the lexical and semantic data fields. Obviously, we would want to retrieve all entries which had a particular word as a synonym or as a collocation, for example. So the Cross-refs relation holds a set of one-to-one links, each one linking a source headword and a target headword. A simplified scheme for the database is shown in Figure 2, with data fields filled for illustration. One additional relation (System) holds housekeeping information for the benefit of the applications programs which access the database, but this can be ignored by the general user.

The database was set up very quickly and simply. Figure 3 shows part of the database definition file which is compiled by MRDS into an empty database. Each relation is defined as a set of fields, one or more of which in combination are designated as the primary key for access. The key fields are indexed for optimum retrieval speed; other fields may be designated for secondary index-ing if retrievals are anticipated, and all other data can be accessed by sequential search.

Applications Software

Almost all applications software was coded in Multics PL/1. This language, in its standard definition, is already a powerful, general-purpose tool, and on the Honeywell it had the tremendous additional advantage of being the language in which the operating system itself is coded. The PL/1 programmer can make use of all the system's subroutines to handle I/O, file storage and manipula-tion, sorting and merging, VDU screen display, 'window' management, etc. Moreover, the compiler supports a number of extra string-handling functions for PL/1 and produces very efficient code.

CATEGORIES

heal 1 to restore to a state of health   V-OD   25476

heap 1 a disorganised pile of objects   N-C   25477

heap 2 to place things in an untidy pile   V-OD   25478

EXAMPLES

heal 1 1 The doctor healed many sick people.
heal 1 2 After six weeks I was fully healed.
heap 1 1 Her clothes lay on the floor in a heap.
heap 2 1 John heaped more potatoes onto his plate.
heap 2 2 I saw bodies heaped in the back of the truck.

CROSS-REFS

cure	1	25476
make better	1	25476
sick	4	25476
wounds	4	25476
pile	1	25477
mound	1	25477
untidy	4	25477

FIGURE 2

relation:

Examples (entry_id* eg_id* eg_num example not_for_dict
gloss syntax style_labels field_labels pragmatics der_word
der_phr),

Categories (entry_id* entry cat_num has_var_spells definition
not_for_dict illustrate infl_forms syntax style_labels
field_labels pragmatics date_in),

Subentries (entry* subentry_of*)

Cross_refs (entry_id* eg_id xref_type* target_entry* target_cat
xp_note),

Var_spells (entry* dict_form),

System (key* value);

index:

Categories (entry),
Cross_refs (target_entry);

FIGURE 3

Data Validation and Entry

The first program required was for data entry. The slip files from the micro-computer had to be validated and then added to the database. I wrote this program to carry out as much automatic checking of the data as was feasible. For instance, the category and slip numbers were sorted and any gaps in the number sequence were reported. Each field was checked to ensure that the format of the data was as expected. The dates which were included in the first record of each slip file were checked to ensure that data was submitted in the correct order, and a slip count, appended to each file by the microcomputer, was cross-checked by the mainframe and any mismatch reported. All these features made it easier to manage the compilation of the dictionary and to avoid loss of data, duplication of effort, and inconsistency in the compiled text. The clerical staff were responsible for looking at the validation phase reports and making corrections. In 90 per cent of cases the errors were mechanical and correction was trivial: in all other cases the lexicographers were consulted about corrections. Normally, no data could be entered in the database if the validation failed.

The Compilation Monitor

The dictionary database was linked to another MRDS database which recorded administrative information about the compilation. This second data-base, the Compilation Monitor, was based on the Headword-Concordance Index and stored, for each headword, details on who compiled the entry on what date, who keyed the slips, who edited the entry, how long the entry was, etc. From this database, the Project Manager was able to produce reports giving comprehensive figures on the percentage of database already com-piled, in process of compilation, keyed, etc. Of particular interest, was the ability to produce statistics on compilation organised by headword group: the group A words were to receive priority attention, while many group F words were rejected as unworthy of inclusion at this stage. The Compilation Moni-tor enabled the team to plan their work so that attention was directed to those areas where it was most required.

As entries were stored in the lexical database they were looked up in the Compilation Monitor. If no corresponding entry was found in the Monitor, the batch of slips was rejected and held for manual checking. This step was designed to prevent misspelt headwords being stored in the database (and inevitably lost, since the primary access key was the headword string). The operator, having verified the rejected headwords would re-submit the slip files after creating entries in the Compilation Monitor for the new headwords which were to be added.

Retrieval

The next major program was for basic retrieval. This program was to provide a means of getting cross-reference information from the database from day to day to accompany the work packs of words to be compiled. For example, if a lexicographer is to compile an entry for the words *true*, *truth*, *truly*, *truism* then the following command is issued:

db_print_entry -wd true truth truly truism -xref -of my_xrefs

The program uses the Cross-refs relation of the database and prints out every entry for which the specified words are target entries. The entries which were the *sources* of these cross-refs are then retrieved from the Categories relation and printed out for the lexicographer in the file 'my_xrefs'. We decided at the inception of the project that this feedback would be a fundamental requirement and, when we set up the database, certain fields of the dictionary slips were designated as cross-reference fields. It was not possible to cross-reference all fields using the one-to-one mapping in the Cross-refs relation since the penalty in terms of increased storage and fragmentation of data was considered too great. Only the fields required for the purposes of compilation were indexed in the separate relation. If data is to be retrieved by searching on other fields, then the search must be done sequentially through each entry in the Categories or Examples relations. This is not an irreversible decision, of course. If demand is such that inefficient sequential searches are frequently being made on the database, then a secondary index can be introduced to speed access, at the expense of more filestore usage and, possibly, further fragmentation of the data.

This cross-reference retrieval was carried out automatically for each headword to be compiled. It is a facility which was extremely valuable for the lexicographers. Many of the inconsistencies and inadequacies of dictionaries compiled without the aid of a computer database were eliminated because of this feature of the compilation process. Near synonyms could be differentiated in their definitions, idiomatic phrases containing more than one fully lexical item were dealt with and cross-referenced consistently, and so on.

The *db print entry* program retrieves entries in a form suitable for printing out on paper. Command line arguments control the retrieval operation, and the following features were programmed:

a) specific headwords to be retrieved could be listed in the command line, or submitted in a file
b) headword and category specification allows retrieval of specific sense categories
c) output may be directed to the VDU or to a file for subsequent editing or printing
d) the -xrefs control argument may be modified with a string of numeric cross-reference types, which limit the retrieval to only the corresponding cross-reference fields
e) a single date or date range may be given instead of an explicit list of headwords. In this case, all entries entered during the specified period are retrieved.

The data entry and retrieval programs provided the fundamental operations, and were used mainly in batch mode. The project clerks were responsible for running regular retrievals, to keep the lexicographers supplied with material and updates as newly compiled entries were entered. The lexicographers had access to terminals in their offices so that they could consult the database whenever they needed to.

Updating

As soon as compilation was running efficiently, we turned our attention to developing an outline browse and update program which was to enable lexicographers to edit database entries at a VDU terminal. We designed and produced a program which made use of the Multics window management subsystem to provide a screen-editor style of database updating. Kumar Tambyraja of CeCCS helped in the design and carried out the programming. The underlying organisation of the data into slips was convenient at this stage, as it had been in designing the data-entry program on the micros. Each screenful of data was laid out, proforma-style, as a slip (similar in layout to the paper slips on which the lexicographers compiled the entries originally). The window management sub-routines allowed protected fields to be defined on the screen, and by the use of the normal cursor-control keys, the user is free to move around the data, inserting and deleting text as required. The aim is to give the users the impression that they are editing free-format text – of course, in practice this is very difficult to achieve. For example, if the user alters a word which occupies one of the cross-reference fields (which generate a special entry in the Cross-refs relation) then that entry must be located, deleted and possibly recreated with a new target. Similarly, the user who wishes to reorder sense categories may simply alter the category numbers on the screen. But as the category number was part of the primary key, used for unique identification of each category entry, then such an alteration would involve inefficient deletion and rehashing of entries. The simple solution was to add an additional data field, not part of the primary key, which contains the visible category number – thereby allowing the hidden, keyed category number to remain constant.

We had to consider, too, the question of data integrity. Allowing the users to alter the text of the entries at whim gave some cause for concern that data may too easily become accidentally corrupted. The software must be very sophisticated and complex if it is to provide sufficient flexibility for the lexicographer while constantly checking the validity of the data and attempting to avoid accidents. In general we erred on the side of flexibility: it was considered intolerable for the lexicographers to be too rigidly constrained in what operations they might perform on the data. We relied on frequent backup of the database and on our own transaction logging routines to restore any accidental loss or misplacement of data.

The final version of the program, *update dict*, was large and put a considerable load on the operating system. We were disappointed at the performance of the program during the prime shift on the Honeywell mainframe. Every character hit on the keyboard has to be interpreted, the window manager is called to adjust the screen display, several retrieve, delete and store operations on the database may be required for one modification and the transaction must be logged. All this activity going on behind the scenes slows the response time for the user and, when the computer is heavily loaded, the on-line update system is frustrating to use. Multics has a very powerful facility for getting an execution profile of PL/1 programs, and we are using this to gain some insight into which operations are consuming the most processor time on average. This information should help us to optimise the program and improve its efficiency.

These three applications programs – *valid slips, db print entry* and *update dict* – constitute the basic dictionary database package. A number of additional PL/1 programs were written during the course of the project in order to facilitate the management of the database.

Dictionary Extraction and Editing

Consistent with Cobuild's design principles, the database, after four years of compilation, was far more detailed and schematic than the planned printed dictionary. The next stage of the project, then, was to convert the database information into a form suitable for publication as a one-volume learners' dictionary. The database entries had not been thoroughly edited to bring them into line with the lexicographic policy as it was finally formulated, so that a complete edit of the data was needed. It was decided that this editing process should be carried out on text extracted from the database, rather than on the database itself. On the one hand we were concerned not to reduce the information contained in the database by editing it down to a specification which was imposed by the constraints of the printed learners' dictionary. On the other, we did not want to spend valuable time editing material in the database which would appear in quite a different form on the printed page. It was agreed, then, that we would write an extraction program to create a preliminary version of the dictionary text in alphabetic sequence.

This program, though very simple in principle, turned out to be fairly complex. For example, the printed book shows all word forms of the head-word lemma in full after the boldface headword and pronunciation. The database records only the irregular inflexions, so that the extraction program had to generate all the regular inflexions by rule. This, of course, threw up many instances of omission in the database! One memorable entry began: *went* /wɛnt/ *wents, wenting, wented . . . . . .*

One interesting feature of the *extract* program was that it made an attempt to convert the definition recorded in the database into the prose style of definition which is to be found in the Cobuild dictionary (for an account of the dictionary definition style see Chapter 6). The computer program used the syntax information associated with each sense category to generate an appropriate phraseology for the formulaic beginning of each definition. If, for example, the database entry for NOMINATE contains the information that this verb takes an object and the object is usually a person, then the computer employs the formula: 'If you *nominate* someone, you . . .' Of course, in many cases the computer would phrase the definition incorrectly, but it was agreed that overall there was a significant saving of manual effort in making these editorial modifications.

The *extract* program inserted appropriate codes into the data files to mark the typographical features of the dictionary text. The fields of the database correspond to the logical units of information in a dictionary article, and the computer is able for the most part to determine which typeface is required for each data field extracted from the database.

The extracted text was only an approximation to the final dictionary layout. For some entries complete revision of the categorisation, rewording of definitions and different placement of idiomatic phrases or figurative meaning extensions were required to achieve the best possible presentation on the printed page. The extracted text had to be reduced in overall length and the details of features such as definition style and centre column layout had to be revised after the preliminary typeset samples had been obtained.

The database entries were extracted into a large number of fairly short text files in alphabetical sequence. These files were edited on-line by the lexicographic team who used the powerful *emacs* text editor to rework the dictionary entries. The *emacs* editor was particularly well suited to the very specialised work of dictionary editing since it allows user-defined macros to be set up and bound to the function keys of the VDU keyboard. These macros are actually short programs (written in LISP style) which may be arbitrarily complex. Using this facility, it was possible to customise the *emacs* editor to perform elaborate editing operations on the dictionary text with single keystrokes.

Although the work of editing out a dictionary to meet the publishers' specification was not carried out directly on the lexical database, nevertheless the computer played an important role in assisting with the management of the editorial process. The Multics electronic mail system was used by the lexicographers to deliver editorial 'notes' to each other, via a central mailbox. An editor wishing to draw attention to some aspect of, say, cross-referencing or grammatical coding would send a message to the central mailbox, with the appropriate headword as its primary access field. Other lexicographers consult the mailbox to retrieve any messages relevant to the entries they are working on.

The computer was also able to carry out a number of exhaustive checks on cross referencing and on the vocabulary of definition and examples in the dictionary text. First a complete list of *all* headwords, lozenge words, inflected forms and compounds was drawn from the dictionary text files. Eileen Fitzgerald wrote a program to process the dictionary text, looking up all the synonym, antonym, superordinate and lexical cross-references from the Extra Column and reporting any which could not be found as headword entries in the dictionary. A second pass through the files performed a similar operation on the definition and example text: the computer would identify and report any entry containing a word in the definition or example which was not found in the lookup wordlist. Of course, the output was checked by a lexicographer whose responsibility it was to assess the error report and to take appropriate editorial action.

Draft typesetting

The project was fortunate to have access to the University's Compugraphic MCS8400 computer typsetting equipment. This phototypesetter is connected to the Honeywell and is driven by the Multics document composition software. The text files of the dictionary already contained embedded codes to mark all the relevant typographical features: bold face, italic, special symbols, small caps, etc. It is a trivial operation to replace these codes automatically with commands to be interpreted by the Compugraphic typesetter, and to send the text file to be phototypeset. The turnaround time can be as low as four hours, but generally typeset dictionary text on bromide paper was available to the lexicographer within 24 hours.

This facility compensated somewhat for the fact that the editing of the dictionary text files had to be carried out on standard, medium-resolution VDU screens without any WYSIWYG (What You See Is What You Get) capability. It also enabled the lexicographers to experiment freely with the typography of the dictionary, to gather the opinions of TEFL teachers about the layout and to make revisions where necessary.

Conclusion

As we anticipated at the outset, using computer techniques extensively to build a substantial corpus of English text, to analyse it objectively and exhaustively, and to capture the insights gained from that analysis in an electronic database has moved the science of lexicography into a new phase. The power of the machine to store, search, classify, sort and otherwise manipulate language data in vast quantities liberates the study of language, much in the same way as the technology of the electron microscope opens new vistas for the researcher into physics and the natural sciences.

The *Collins Cobuild English Language Dictionary* is only the first fruit of a project which has developed a range of computer-based resources for processing English language corpora and has built a comprehensive database which has great potential as the foundation for many reference and language teaching publications.

References

Berry-Rogghe, G. L. M. 1973. 'COCOA: A Word Count and Concordance Generator'. *ALLC Bulletin* Vol. 1.

Hockey, S. and **I. Marriott**. 1979. 'The Oxford Concordance Project', *ALLC Bulletin*, Vol. 7 and Vol. 8 (1980).

Johansson, S. 1980. 'The LOB Corpus of British English Texts: Presentation and Comments', *ALLC Journal*.

Kucera, H. and **W. Nelson Francis**. 1967. *Computational Analysis of Present Day American English*. Brown University Press, Providence, Rhode Island.

Reed, A. and **L. Schonfelder**. 1979. 'CLOC: A General-Purpose Concordance and Collocations Generator' in *Advances in Literary and Linguistic Research*, D. Ager, F. Knowles and J. Smith (eds). Department of Modern Languages, University of Aston in Birmingham.

CHAPTER 3: **The Process of Compilation**

Ramesh Krishnamurthy

Although this paper is intended to be a factual account of the process of the compilation of the *Collins Cobuild English Language Dictionary* as it actually happened, and not a discussion of theories about how best to set about compiling a dictionary, it may be useful to look briefly at the following passages, in order to place our methods and decisions in some kind of context.

Zgusta (1971) gives us a theoretical model for compilation when he breaks down 'the work to be done by the lexicographer' into four main tasks: '1. the collection of material 2. the selection of entries 3. the construction of entries 4. the arrangement of the entries.'

For the details of the tasks involved, we can compare the following two accounts, widely separated in historical terms:

In 1791, Boswell gave the following description of how Johnson put together his dictionary: 'The words, partly taken from other dictionaries, and partly supplied by himself, having first been written down with spaces left between them, he delivered in writing their etymologies, definitions, and various significations. The authorities were copied from the books themselves, in which he had marked the passages with a black-lead pencil . . .'

Kipfer (1984) outlines the practicalities of current techniques of dictionary-making: 'Most users believe that the lexicographer simply sits down and "writes" a dictionary. This is far from true! The dictionary editors conduct a reading program, excerpting quotations (citations) from . . . written . . . and . . . spoken sources. These citations . . . may be stored in computer . . . The editors take all the slips for the word and divide them into the different senses, then use them to write the actual definitions . . . A dictionary is a record of actual usage.'

Apart from the reference to 'etymologies' in the quotation from Boswell, which is a feature not relevant to synchronic learners' dictionaries such as the Cobuild dictionary, the main elements of the process of compilation have remained constant since his time. Kipfer, with her reference to a rudimentary computer-held corpus of data, comes closer to describing the process of compilation as it actually occurred at Cobuild.

For the purposes of this paper, I propose to consider the process of compilation in two main sections: resources and process. Some illustrations of output are given in the Appendix.

Resources

The Cobuild lexicographer had at her or his disposal the following major resources: the corpus, policy papers, works of reference, expert linguists in the Birmingham University English Department, native-speaker informants, and the computer.

The Corpus

In the Cobuild Dictionary project, the first of the tasks listed by Zgusta, 'the collection of material', remained largely out of the hands of the lexicographers throughout, because a concordanced corpus of 7.3 million words (six million words of written text and 1.3 million words of transcribed speech) was extracted from the Birmingham Collection of English Text and made available to lexicographers in the form of microfiches and 'hard copy' (printed pages). A more detailed description of the corpus and its development is found in Chapter 1.

The concordances, representing the 'authorities' in Boswell's terms or the 'citations' in the quote from Kipfer, were the primary tool of lexicographers on the Cobuild project and where the evidence of the corpus was clear, its influence on the dictionary entry was always decisive. Not only were the concordances unique to Cobuild, but the project was the first to work directly from such a large body of evidence stored in this form.

In the later stages of compiling and for both of the on-line editing phases, fiches of concordances were available from a corpus of about 20 million words for forms with fewer than 50 occurrences in the 7.3 million word corpus (for example, for the form *bereaved*, there were only six concordance lines in the 7.3 million corpus, but a further 25 lines came from the larger corpus).

In addition, where further guidance was required on the way in which a particular lexical item was commonly used in EFL coursebooks, etc., access to the TEFL Side Corpus was provided (for example, there were 11 lines for the word 'adjective' in the 7.3 million, 23 more in the 20 million, and 65 in the TEFL Side Corpus; the comparable figures for the form *illustrating* were 7, 17, and 26).

Frequently occurring words present a great problem for lexicographers in trying to analyse the evidence. As Murray (1888) says, '. . . with the larger articles, as those on *at, by, but, be, bear, break* . . . the mere study of the result, arranged in some degree of order, gives little idea of the toil and difficulties encountered in bringing into this condition what was at first a shapeless mass of many thousand quotations.'

At Cobuild, this problem was greatly reduced by the creation of a sampling program that provided any specified proportion of concordance lines on an 'every nth line' basis for any frequently occurring items for which the total concordances were too numerous to be easily analysed by lexicographers.

The standard concordance line consisted of 100 characters with the keyword in the middle, and the lines were normally presented in alphabetical order of the first character of the word following the keyword. A set of codes at the left of each line indicated whether the line was from the spoken or written part of the corpus, the nationality of the author and the country of publication, and the specific text or transcript from which the line was taken. Thus the lexicographer was given some guidance as to the language mode, register, and possible regionality of each line.

However, for words such as conjunctions, discourse organisers, or signal words that required a longer context for proper analysis or appropriate exemplification, a program was written to produce a selection of longer concordances from a one million word sub-corpus. For the word *as* therefore, the longer concordances produced the following long examples which eventually found their way into the dictionary text: 'Napalm should be banned, as should the development, production, and stockpiling of all chemical weapons.' 'He was totally unprepared, as is the way with American he-men, for anything that could not be settled with a fist or a gun.' 'He thinks he would like to teach, but as his subjects are Greek and Moral Philosophy he's not likely to find a job.' 'The mother (as if she didn't have enough to do already!) has to remember to pay some attention to her husband.'

For some indication of lexical words that might fall into this group, see Eugene Winter's list of 'Vocabulary 3' items: *Proposed Lexical Items of Connection* (1978) which includes such words as *basis, case, cause, compare, condition, distinction, matter, instance, point, reason, way,* etc. Examples selected for the final dictionary text again show the advantage of being able to have available the longer concordance lines: for *reason*, 'Public pressure is towards more street lighting rather than less: the reason is, of course, that people feel safer in well-lit streets.'; and for *way*, 'I've been given six months to do the job. A week one way or the other will make no real difference.' The longer examples preserve the naturalness of the type of discourse in which these 'Lexical Items of Connection' operate.

The same program that produced the longer concordance lines also offered the facility for alphabetically ordering the concordance lines by the character string to the left of the keyword, so that leftward collocations such as preceding prepositions, determiners, quantifiers, modifiers, or other lexical items were more easily identified.

This was very useful in the analysis of a word like *time*, for example, which often figures at the rightmost end of phrases and prepositional groups. There are 9,481 lines for *time* in the 7.3 million word corpus (which is in itself a daunting number of lines for any lexicographer to scrutinise), and 1,594 in the one million sub-corpus. By selecting just 300 of these, the following leftward collocations emerged: 16 lines for *at the same time*, 14 for *all the time*, 13 for *at the time*, 13 for *a long time*, 11 for *for the first time*, and so on. Phrases such as *once upon a time* and *one . . . at a time* were also easier to spot, even when there were only one or two lines for them.

Finally, concordances were produced for second elements in compound words where a hyphen provided the element-break marker, so that entries for combining forms such as *-toothed, -looking,* etc. could be compiled.

The optical scanning process, by which much of the corpus was input to the computer, produced a fair number of misreadings (e.g. 200 concordance lines for *going* were found under the form 'gong', lines for *well* under 'weli' and for THE under 'thc'). Proof-reading has been carried out subsequently.

The lexicographer was still left facing the problem of identifying multi-word items in which the words did not appear consecutively in the text, such as phrases with considerable lexical variation (e.g. 'shake someone by the hand, shake someone's hand, shake hands with someone, etc.') or phrases with 'open slots' into which any of a set of lexical items can be inserted (e.g. 'a fisherman's **dream**, a footballer's **dream**, a politician's **dream**, etc.'), and, of course, separable phrasal verbs (e.g. *put off* as in lines such as 'some deliberate ploy to put the reader off', 'They decided to put the whole thing off until the following day', etc.)

Policy Papers

Lexicographic policy had been developed from 1981 onwards by experimentation and trial compilation. A set of policy papers was gradually established which encapsulated the Cobuild house style.

In the latter half of 1983, a thorough review of policy was undertaken and the results incorporated in a revised set of policy papers. These aimed to deal with the problems raised by the old policy papers, to clarify policy where divergent interpretations or ambiguities had become apparent, to bring the compilation of the dictionary database more into line with the requirements of the dictionary itself, and to fill gaps in policy and make explicit policies that had developed over the previous two years.

These new policy papers formed the basis for all subsequent compilation and policies remained fairly fixed from this point on, apart from a few minor modifications (e.g. the addition of swh as an abbreviation for *somewhere* in phrases that required a following adjunct of place or direction) and a few architectural changes in the dictionary database which were effected by program (for example two-word compounds such as *driving licence* and *green belt*, previously held as phrases, became headwords in their own right, and phrasal verbs such as *drive off* and *swear by* held as 'phrases' became categories and were tagged in a look-up table that enabled the phrasal verbs to be output as sub-entries).

Eventually, in 1985–6, many of the entries that had been compiled under the old policy were recompiled so that the whole of the database reflected a consistent policy.

The policy papers issued in late 1983 consisted of 32 papers, each dealing with a particular topic:

1. The headword list and selection of senses. The main criterion for inclusion or exclusion of headwords and senses was the strength of the corpus evidence.

2. The slip The type of information to be recorded on the computer input slips and the number of characters available in each field was explained as well as the mechanics for arranging and numbering the slips in a sequence (see Appendix 2 for slip formats).

3. Headwords, lozenge words, and second alpha order. The criteria for treating lexical items as headwords, derived words (lozenge words in Cobuild terms because of the symbol that was generated to indicate such words in the dictionary), or phrasal verbs (which were to appear in a subsidiary alphabetical order at the end of headword categories, hence 'second alpha order') were set out. There was a list of acceptable suffixes (e.g. *-ly, -ness*, etc.) for items treated as derived words, and rules for when such derived words were to be treated as headwords.

4. Categorisation. The categorisation of a word was primarily based on semantics. Differences of word-class and syntax were used as the basis for creating sub-categories. Ordering of categories depended mainly on frequency of occurrence in the corpus data, with concrete or literal senses preceding abstract or metaphorical ones, while maintaining some cohesion in the semantic flow through the entry.

5. Definitions. Definition style was fairly rigorously laid down, with the main emphases on accuracy and clarity while avoiding difficult vocabulary and constructions. The main principle of definition consisted of providing a genus word and then supplying sufficient differentiae to distinguish the headword from its near-synonyms. For further details see Chapter six.

6. Usage restrictions that affect definitions. Where there were severe syntax restrictions on a word or sense, for example a verb that was only used in the passive, the commonest syntactic structure was defined rather than the headword form.

7. Examples. Examples for a word or sense were selected in order to show typical usage, involving syntactic patterns, regular collocations, and appropriate contexts, rather than to clarify or extend the definition. They were taken from the concordances wherever possible, but slight modification was permissible.

8. Phrases. Three basic types of phrases were isolated: fixed phrases (e.g. *by and large* and *once in a while*), syntactic phrases (e.g. *on ONE'S own* and *give SB the pip*), and lexical phrases (e.g. *now and then, now and again* and *a good deal, a great deal*). Multi-word items functioning as prepositions (e.g. *in relation to*) or subordinating conjunctions (e.g. *on the grounds that*) were also covered.

Guidance was given on how to define phrases, at which element to place them, and where to place them within an entry. Polysemous phrases and phrases with pragmatic import were discussed. The distinction between phrases, compounds, and collocational or syntactic patterns was indicated.

9. General syntax. The system of syntax notation was specially developed to allow lexicographers to record not only word-classes and paradigmatic syntactic variations, but also individual syntagmatic sequences. This was achieved by the use of a number of labels or 'primitives' linked by a small set of logical or relational symbols or 'connectors' according to fixed conventions.

The labels included the usual vb for verb, n for noun, adj for adjective, etc., but also QUAL-BRD for broad qualifiers (including demonstratives, possessives, modifying adjectives, and qualifying adjuncts or clauses), NEG-BRD for broad negatives (including strict negatives such as *no* and *not*, adverbs like *seldom*, and some uses of items such as *few* and *only*), etc.

The connectors included such symbols as:

+ = followed by or having in its environment

~ = usually used in a particular tense, functioning as a particular syntactic unit, etc.

/ = realised lexically as

( ) = optional feature or element

< > = composed of or functioning as.

Thus, typical notations for items included such strings of labels and connectors as:

N-AN//S = noun always with the determiner *a* or *an* and never used in the plural

V+PREP/FOR = intransitive verb always followed by the preposition *for*

PHR-VB<V-OD+ADV> = phrasal verb composed of a transitive verb and an adverb and

ADJ-EAP+NEG-BRD = qualitative adjective used in both attributive and predicative positions and always having a broad negative in its environment.

To ensure maximum flexibility, wherever the syntax notation system or indeed any other aspect of policy was felt to be inadequate to cope with a particular piece of information, the letters XP were written on the appropriate part of the computer input slip and a note written within square brackets wherever on the slip there was sufficient space.

10. Nouns. The syntactic coding for a noun involved compulsory recording of information regarding number, use with determiners, and countability. Syntactic requirements (e.g. always followed by the preposition *of* or a *that* clause) were also a matter for compulsory recording.

Additional syntactic information could be recorded by using labels indicating that it functions as an itemiser or quantifier, refers to a container or to the amount contained, is a proper noun, is used in titles or forms of address, etc.

Guidance was also given on the treatment of plural nouns, the nominal use of adjectives and participles, and nouns that typically occur in a particular clause position or that can be used in the singular or plural with no semantic difference and no real denotation of number.

11. Compounds. The distinction was drawn between nominal compounds, phrases, and nouns used to modify other nouns. The criteria included the transparency of the combination, given the individual meaning of the elements, and whether a clear paradigm operated at both slots. The commonest orthographic form of a compound (i.e. one word, two words, or hyphenated) was always indicated.

12. Adjectives. The primary sub-divisions of adjectives was into qualitative adjectives, colour adjectives, and classifying adjectives. The positions they could occur in (i.e. premodifying, predicative, and postnominal) were an essential part of their syntax notation.

Adjectives commonly used as the head of verbless clauses (e.g. *nervous and trembling, he opened the letter*), after *it is*, or before a clause introduced by *that, who, if*, etc. were given a separate notation.

The use of adjectives in the comparative and superlative, as nouns, or as object complements (e.g. *He cut the bread thick*), and the recording of adjectival inflections were also dealt with.

13. Adverbs. Only four main types of adverb were recorded for the database: adverbs that could modify an adjective, another adverb, or a verb; adverbs of degree; sentence adverbs (or disjuncts); and broad negative adverbs (e.g. *hardly* in *He was hardly able to speak*). Further information could be recorded by using the general syntax notation (e.g. to note that *asunder* always follows the verb it modifies) or adding a special note, for example to indicate aspective adverbs such as *technically* and *financially*.

14. Verbs. Verbs probably have the widest range of syntactic variability in their environment and this was reflected in the policy paper on verbs. Transitivity was obviously one of the key features to record, and the basic symbols used were v for intransitive verbs (or, to be more precise, verbs which cannot take a lexical object, but may take a clause, infinitive, or participle as object or be followed by a complement) and v-OD for transitive verbs.

In addition to these, labels could be added to specify di-transitives, ergatives, reflexives, performatives, reporting verbs, modals, auxiliaries, verbs that have impersonal subjects (such as *it, there* or *what*), cognate objects, etc.

Problem areas such as delexical verbs (e.g. *heave* in *heave a sigh*) and compound verbs (e.g. *bulk buy*) were also discussed. Features of the syntactic environment, for example infinitives, participles, complements, *that* clauses, adjuncts, etc. could be indicated using the general syntax labels. Usage restrictions such as for verbs never used or always used in a particular tense or mood were also coded, as well as syntactic patterns. Inflections were dealt with in paper 21.

15. Phrasal verbs. Distinguishing phrasal verbs from literal combinations (e.g. *refer to* and *face forward*) and completive combinations where the adverb simply added a sense of 'completely', 'repeatedly', or 'intensively' (e.g. *deal out* (*cards*)) was a problem, and depended on such criteria as whether the same verb occurred in the same meaning independently or with a range of other particles or adverbial phrases, and whether the particle occurred in the same meaning with other verbs.

Phrasal verbs were held as categories in their own right at the end of the main entry for the headword. Restrictions on the separability of the particle from the verb or on the possibility of passivization were also noted. Infrequent combinations such as *throw overboard* and *throw open* were treated as phrases.

16. Participles. Participles were also a problem area, and the paper discussed how to deal with the adjectival use of a present or past participle, when to treat it as a main entry, a derived word, or merely as an example within a verb category. The distinction between adjectival past participles and passive verbs was discussed. Guidance was also given for dealing with participles used as combining forms or nouns.

17. Combining forms. Lexical items (e.g. *-toothed* and *-looking*), often participles, that were used productively in the formation of compounds were treated as main entries. Different information was recorded at each element, depending on which was the productive one.

18. Prepositions. Most of the common, single-word prepositions were compiled as a set in a separate special operation. Prepositional phrases (e.g. *on account of*) and prepositions derived from other lexical items (e.g. *considering*) were treated as separate categories or as main entries.

19. Conjunctions. All the co-ordinating conjunctions and most of the single-word subordinating conjunctions were compiled separately as a set, so only phrases functioning as conjunctions (e.g. *on the grounds that*) and conjunctions derived from other lexical items (e.g. *considering* when followed by *that*) were discussed.

20. Interjections. The label for interjections could be used for categories, phrases, or individual examples.

21. Inflections. Inflections for verbs, nouns, adjectives, and adverbs were discussed. For each word-class, the regular inflections were prescribed and needed no notation. Common but irregular inflections and variations between American and British English forms (e.g. *traveling* and *travelling*) were coded. Highly irregular inflections were given in full (e.g. for *go*) and any alternatives were noted (e.g. *learned* and *learnt*).

Inflectional information was only given for the first category of each word-class in an entry and was assumed to be the same for all other categories having the same word-class unless new information was supplied. If it was, it only applied to the category for which it was given and had to be repeated if it applied to more than one category.

The last element of a compound was assumed to inflect, and the information given depended on the policy for its word-class. Any irregularities were given in full. Phrasal verbs were not given inflections unless there was any change from the inflections given in the main entry.

Irregular inflected forms were treated as main entries (or categories in the case of homographs such as *bore*) and cross-referred to the uninflected form.

22. Pronunciation. Although lexicographers were not responsible for supplying the phonetics at the compilation stage, we had to indicate any change in pronunciation within an entry at the relevant category (e.g. for *contest*, at the first verb category after the noun categories or vice versa). For abbreviations, truncated forms, acronyms, etc., a note was required about whether the form was pronounced as individual letters, as a word, as the expanded form, etc. Alternative pronunciations were noted.

23. Synonyms, antonyms, and superordinates. We were given guidance on the selection and recording of these semantically related items for a category, phrase, derived word, or for an individual example. Database cross-references were made to the individual elements of any multi-word items entered.

A crude notion of core meaning elements in definitions was established and synonyms were expected where possible to share, and antonyms to be antonymous to, most of the core elements, to be the same word-class or phrase type, and close in register. Synonyms would therefore be near-synonyms of each other, but antonyms might be antonymous to different core elements.

Given any necessary syntactic adjustments, synonyms for an example were to be substitutable for the headword in it without much change in register. Antonyms were to be substitutable for the headword plus a negative.

The principle of superordinateness was founded on an equally crude model of lexis in which, for example, *scottie, terrier, dog, canine, and mammal* belong to adjacent levels in a hierarchy, and therefore *terrier* is the superordinate for *scottie, dog* for *terrier* and so on.

Only one superordinate was allowed for each category or example and had to be the same word-class as the headword, could not also appear as a synonym, but could also appear as a semantic field label.

24. Field. The term *field* referred to the semantic field of a word. Items entered under this heading were to be nouns or nominal groups, for ease of retrieval and future use. The number of items was restricted by the number of characters available on the computer input slip. Field labels were chosen from the next level up in the hierarchical notion of lexis used for superordinateness.

Thus for *bad-tempered*, field labels would probably include *people, charac-ter, behaviour, and irritation*. Despite the freedom allowed to us in the selection of field labels, early reviews of the database revealed that we were being remarkably consistent in our choices.

25. Style. Style labels indicated how a word was used, for example whether its use was more prominent in a particular geographical region, in speech or in writing, in formal, informal, or intimate situations or contexts.

Some labels indicated the attitude of the user (e.g. rude, pejorative, offensive, euphemistic, approving, or humorous), others the likely type of user (e.g. children, or a particular group or profession, such as criminals, journalists, sportsmen, computer staff, doctors, lawyers, or poets). Archaic, old-fashioned, current or neologistic uses were labelled, as were trademarks, proverbs, cliches, metaphoric usages and non-standard usages. Multiple labels could indicate simultaneous or alternative features.

26. Pragmatics. During the early stages of compiling, the need to record the pragmatic force or effect of a word or utterance became evident, and a range of methods was developed to allow this. Explicit performative verbs (e.g. *object, agree, promise and predict*), concealed performatives (e.g. *Please accept my sincere apologies = I apologise sincerely*), and implied performa-tives (e.g. *I didn't mean to be rude = I apologise*) were identified and labelled.

Where the pragmatic function of an utterance was not so evident, but the pragmatic effect on the listener or reader could be assessed, this was noted (e.g. the persuasive effect of *I'd be really grateful if you could help me*). Other such effects included dissuasion, deception, encouragement, and bribery.

Utterances indicating the relationship of a speaker or writer to their discourse, e.g. commenting on it, structuring it, or moving it from one idea or subject to the next were also noted. These were often signalled in written text by occurring at the beginning of a sentence or between commas or dashes (e.g. *actually* in *Actually, I don't think that's quite right* politely signals the correction about to be made). Phrases such as *by the way, so to speak*, or *and so on*, and closed-set turns such as *Thanks* and *Do* were also noted for their pragmatic effect.

27. Collocates. The definition of regular or significant collocates was 'lexical items occurring within five words either way of the headword with a greater frequency than the law of averages would lead you to expect'. The impor-tance of collocation was stressed and we were asked to record these items in dictionary examples. Function words such as prepositions, determiners, pro-nouns and auxiliaries were ignored, but delexical verbs were significant. Collocation was established only on the basis of corpus evidence.

28. + box. The '+ box' on the computer input slip was used to record collocates, related words (e.g. *night* and *nocturnal*), items other than the headword in phrases, compounds, and combining forms, and elements of multi-word items recorded as synonyms, antonyms and superordinates. It could also be used to generate a cross-reference to any item whose compiler might benefit from information recorded at the source entry.

29. Cross-references. This summarised the information on cross-references given in other papers and gave a few more cases where they were needed. For example, internal database cross-references were automatically generated by any item entered as a synonym, antonym, or superordinate, and any item in the '+ box' (see 28 above).

Surface or text cross-references were intended to appear in the dictionary text to indicate to the user where a particular word, phrase, or sense was treated. Where known, the particular category of the target word was given. A less common synonym or synonymic multi-word item could be defined simply as 'another word for . . .' or 'another expression for . . .'. Stylistic or regional restrictions could be specified (e.g. 'a formal word for . . .', 'an American word for . . .'). Headwords also appearing as derived words in another entry had to cross-refer to them. Polysemous phrases in different categories of an entry cross-referred to one another. Semantic confusables (e.g. *foetus* and *embryo*), irregular inflections, and alternative spellings and forms required cross-references, as did phrasal verbs and their nominalizations (e.g. *take over* and *takeover*).

30. Alternative spellings and forms. The full entry for a word appeared at its commonest spelling or form and a cross-reference was placed at the other spelling(s) or form(s). Concordance lines selected as examples retained the original spelling or form. No examples were given at the less common spelling(s) or form(s).

Details were given for alternatives of the *despatch/dispatch* type, for American spellings (e.g. *color* for *colour*), for British spellings (e.g. *gaol* for *jail*), for polysyllabic verbs ending in *-ise* and *-ize* (with a few exceptions, *-ize* was the preferred main form), and initial capitals (merely exemplifed if infrequent, but treated in a separate category where always capitalised in a particular sense). Derived words and phrasal verbs did not show any alternative spellings. Items written as one word, two words, or hyphenated, were compiled at their commonest form and the alternatives mentioned if common. A compound and one of its elements (e.g. *scuttle* and *coal scuttle*, *thermos flask* and *thermos*) or a shortened and unshortened form (e.g. *bra* and *brassiere*) were treated as synonyms where appropriate.

31. Abbreviations and acronyms. No distinction was made between abbreviations and acronyms. Most abbreviations were compiled in a separate operation, so we needed only to attend to extremely common ones (e.g. TV) or homographs of items being compiled (e.g. salt and SALT). The presence or absence of full stops was ignored. Pronunciation was indicated (i.e. whether an abbreviation was pronounced as letters, as a word, or as the expanded form). Definitions were supplied if the abbreviation was the commonest form, otherwise only a cross-reference was needed. Inflections (e.g. *pp* as the plural of *p* meaning page) and syntax were stated as for any other item and polysemous abbreviations were categorised as any other headword.

32. Illustrations. At the compilation stage, the dictionary was expected to have illustrations, so wherever an item was felt to need one, it was so marked.

Works of Reference

These included most of the reference tools that any linguistic project in the English language might need to consult on occasion.

At our disposal were the major international dictionaries such as *The Oxford English Dictionary* and its Supplements, various editions of Webster, a range of dictionaries produced by Oxford University Press and Longman for native-speakers and EFL learners, and of course, as funding publishers, a large selection of Collins dictionaries, including bilingual ones (as many of the lexicographers had a foreign language at degree level) and especially the *Collins English Dictionary*.

We also had recourse on occasions to various grammars of English, especially Quirk et al., as well as to thesauri, usage books, and EFL coursebooks. There was a reasonable selection of encyclopedias, specialist dictionaries such as the Penguin series, volumes on sport, wildlife, and other technical subjects. We had numerous works, including journals, articles and papers, covering the theoretical aspects of lexicography. Any gaps in our in-house collection were usually readily filled by the University Library.

All of these were, of course, secondary tools, and consulted only after inspection and analysis of the corpus data.

Expert Linguists in the Birmingham University English Department

The project was part of English Language Research (ELR) within the English Department of the University, and consequently we could call on assistance from colleagues in the department. They conducted seminars in various aspects of syntax, lexis, and discourse, and lexicographers attended specialist seminars at ELR. Various members of ELR also gave us guidance on specific types of lexical item such as discourse organisers, disjuncts, etc. Numerous visitors to the project and outside speakers gave us valuable insights into different areas of language, both theoretical and practical.

Native-Speaker Informants

Under this heading I would include not only the informal and frequent consultations between fellow-lexicographers on the Cobuild project, during which personal intuitions could be tested and confirmed or rejected, but also the various forms of language input that we all encounter in daily life. Newspapers, radio and television programmes, advertising material, overheard conversations, etc., often helped to fill the occasional gaps in the corpus data.

Information acquired in this way always remained a minor and usually secondary input, but was extremely useful in the area of neologisms or new senses of existing items (e.g. *massage* in the expression *massaging statistics*), or for the more colloquial and spoken lexical items. For a period of time, a 'neologisms file' was maintained and regularly updated to provide references for words that had acquired recent importance.

However, queries on some items could not be resolved even from data of this kind: for example, when trying to ascertain whether the term *L plates* (for the signs required to be displayed on a car being driven by a learner driver in Britain) was normally written with a hyphen (*L-plates*) or not, a thorough scrutiny of *The Highway Code* and *Advice for Learner Drivers* (the two official HMSO publications that might have yielded some evidence) failed to provide even a single occurrence of the term, although the displaying of *L plates* is a legal requirement!

The Computer

As already mentioned in the section headed The Corpus, the computer allowed us to gain access to the data in the corpora in various different ways.

As compiling progressed and data was input to the dictionary database, programs were written to provide screen or printed output of database entries. Thus increasing evidence became available from words already compiled by fellow-lexicographers.

Eventually, the computer was used to generate automatically, for any word about to be compiled, printouts of cross-references from other related items together with the relevant parts of the database entries for those items (for example, for the other elements in a phrase, for collocates, for synonyms, etc.), and these were issued to lexicographers with each batch of words to be compiled and the relevant concordances.

Facilities for interrogating the dictionary database using almost any item (e.g. a syntax pattern, a particular lexical item entered as a synonym, etc.) were made available from an early stage and these facilities were refined and extended as the need arose. They proved invaluable in standardising syntax notation during the extraction of the dictionary from the dictionary database.

Information could also be retrieved from the compilation monitor database, such as the headword list itself, or details about which lexicographer had compiled a word and when, how many concordance lines there were for a headword in the 7.3 million word corpus, and in which of the three dictionaries and three TEFL sources (from which the headword framework had been created) the headword occurred.

The computer was used to overhaul the dictionary database prior to extraction of the dictionary, and became the central tool of the project during the editing stages, when most of the work was carried out on-line. Fuller details of the role of the computer in the Cobuild project are found in Chapter 2.

Process

The following two sections roughly cover the second area of the lexicographer's task as defined by Zgusta, namely 'the selection of entries'.

Allocation of Items to Lexicographers

The creation of a headword list for the dictionary database and its use as the basis for the compilation monitor database (for details see Chapter 2) meant that words could be allocated to lexicographers with a great degree of flexibility and efficiency. Batches of words could be selected from an alphabetic sequence, or on the basis of semantic similarity, or because they belonged to a closed or restricted set. Words could be selected by the project controller or by the lexicographer, and the risks of omission of a headword or duplication of effort were vastly reduced.

Concordances: ('First catch your hare, hares, haring and hared')

For each item allocated to lexicographers, concordances were issued to them or could be selected by them from the 'hard copy library'. The first task of the lexicographer was therefore to ensure that concordances for all the relevant forms of the headword being compiled were to hand. For example, the singular and plural forms for nouns; base, comparative, and superlative forms for adjectives; all tense and participle forms for verbs.

This was especially important for irregular words such as *child/children*, *buy/bought*, etc. Forms ending in apostrophe and *s* were separately concordanced, as the computer notion of keyword was a simple 'string of characters between spaces'. An initial capital letter was not a problem as such occurrences were concordanced along with initial lower case ones. Nominal compounds presented a further problem, as they could appear in three separate sets of concordances (i.e. as one word, hyphenated, or as two words). Alternative spellings such as words ending in *-ise* and *-ize* were obviously concordanced separately, but the lexicographer had to be constantly on the alert to recognise the possibility of variant forms and to check the concordances for evidence of those forms as well.

Before compiling an abbreviation or truncated form, or a headword that the lexicographer knew had an abbreviation or truncated form, it was necessary to check two or three sets of concordances in order to ascertain which form had the highest frequency. This was in order to ensure that the item was given the fullest treatment at its commonest form, and cross-references placed at the less frequent ones. Occasionally, for example at the entries for *MP* and *Member of Parliament*, both forms received full treatment because both occurred with very high and almost equal frequency.

If no concordance evidence was available for a headword, in most cases the word was rejected for compilation, and this was recorded in the compilation monitor database. Occasionally, if the lexicographic team agreed that an item should nevertheless be compiled, for example if it appeared in another EFL dictionary or was a very colloquial usage that just happened never to have been used in the corpus texts, this was done, but the item was usually marked in the dictionary database as being held for the database only. Such items were not extracted for inclusion in the dictionary text. The same procedure was sometimes carried out on rarer senses of a headword.

Neologisms that were felt to be likely to remain in use for some time were compiled and the word was inserted into the compilation monitor database at the same time as the entry for it was keyed into the dictionary database.

Concordances: Analysis

This section begins the third phase of a lexicographer's task in Zgustan terms, i.e. 'the construction of entries', but in fact Zgusta fails to specify what is in fact surely the central core of the lexicographer's art, the analysis of the material collected.

In checking that the concordances for all the possible forms of a word had been gathered together, a comparison of the relative frequency of the various forms gave an early indication of prominent word-classes or the potential sub-types of word-class. For example, a noun with no -s form concordances might indicate its uncountability. A verb with mainly -ing or -ed form evidence might indicate that its verbality had declined and its main use was as an adjective (e.g. there were no lines for *encrust* or *encrusts*, one for *encrusting* used as an adjective, and 45 for *encrusted*, only two of which could be construed as active past tenses of the verb, the rest being adjectival uses) or noun (e.g. 11 lines for *backsliding* as a noun and none for any form of the verb), etc.

In the early stages of compiling, coloured felt-tip pens were used to mark concordance lines in which the word (in whatever form) was used with a particular area of meaning. This was in order to facilitate subsequent grouping of examples drawn from concordances for different forms into the same semantic category, and also the ordering of the categories of an entry into frequency order. Later on, as lexicographers got used to working with concordances, this technique was largely dispensed with.

Collocational evidence was of great usefulness in an analysis of the corpus data. The concordance lines were arranged in alphabetical order of the first character after the space following the keyword. This meant that some features of the behaviour of a lexical item in text became immediately apparent.

A frequently occurring following preposition probably indicated a syntactic requirement or pattern for the word or a particular sense of the word (e.g. 70 of the 96 lines for the form *refer* were immediately followed by *to*), many lines for the same following noun might suggest a nominal compound (e.g. five lines out of 19 for *staple* in the 7.3 million corpus were followed by *diet* and 12 lines out of 62 in the larger corpus). Verbal forms often followed by nouns might, on closer inspection, give evidence of a typical object or type of object for a transitive verb. Pronominal items occurring in the following slot might indicate a phrase or pragmatic utterance (e.g. 50 lines for *mind* followed by *you* indicated the use of the expression *mind you* to introduce an after-thought, modification, or warning). Reflexives might suggest a reflexive verb.

Collocates occurring in other positions with respect to the keyword were often a little more difficult to recognise, but lexicographers soon became adept at registering these as well.

The distinction between a regular collocation for a particular word or sense and the more rigid pattern of a set phrase was sometimes very hard to make, because there is a continuum between them.

Concordances: Selection of Examples

After an initial survey of all the concordances, the next task was the selection of examples. A more detailed discussion of the principles behind the selection of examples will be found in Chapter 7. The first example selected for any word or sense of a word was intended to show typical usage in terms of syntactic behaviour and collocation. Subsequent examples registered syntactic patterns, further collocations, etc.

Wherever possible, examples selected from the concordances were not altered in any way. However, some modifications were sometimes necessary. For example, a very long sentence might contain a great deal of material that was felt to be extraneous, irrelevant or confusing to a learner, and might be shortened to focus attention on the keyword and essential syntactic and collocational features.

Concordances from the spoken section of the corpus might contain false starts, revised sentence structures, hesitations, repetitions, etc. which could be omitted without affecting the integrity of the example (e.g. in the concordances for *bit*, there is a line *er no you feel a bit dizzy afterwards yes feel a bit and you have to take it easy for a bit you lie*, which might be amended to *You feel a bit dizzy afterwards and have to take it easy*).

Sometimes, an author may have inserted a word of a very different register from the keyword in order to create a particular stylistic effect. If the word could be replaced by one more compatible with the register of the keyword, this may have been done (e.g. in the concordance line for *vermin*: *In Scotland, feral cats are treated as vermin, and so poisoned, feral* was changed to *wild* for the dictionary example). If the keyword was used twice within a sentence, but used with different meanings, it might be appropriate to delete one of the occurrences (e.g. *for a bit* in the example given a few lines above).

If any such changes were made to the actual concordance line, this was noted on the example slip. Some examples were felt to be of interest for future research but did not warrant inclusion in the dictionary, and these were marked accordingly, with notes on the reasons for holding them.

Only on very rare occasions, when the corpus evidence was exceptionally limited or idiosyncratic in some way, did lexicographers actually make up entire examples.

Categorisation

This section commences the third task ascribed to lexicographers by Zgusta: 'the construction of entries'. The practical criteria involved in the process of categorisation are more fully discussed in Chapter 4.

Once the examples had been selected for a headword, they were grouped together in categories on the basis of semantics and sub-categories were created where differences of word-class or syntax required them. This often involved drawing the distinction between syntactic requirements and syntactic patterns (cf. policy paper 9 in section 1.2).

The ordering of categories depended on frequency of occurrence and

precedence of concrete over abstract senses, with due regard for the maintenance of semantic flow within the entry (cf. policy paper 4 above).

Definitions

Murray (1888) declares: 'A Dictionary . . . is not a Cyclopaedia: the Cyclopaedia *describes things*; the Dictionary *explains words*, and deals with the
description of things only so far as it is necessary in order to fix the exact
significations and uses of words.'

Once the examples for an entry had been grouped into categories and sub-
categories, and these had been ordered, definitions had to be written for each
category and sub-category. Cobuild definition style aimed at accuracy and
clarity, and the structural requirements were a genus word and sufficient
differentiae to distinguish the headword from any near-synonyms. Esoteric
vocabulary, highly idiomatic expressions and complex constructions were
avoided. For further details see policy paper 5 and Chapter 6.

Additional Information

By the time the lexicographer had reached this stage in compiling a word,
much of the lexical (collocational) and syntactic environment had already
been noted on the example slips. If it had not been done already at the time of
categorisation, the essential syntactic requirements for each category and sub-
category had to be established, with the aid of the examples within it.

The compiler had now to check that, for each category and sub-category,
any relevant information concerning the inflections, pronunciation, style, and
pragmatics had been entered. A superordinate had to be supplied, and
synonyms, antonyms and field labels sought. If an illustration was felt to be
desirable, the pink slip was appropriately marked (see the relevant sections of
'Policy Papers' for details).

All that remained was for the ordered categories and sub-categories to be
numbered according to a fairly basic decimal notation system, and for each
slip within the entry to be numbered consecutively. Various procedures were
available for subsequent insertion or removal of slips before keyboarding.

Compilation Phases at Cobuild

At Cobuild, the overall process of compilation took place in four major steps:

Compiling on Computer Input Slips

Lexicographers analysed the corpus evidence, mainly from the 7.3 million
word corpus, and compiled entries on slips of paper that were specially
designed to hold the information in a format suitable for computer input to
the dictionary database. The entries were reviewed by senior colleagues and
revised where necessary after due consultation with the compilers. Various
groups of words, for example abbreviations, particles, auxiliaries, and modals
were compiled separately in special operations.

Input to Database and Other Computer Processes

The entries were keyboarded from the slips into the dictionary database as compiling progressed. Later, computer programs were run over the database to achieve a greater degree of standardisation of entries, to clean up certain recurrent errors, etc. Some manual editing of the database was also carried out. Trial editing to produce dictionary text from the database was carried out and numerous typeset samples prepared and reviewed. The preliminary dictionary text was then extracted from the database by computer programs, which also inserted the relevant typeface codes.

On-line Editing of Dictionary Text

By this stage, it was necessary to introduce considerations relating to the desired shape and style of the actual dictionary entries. Each entry was to be introduced by a full list of the forms of the lemma involved. These were generated by programs, which, however, often proved inadequate to deal with the idiosyncrasies of the English lexicon, and a great deal of manual correction was required by lexicographers.

The database concept of 'category' and 'sub-category' was superseded by the 'dictionary as prose' units of paragraph and sub-paragraph (see Chapters 4 & 6). This entailed a major change in policy as regards the ordering of the information within an entry. The semantic ordering of categories in the database was found to lead to a considerable fragmentation of the structure of a dictionary entry as, for example, a verb category was followed by its related noun and then by another verb category and another noun, etc. Hence, for the dictionary, it was decided to reorder the categories on a syntactic basis. Again, computer programs were used to do this automatically, but only partially succeeded.

However, to accommodate cases where it was felt unnecessary to create a separate paragraph to illustrate the less frequent use of a word in the same meaning but in a different word-class, a new strategy was developed. This involved the generation of a new symbol for the printed text (▶) followed by an indication of the change of use: *used as a noun, used as an adjective*, etc. The same strategy was adopted for minor changes in the semantic application of a word in a particular sense, as for example an adjective that commonly described people but could also describe their behaviour, or a noun that referred to a container but could also refer to its contents.

Another major change involved the shift of emphasis from the traditional dictionary concept of 'definition of meaning' to the principle of 'explanation of usage', which considerably altered the style of language and structures used. (See Chapter 6 for further details.)

Information about syntax and synonyms, antonyms, and superordinates was to be placed in an extra column to the right of the main dictionary text, to highlight the information and to avoid breaking up the flow of prose.

Phrases were grouped together after the main senses of a word, except where a phrase was felt to draw specifically and only on a particular sense. Polysemous phrases were grouped together in a paragraph, as it was realised that a learner could not be expected to know which senses of a word gave rise to phrases identical in form.

During this on-line editing phase, as the fiches for the larger corpus were now available, we attempted to replace any made-up or greatly amended corpus examples with real extracts from the corpus. The larger corpus also gave us valuable new insights into many words, which changed some entries radically from the database ones. For example, the metaphoric use of the word *graveyard*, (as in *Elections are the graveyard of the political prophet*) signalled by the following preposition *of* was represented by only two lines out of 20 in the 7.3 million word corpus, and therefore had not been included in the database entry, but gained an additional nine out of 65 in the 20 million word one, and was admitted to the dictionary entry itself.

Senior colleagues, as in the database compilation phase, reviewed the edited dictionary text and it was revised accordingly. The phonetic symbols to be inserted into the text to indicate pronunciation were automatically input to the appropriate part of each entry during this phase.

Second On-line Edit and Final Checks on Dictionary Text

The resulting text was read and commented on by outside experts who had not been involved in the compiling. These comments were incorporated into the dictionary text if they were supported by the evidence, again by on-line editing. Style checks helped to increase consistency of presentation within the dictionary. Checks were made to eliminate spelling errors and to increase consistency in spelling where variants existed. A cross-reference check was instituted to ensure that dictionary users were not sent on fruitless hunts. A sensitivity check was also carried out to minimise undue or inadvertent offence. Some proofreading corrections were also carried out on-line.

Conclusion

The procedures described in this paper show a blending of traditional lexicography with modern technology. Much of the time and energy was spent in coping with unexpected events, because the methodology was quite untested. Progress was slow initially and accelerated as areas of the work stabilised, so that the final stage of extracting and editing the dictionary from the database was done in little over one year. We think we can say with Murray [1888]: 'Our own attempts lay no claim to perfection; but they represent the most that could be done in the time and with the data at our command.'

Appendix

The appendix is intended to display the different formats in which information about a word was held at different stages of the Cobuild dictionary project.

[1] **Concordances from 7.3 million word corpus and larger (c.20 million word) corpus**: the format of concordances showing alphabetic ordering by first

character to the right of keyword and codes identifying spoken or written source, nationality of author, and place of publication.

[2] **Slips**:the format and typical information contained on the computer input slips (for details of actual input procedures, etc., see Chapter 2).

[3] **Dictionary database**: the format of printed output from the database using the 'dbpe' program (for details see Chapter 2).

[4] **Machine-extracted dictionary text**: the format of printed output of computer files containing such text, with typesetting codes.

[5] **Page proof of dictionary text**: the format of the final dictionary page at the proof-reading stage.

References

Boswell J. *The Life of Samuel Johnson LLD*, reprinted in Everyman's Library, Dent 1906.

Kipfer, B. A. 1984. 'Work on lexicography' in R. R. K. Hartmann (ed.): *Exeter Linguistic Studies: Vol. 8.*

Murray, J. A. H. 1888. Preface to *A New English dictionary on Historical Principles: Vol. 1 A and B*. Clarendon Press, Oxford.

Winter, E. 1978. 'A look at the role of certain words in information structure' in K. P. Jones and V. Horsnell (eds) *Informatics 3*. ASLIB, London.

Zgusta, L. 1970. *Manual of Lexicography*. Mouton, The Hague.

APPENDIX 1: Concordances from 7.3 million word corpus and larger (c. 20 million word) corpus

```
=== RES verit-

GW0185    14   rdinary life, and need, was immensely important, a verit- able life-line. And when later, I heard that s


=== E7 veritable

                                                                         11

GW0085  AH BR   gift--a jewel beyond the dream of Scheherazade.  "Veritable?" Arenskaya asked briskly. "Mais si," se
GW0076  BR BR   ble pieces had a golden sovereign in its midst! A veritable God-send! We really lived for a week. As
GW0033  BR BR   urt on earth, or the ugliest; the worst slut or a veritable Mrs Beeton; a mad and nagging witch or t
GW0072  AH BR   with his liquor, and his toilet descended like a  veritable Niagara, immediately beyond our bathroom
GW0072  AH BR   was still with us,..in this or that rented car. A  veritable Proteus, of the highway, with bewildering
GW0085  AH BR   elf to the shadows. "Is small," she said. "Must be veritable. She retired with her pinpoint definite
GW0007  BR BR   will be surprised to see that his hands perform a  veritable ballet of airborne movements and shiftin
GW0264  AH BR   celebration in town judging by the firecrackers,   veritable bombs, that ex- ploded all the time, and
GW0022  BR BR   msleigh Village Hall I'm sure the audience has a   veritable host of fascinating questions for our te
GW0033  BR BR   irst troubadour Guillaume, Count of Poitou, the    veritable love breviary woman de la Rose, begun i
GW0072  AH BR   xample. Lo at the time still had for the cinema a  veritable passion (it was to decline into tepid co


=== RES veritable

                                                                         18

GW0264    221   reakdown, then all we have to look forward to is a veritable 'technocracy of the ruins'. Political perti
GW0089    176   or some rich and precious metal. In this shrine, a veritable Byzentine Fort Knox, the Mandylion had join
GW0251      4   n in most families. You may also need to marshal a veritable array of friends and relatives to help out
GW0114     32   man, woman and child, whilst to invalids it is a   veritable boon." Artists like W. R. S. Stott and C. E
GW0222     91   t dull from young men's point of view, although a  veritable brick so far as pulling her weight in the f
GW0177     15   f terminal acne. She could see the factory now, a  veritable city of red brick build- ings, their hundre
GW0089     15   a devout Catholic, Mr David Willis, the last of a  veritable dynasty of English physicians named Willis
GW0264      6   tion growth has been a brief, abrupt phenomenon, a veritable explosion. Professional ecologists draw a c
GW0104    257   ol and was drenched in the wind-borne spray of the veritable fountain. The fountain was the fountain of
GW0255    269   of the older <ikibbutzin,>I had been turned into a veritable garden. As senior member and one of the fou
GW0101    209   dressed mainly in a valuable scroll would appear a veritable gift from Allah. I came out on to the dark
GW0062    377   nted from voting, Pakistan's 1977 elections were a veritable jamboree of fraudulent practices, and the e
GW0041     74   from his house to school, getting to us would be a veritable marathon. Within a week we ex- pected Percy
GW0216    170   ejected sperm of a hanged man, and also we had a   veritable mermaid, pretty ratty by now, but cleverly
GW0229    348   n With No Name (plexus, £4.50 pounds) is a <p 348> veritable one-man movie industry compared with such h
GW0177     66   ed by an iron triangle that forms her flesh was a  veritable prison cell. One side of this triangle is t
GW0104     87   egenerated capillaries reruptured. Her flesh was a veritable rainbow. She could have provided a perfect
GW0104    222   after-hour post-mortems. By comparison, Lee was a  veritable tape recorder. It soon developed that they


=== RES veritably

                                                                          1

GW0042    37   hantine fecundity, to be capable of kicking with a veritably rauniike flourish. It was, however, one of
```

APPENDIX 2: **Slips**

HEADWORD *veritable*		CATEGORY NO φ		SLIP NO 10

DEFINITION real or proper. used especially when comparing two things or two people in order to emphasize that they really are similar [used as intensifier]

INFLECTED FORMS

SYNTAX *ADJ-EA:XP*

FIELD	STYLE	=		↑
authenticity comparison		absolute proper		real
	+			**PRAGMATICS** exaggeration (awareness of exaggeration)
		≠		

EXAMPLE	SLIP NO 20
< the water > descended like a veritable Niagara	

SYNTAX

DER WD	+	= ⊘	↑ ⊘	STYLE *Simile*
DER PHRASE			FIELD ⊘	PRAGMATICS
		≠		

EXAMPLE His hands perform <ed> a veritable ballet of ## movements.	SLIP NO 30
EXAMPLE < She was > a veritable Mrs. Beeton < in the kitchen >.	SLIP NO 40
EXAMPLE I'm sure the audience has a veritable host of ## questions for our < speaker >.	SLIP NO 50
EXAMPLE a veritable God-send!	SLIP NO 60
EXAMPLE # #	SLIP NO 70

SYNTAX *ADV*

DER WD *veritably*	+	=	↑	STYLE O
DER PHRASE			FIELD	PRAGMATICS
		≠		

APPENDIX 3: **Dictionary Database**

```
veritable   0.00       10
DEF:   real or proper; used especially
       when comparing two things or
       two people in order to
       emphasize that they really are
       similar.
SYN:   ADJ-EA:XP [used as intensifier]
FLD:   authenticity; comparison
=  :   absolute; proper
↑  :   real
PRG:   awareness of exaggeration;
       exaggeration
veritable   0.00       20
EX :   <The water> descended like a
       veritable Niagara.
SYN:
STY:   SIMILE
FLD:   authenticity; comparison
veritable   0.00       30
EX :   His hands perform<ed> a
       veritable ballet of ##
       movements
SYN:
veritable   0.00       40
EX :   <She was> a veritable Mrs
       Beeton <in the kitchen>.
SYN:
veritable   0.00       50
EX :   I'm sure the audience has a
       veritable host of ## questions
       for our <speaker>.
SYN:
veritable   0.00       60
EX :   A veritable God-send!
SYN:
veritable   0.00       70
DERWD:  veritably
EX :
SYN:   ADV
STY:   0
```

APPENDIX 4: **Machine-extracted dictionary text**

```
.unl   1.5
.ur    |1| veritable |9| ~p~ |5|
.ur    |8| veritable |5| means
.ur    |5| real or proper; used
       especially when comparing two
       things or two people in order
       to emphasize that they really
       are similar.
.ur    |7| <The water> descended like
       a veritable Niagara...
.ur    |4| [SIMILE;]
.ur    |7| His hands perform<ed> a
       veritable ballet of
       movements...
.ur    |7| <She was> a veritable Mrs
       Beeton <in the kitchen>...
.ur    |7| I'm sure the audience has a
       veritable host of questions for
       our <speaker>...
.ur    |7| A veritable God-send!
----------------------------------------
CCOL   veritable
.ur    |2| ADJ-EA:XP [used as
       intensifier]
.ur    |C| ↑ real |C| = absolute,
       proper |C|  PRAGS awareness of
       exaggeration, exaggeration
----------------------------------------
```

Note: in the examples in appendices 2, 3, and 4, alterations to authentic corpus data are put in angle brackets: ⟨ ⟩.
Omissions and ellipses are marked by double hashes: ##.

For example *peas* is the object of the transitive verb *freeze* in *You can freeze peas* and it is the subject of the intransitive verb in *Peas freeze well.* Other examples are **open** and **boil.** EG *We couldn't* **open** *the window... The window* **opened** *easily... He had* **boiled** *the kettle... The kettle* **boiled.** Some verbs are described as v or v-ERG. Verbs described in this way have a transitive and intransitive use in the same way as the examples shown above and, in addition, they have an intransitive use with a subject which is different from the object of the transitive verb. An example is **sail.** EG *He* **sailed** *the boat towards Dover... The boat* **sailed** *towards Dover... He* **sailed** *towards Dover.*

verge /vɜːdʒ/, **verges, verging, verged. 1** If you are **on the verge of** something, you are going to do it very soon or it is likely to happen or begin very soon. EG *...people living on the verge of starvation... West Germany's unions appear on the verge of settling their latest pay dispute.*
PREP ⫶ near = close to

2 The **verge** of a road is a narrow piece of ground by the side of a road, which is usually covered with grass or flowers. EG *The two of us began walking together along the grass verge.*
N COUNT ⫶ border = roadside

verge on. If a particular quality **verges on** or **verges upon** another, it is almost the same as it. EG *I had a feeling of distrust verging on panic... It was the kind of smile that verged on laughter.*
PHRASAL VB : V + PREP = border on

verger /vɜːdʒə/, **vergers.** In the Anglican church, a **verger** is someone whose job is to look after the building and contents of a church.
N COUNT

verifiable /verɪfaɪəbəl/. Something that is **verifiable** can be proved to be true. EG *...verifiable evidence.*
ADJ CLASSIF = provable

verify /verɪfaɪ/, **verifies, verifying, verified. 1** If you **verify** something, **1** you check that it is true by careful investigation. EG *...evidence that could be tested and verified... I remember one story, which I have never verified, but which rings true.* ◊ **verification** /verɪfɪkeɪʃən/. EG *Any hypothesis must depend for its verification on observable evidence.* **2** you state or confirm that it is true. EG *She was asked to verify his statement.* ◊ **verification.** EG *He looked at his daughter for verification.*
V+O = substantiate
◊ N UNCOUNT
V+O
◊ N UNCOUNT

verily /verɪli/ means really or truly; an old-fashioned word.
ADV SEN

verisimilitude /verɪsɪmɪlɪtjuːd/ is the quality of seeming to be true or real; a fairly formal word. EG *...the American theatre's obsession with social verisimilitude.*
N UNCOUNT = authenticity

veritable /verɪtəbəl/ is used to emphasize a description of something and to suggest that, although the description might seem exaggerated, it is really accurate. EG *The water descended like a veritable Niagara... I'm sure the audience has a veritable host of questions... ...a veritable passion for the cinema.*
ADJ CLASSIF : ATTRIB ⫶ real = positive, absolute

verity /verɪti/, **verities.** The **verities** of something are all the things that are believed to be true about it; a formal word. EG *...scientific verities.*
N COUNT : USU PL

vermicelli /vɜːmɪseli/ is very thin spaghetti.
N UNCOUNT

vermilion /vəmɪljən/. Something that is **vermilion** is bright red in colour. EG *They don their resplendent vermilion robes.*
ADJ COLOUR

vermin /vɜːmɪn/ are **1** small animals such as rats and mice, which carry disease and damage crops or food. EG *In Scotland, wild cats are treated as vermin, and so poisoned.* **2** people who are regarded as harmful to others or dangerous to society. EG *He says that football hooligans are vermin.*
N PLURAL = pests
N PLURAL

verminous /vɜːmɪnəs/. Something that is **verminous** is covered with or full of insects such as lice and fleas.
ADJ CLASSIF ⫶ infested

vermouth /vɜːməθ/, **vermouths.** Vermouth is an alcoholic drink made from red or white wine flavoured with herbs.
N MASS

vernacular /vənækjələ/, **vernaculars.** The **vernacular** of a country or region is the language that is most widely spoken there. EG *Wherever we go for our holidays, he never seems to have any problem with the local vernacular.* ▸ used as an adjective. EG *...the vernacular programmes for new citizens of the UK.*
N COUNT : USU the+N IN SING
▸ ADJ CLASSIF : ATTRIB

A **vernacular** is a style of architecture in which ordinary people's houses are built, for example using local building materials and having low ceilings, rather than copying the grand architecture of palaces and churches; a technical term. EG *Architects are consciously trying to re-create a true English*
N COUNT : USU SING, OR N UNCOUNT

vernacular. ▸ used as an adjective. EG *...the vernacular architecture of Britain.*
▸ ADJ CLASSIF : ATTRIB

verruca /vəˈruːkə/, **verrucas.** A **verruca** is a small, hard, infectious growth on the skin rather like a wart, which most commonly occurs on the sole of the foot.
N COUNT

versatile /vɜːsətaɪl/. **1** Someone who is **versatile** has many different skills and is able to change quickly from using one to using another; used showing approval. EG *He's the most versatile of actors.* ◊ **versatility** /vɜːsətɪlɪti/. EG *He had impressed us with his versatility as a journalist.*
ADJ QUALIT ⫶ talented = adaptable
◊ N UNCOUNT = skill

2 Something such as a tool, machine, or material that is **versatile** can be used for many different purposes. EG *...this extremely versatile new kitchen machine... ...silicon, a highly versatile substance.* ◊ **versatility.** EG *...the versatility of plastics and other new materials.*
ADJ QUALIT ⫶ useful
◊ N UNCOUNT

verse /vɜːs/, **verses. 1** Verse is writing which is arranged in lines which have a pattern of beats and which often rhyme at the end of the lines. EG *He has published an anthology of verse... She used to write plays in verse.* ● See also **blank verse.**
N UNCOUNT = poetry

2 A **verse** is **2.1** one of the parts into which a poem or song is divided. Usually, each verse of a song has the same metre and rhyme structure. EG *He sang a verse of 'Lili Marlene'.* **2.2** one of the short sections into which chapters of books of the Bible are divided. EG *...the Second Book of Kings, Chapter 6, verse 25.*
N COUNT ⫶ section = stanza
N COUNT

versed /vɜːst/. If you are **versed in** something, you know a lot about it. EG *She is well versed in French history.*
PHR + NG : USED AS C

version /vɜːʃən, -ʒən/, **versions.** A **version** of something is **1** a form of it in which certain details are different or have been changed from previous forms. EG *There are two versions of this statue... She asked a different version of the question... ...from the first draft to the final printed version.* **2** a play, film, or other production based on a story or other work that had been been previously written in another form, for example as a novel. EG *...the 1939 film version of 'Wuthering Heights'... ...a concert version of Telemann's opera.* **3** a description of an event or idea by a particular person, especially when this disagrees with another person's description of the same event or idea. EG *Each of the women would have a different version of what actually happened that day... The committee accepted Carleson's version of the incident.*
N COUNT + SUPP : USU + of
N COUNT + SUPP : USU + of = adaptation
N COUNT + SUPP : USU + of ⫶ account

versus /vɜːsəs/. You use **versus** to say **1** that two ideas or things are opposed, especially when a choice has to be made between them. EG *...the problem of determinism versus freedom... We argued about pipes versus cigarettes.* **2** that two people, groups of people, or teams are competing against each other, for example in a sporting event or a case in law. EG *The big match tonight is England versus Spain.*
PREP : NG + PREP + NG = against
PREP : NG + PREP + NG

vertebra /vɜːtɪbrə/, **vertebrae.** Vertebrae are the small circular bones that form the backbone of an animal or human being. EG *...a painful stiffness in the upper vertebrae.*
N COUNT : USU PL

vertebrate /vɜːtɪbrɪt/, **vertebrates.** A **vertebrate** is a creature which has a backbone. Mammals, birds, reptiles, amphibians, and most fishes are all vertebrates; a technical term. EG *The insects colonised the land before the vertebrates.* ▸ used as an adjective. EG *...the bones of those first vertebrate inhabitants of the land, the amphibians.*
N COUNT
▸ ADJ CLASSIF : ATTRIB

vertical /vɜːtɪkəl/. **1** Something that is **vertical** stands or points straight up from a flat surface, or goes straight up from the bottom to the top. EG *The monument consists of a horizontal slab supported by two vertical pillars... A vertical line divides the page into two halves.* ◊ **vertically.** EG *The human brain is divided vertically down the middle into two hemispheres.*
ADJ CLASSIF ⫶ upright ≠ horizontal
◊ ADV WITH VB

2 Vertical is used to describe a cliff or drop which is so steep that it goes straight up or straight down without sloping at all. EG *The cliff plunged in a vertical drop to the bottom... ...a bay surrounded on three sides by vertical cliffs.* ◊ **vertically.** EG *The slope drops off almost vertically.*
ADJ CLASSIF = sheer
◊ ADV

3 The **vertical** is the direction that points straight up, at an angle of 90 degrees to a flat surface. EG *The sun had swung over the vertical and the afternoon heat was closing in.*
N SING : the+N = perpendicular

CHAPTER 4: **The Analysis of Meaning**

Rosamund Moon

Introduction

> I do not expect that my treatment of words, especially difficult words, will strike other people as that which they would have adopted . . . the most that can be expected is 'this is not an unreasonable way of exhibiting the facts'. (Murray: 1883)

Reasonableness is the most to be expected from descriptions of meaning. Dictionaries present consensus views about meaning, records of shared beliefs, and they attempt to make objective statements. The basis for these statements may be hard evidence, as with *The Oxford English Dictionary* and the *Collins Cobuild English Language Dictionary*, or the 'consensus' analyses set out in other dictionaries. Intuition and introspection nevertheless play a part, since meaning is a subjective experience, and descriptions in dictionaries need to satisfy intuition in order to be satisfactory overall.

It has been a central tenet of work at Cobuild that observations and statements should be based on the evidence of the Birmingham Collection of English Text. Each analysis of each word was intended to be 'new': in fact, in many cases it was forced to be 'new' because the evidence failed to fit existing frameworks. By concentrating on textual evidence for word meaning, we hoped to make statements about it that were neither subjective nor derivative. It is a reflection of the complexity of language that even hard evidence does not rule out pluralities or diversities of analysis: that there are no final or absolute answers to the question of how many senses[1] words have, or how they should be divided. Our analyses are attempts to make coherent interpretations of words as they appear in text, using, as far as possible, formal criteria.

Meaning: The Theoretical Underpinnings

> The meaning of a word, expression, or gesture is the thing or idea that it refers to or represents and which can be explained using other words. (definition, *Collins Cobuild English Language Dictionary*: 1987)

Significant about this definition is not only the fact that it suggests a criterial feature of *meaning* is its explicability in another mode, but that it also explains the word in context. Dictionaries traditionally record vocabulary as if meaning is something independent, inherent and unique to an item, and serving to distinguish it from all others. Words and phrases are treated in isolation for the most part, with occasional indications of restricted collocation such as *auburn* (of hair) . . . or *ajar* (of a door), or of restricted structure, such as 'always with *the*'. This may be inevitable, given the word-based structure of the dictionary, but it has the consequence that words and their meanings are decontextualised and so seem autonomous and fossilised, like flies caught in amber.

The role of context

The role of context is crucial to the lexicography done at Cobuild: context disambiguates. In continuous discourse, whether written or spoken, true ambiguity occurs rarely, except where a writer or speaker deliberately wants to be ambiguous – for example when punning or telling jokes. A whole battery of given or shared information means that a particular word is unlikely to be ambiguous at the moment of utterance, irrespective of how many different senses for it are recorded in a dictionary.

If dictionaries are to achieve reasonableness, one point about meaning should be made. Sinclair has said (1986: 60):

> The message of a conventional dictionary is that most of the words in daily use have several meanings, and any occurrence of the word could signal any one of the meanings. If this were actually the case communication would be virtually impossible.

The opposite case is that context restricts interpretation and thereby resolves ambiguity. Meaning is the product of context. In order to represent meaning in a reasonable way, we need to recognise the importance of context and to avoid unnecessary and unsatisfactory distinctions in meaning. The use of evidence and of formal criteria in analysing meaning should enable us to achieve the desideratum of reasonableness.

In terms of Cobuild lexicography, context is realised by concordances. For most words, the 50 or so characters that appear on either side of the keyword are sufficient for disambiguation. (For a few words, longer contexts are needed, and this is discussed below.) The context provided by the concordance line gives clear signals of meaning in most cases, in particular through syntax and collocation, and an interplay of these permits disambiguation.

Polysemy[1], homonymy[1], and metaphor

Lexicographers are concerned with theoretical issues such as polysemy in a way that linguists are not. To linguists, polysemy is a phenomenon that may be linked with homonymy on the one hand and metaphor on the other. It is an abstract issue of whether or not a given item is ambiguous: that is, whether it can be interpreted in more than one way, and if so, how related these meanings are. If they are unrelated, then the item may be considered homonymic; if closely related, then one may be an extension of or metaphor for the other. Thus *page* = 'sheet of paper', and *page* = 'retainer' are homonymic, whereas *page* = 'the writing on a sheet of paper' may be seen as an extension of *page* = 'sheet of paper'.

Now, of course homonymy and metaphor are issues with which – at a very basic level – lexicographers must contend. One of the decisions that needs to be made when designing a dictionary is how to handle homonymy. A common reason for treating a single sequence of letters in two or more dictionary entries is that it has two or more discrete etymological roots. The word *page* = 'sheet of paper', has a different history from that of *page* = 'retainer': so too with *lock* = 'device for fastening something securely', and *lock* = 'tress of hair'. This may further be supported by diversity of pronunciation, as with *wind, row,* and *bow*, or of inflection, as with *lie* and *can*. Another reason may be membership of two or more word-classes: *tread*, for example, is both a verb and a noun, and *back* can be a noun, verb, adjective, adverb, and, in some varieties of English, a preposition. Yet some speakers make links between homonyms that are discrete in terms of etymology: Lyons (1977: 552) discusses, for example, the case of *ear*. Many speakers make links across word-class boundaries: they are at least as likely to connect the noun *tread* = 'footstep' with the verb *tread* = 'to step', as they are to connect that noun with the sort of tread that tyres have. But many dictionaries put the nouns together and the verb in a separate entry.

The Cobuild database was structured on a synchronic, semantic basis. It therefore seemed undesirable to treat as homonyms noun and verb forms – or other combinations – of the same word. Words such as *back, tread*, and *daily* were treated as single headwords. Very often, senses of nouns were dealt with in sub-categories adjacent to associated verbs, and so on. Because access to an item is through its orthographic form and because etymological homonymy depends on knowledge that is not available to the dictionary user before he or she locates the word in the dictionary, it was decided to ignore homonymy completely when compiling the database. There are therefore single entries for words such as *page, bank, ear, can, row, may*, and *lie*, regardless of the number of roots. The Cobuild dictionary follows the same policy, with the exception that *a*, the indefinite article, and *I*, the personal pronoun, appear in separate entries from *a* and *i* the letters of the alphabet. Some acronyms and abbreviations were also treated in separate entries from morphologically similar words. Thus *aid* and *AIDS*, *salt* and *SALT* appear as separate headwords. We also made use of a symbol ▶ in the dictionary in order to introduce a change in syntax where there is no semantic change and where separate treatment of the new word-class would necessitate the repetition of the original definition or explanation almost verbatim.

As significant as the issue of homonymy is that of metaphor and meaning extension. It is the case that most senses of most words may be used metaphorically, or may be extended in meaning and used in a new or novel collocation. Thus while *duck-billed platypus* has only one meaning – the referent being a certain Australian monotreme – the word may conceivably be used in other ways. It would be possible to refer to 'a duck-billed platypus of a curriculum' or to say to someone 'You're just a duck-billed platypus': it might not make a great deal of sense, but the hearer could probably hazard an interpretation for the utterances, and given a wider context, a surer interpretation would be made. This process of metaphorisation is fundamental in poetry and literary writing. Only *The Oxford English Dictionary*, currently in sixteen volumes, and with fewer space constraints than any other dictionary, can record formally the one-off figurative uses that it finds: it typically does so by adding them to the exploited sense with the comment 'also *fig.*' or 'also *transf.*'. Most dictionaries merely record institutionalised metaphors and extensions of meaning.

The extent to which one sense is considered metaphorical varies according to both word and individual perceptions. For example, some speakers may associate *foot* = 'part of the leg', with *foot* = 'unit of measurement', though few people have feet that are twelve inches long: most will associate to some degree *jacket* = 'garment', and *jacket* = 'lagging for a boiler'. A few may associate *leaf* = 'part of a plant', and *leaf* = 'sheet of paper'. There is a relatively clear link between *bark* as a verb describing the noise a dog makes and *bark* as a verb describing a way of speaking. Different sets of collocates found with these different senses pinpoint the fact that they *are* different senses. This issue of meaning relatedness is of great importance to dictionary design, especially where a dictionary, like the Cobuild dictionary, does not recognise homonyms.

How should senses be ordered? Simply by frequency? In order to demonstrate syntactic links, or collocational or contextual links, or processes of metaphorisation? These frequently conflict. The choice of a particular meaning as the first sense to be given may be straightforward, where one meaning is commoner than others: there is occasionally a need to put a 'core' meaning first, even if it is less common. For example, the commonest use of *know* in the concordances is in the expressions *you know* and *I know*, but the first sense explained in the Cobuild dictionary is the cognition sense of the simple verb. *Blend* as a verb is used slightly more often to refer to the mixing of sounds, sights, emotions, etc. than it is of substances, but the idea of mixing substances seems more 'literal' and therefore worth describing first: it underlines the other senses, both verbal and nominal. The linear nature of a dictionary entry makes it difficult to show graphically meaning relations, especially where different features or elements of one sense reappear in subsequent senses. The complete break in relatedness that occurs with many cases of homonymy – such as between *page* = 'sheet of paper', and *page* = 'retainer' – may not be distinguishable from other less dramatic distinctions in meaning. There are cases in the Cobuild dictionary where we indicate major splits by means of an introductory note, for example the entries for *like* and *mean* (which has to deal with *means*), but usually such gulfs are shown implicitly rather than explicitly. We make use of the symbol ▶ to introduce very minor changes in meaning that we do not wish to raise to the status of separate sense: this has allowed us to indicate close relatedness of meaning.

Lexicography is applied semantics, and involves a very specialised form of applied polysemy. There are other partial solutions to the problems: we adopted ones that seemed most reasonable to us.

Criteria for Sense Distinctions

> Every distinct sense of a word is associated with a distinction in form.
> (J. M. Sinclair[2])

By concentrating on the formal features of an item and the contexts in which it appears, we hoped to arrive at a reasonable analysis. These formal features relate to syntax, collocations, morphology, etymology, and phonology: they are all measurable to some extent, and they signal, to varying degrees, distinctions in meaning. There are of course other factors that we took into account. The crucial point is that lexicographers both need and use a whole host of techniques in order to carry out an analysis of meaning. No single method or criterion suffices: words vary too much in kind.

In considering these criteria, I shall be making use of evidence from the Birmingham Collection of English Text, and looking briefly at a number of different words. The full relationship between the evidence and the database and Cobuild dictionary entries for a word has been documented in the Appendix to Chapter 3. The database contains fairly detailed analyses of the words in the corpora, far more detail than we required in the dictionary where we concentrate on principal uses. Pragmatic decisions have to be made in editing: a different dictionary would have made different use of the information in the database.

Formal Criteria

Syntax

Syntax is one of the clearest criteria of all. Primary distinctions may be made simply according to word-class. Thus we can immediately make a distinction between, say, the verbal and nominal uses of *tread*. Obviously, this is insufficient for most words: an entry for the word *light* that divided it simply into noun, verb, and adjective would be inadequate. There are entries in the Cobuild Dictionary where we ignore even word-class, or use the ► convention, feeling that word-class distinctions are not as important as semantic similarity. However, a crude division according to word-class remains a basic.

Equally critical is the syntactic division at a level more delicate than that of word-class. Sinclair (1987) discusses in detail the relationship between syntax and meaning with respect to *yield*: Stock (1984) discusses it with respect to *culture*. Distinctions between the meanings of nouns are often reflected in countability. Consider the meaning of *quality* as shown in these uncountable uses[3]:

1a . . . a satisfactory agreement on price and quality.
1b These tracks vary in quality from a corrugated bulldust-covered, well-defined and well-used road to something which you can barely discern.
1c We are not able to comment on the quality and effectiveness of the courses.
1d 'Magnificent quality,' he said. 'Fine colour, too.'

as against these countable ones:

1e . . . his admiration for her mental and spiritual qualities.
1f These indeed are the qualities that give Morris's work such appeal today.
1g The most notable quality of a convention is its sheer tedium.
1h But happiness is an elusive quality, not easily imposed through legislation.

The word *quality* is more complex than this suggests, but syntax supports a basic distinction between the meaning of 'standard' on the one hand and 'attribute' on the other.

Transitivity and patterning of verbs are other useful markers of meaning distinctions. This may be fairly crude, as in a simplistic distinction between the following uses or meanings of *keep*:

2a She kept complaining . . .
2b They had been kept awake . . .
2c She kept a sweet-shop.
2d We kept a bit behind the two of them.
2e She kept a tiny piece of material between her hands . . .
2f He gets the first four pounds to keep himself.
2g *Soft cheeses do not keep as well as hard varieties.

It may be more subtle, as with these examples of *transform*:

3a An area of sandy pastureland can be transformed into a barren dune landscape.
3b . . . and when she saw him, she was transformed.

Transform roughly means 'change'. The new state is typically expressed in an adjunct, and where there is no adjunct, the new state is typically a more positive one. Similarly with *rate* = 'evaluate': something can be rated high or low, but if it is just rated, then it is evaluated favourably. Meaning distinctions in adjectives may be reflected in their gradability. *Hollow* = 'not solid', is ungradable: when it means 'worthless' or 'insincere', it is gradable. In all these cases, other factors reinforce the meaning distinction shown by syntactic distinction, but syntax remains a fairly clear guide. Different meanings may also be associated with different following structures: with *answerable*, you are answerable *to* a superior in a hierarchical organisation, but answerable *for* your actions.

Particular senses of verbs may require particular types of adjunct. *Put* is often cited as an example of a verb that requires an adjunct, but the realisation of the adjunct differs according to sense. The first three senses explained in the Cobuild dictionary refer respectively to the moving of something into a particular place or position ('She put her hand on his arm'), the committal of someone to an institution, etc. ('They had to put him into an asylum'), and the expressing of an idea or remark in a particular way ('He didn't put it quite as crudely as that'). Quite clearly, the first requires an adjunct describing place or position, the second an adjunct describing place, and the third an adjunct describing manner. These distinctions, like the distinctions in the realisation of the object, are shown up in the dictionary by the different ways that the explanations are formulated and by the examples.

A significant feature of senses which might be considered by some as meaning extensions of a core sense is that they very frequently show some restrictedness or defectiveness in syntax. For instance, *line* is highly polysemous, as may be attested in most dictionaries. It arguably has two main strands of meaning: something with length but no width, such as a long mark, and a piece of rope/wire/cable/etc.: these two may be linked conceptually. Virtually all other senses may be tied into these, and many are marked syntactically, typically by means of a modifier or a qualifying phrase, or by a strong preference for being used in the singular or plural or in a particular clause position. A glance at the syntax information in the entry in the Cobuild dictionary for *line*, shown on page 93, demonstrates this coincidence of sense and syntax.

It is typical of nouns which develop new or metaphorical senses that these senses are marked syntactically as well as collocationally. For example, the corpus evidence for *treadmill* provides 30 instances of the word. Only three of them refer to a physical object:

4a . . . a scuttering white mouse in a treadmill, a tank of water-snails and sticklebacks.
4b . . . solemnly 'jogging' on a $276 aluminium treadmill . . .
4c . . . inside the wheel, in order to turn it on the treadmill system.

Two further examples include *treadmill* in similes:

4d . . . over and over in the night . . . as if committed to a treadmill . . . Keith's mind laboured on, self-torturing . . .
4e The road raced wetly beneath the bus, like a treadmill.

Metaphoricity is explicitly signalled by *as if* and *like*. All other instances of the word pick up on the connotations of treadmills, either in a physical way:

4f . . . through transparent tubes into the slow-revolving treadmill of her arteries and veins . . .

or in a psychological way:

4g No one should waste her life on the treadmill of housework.
4h More and more farmers are coming off the chemical treadmill.
4i . . . but they're caught on a sort of treadmill and they'll not earn much over the next . . .
4j We are thus trapped on a treadmill by the very logic of expansionism.

Of these other instances, four show the structure 'the treadmill of . . .' and in another fourteen, *treadmill* is preceded by an adjective or noun modifier: i.e., two-thirds of the examples signal their metaphoricity through syntactic structure.

Many other nouns show similar patterning with 'extended' senses: *blanket* seems always to require support in the form of a modifier or qualifier when it means anything other than a fabric covering. In addition to the idiom 'wet blanket', the corpora provide such examples as 'a blanket of ordinariness', 'a thick blanket of the stuff', and 'the blanket of massive retaliation'. *World* is frequently used to mean an area of involvement with a particular thing – 'the film world', 'the world of film'. It cannot be used in this way without either a preceding modifier or a following qualifier. Syntax as well as collocation marks out these meanings, and there are clear grounds for classifying them as separate senses, although such meanings seem to represent a half-way stage between explicit simile and discrete sense: that is, they are only half metaphors.

Collocation

One way of considering the collocations of a word is as the lexical realisation of the situational context. *Skate* as it refers to a sporting activity has fairly strong collocates of *ice* and *roller* which indicate clearly the distinction

such as rugby or American football is the row *the*+N IN SING
formed by the players of each team when the game ⇑ group
begins or is started again, for example after the ball
has gone out of the playing area.
3 Line is used in the following ways to refer to
groups of words, numbers, etc in a piece of work
such as a book, speech, song, or film. **3.1** A **line** in a N COUNT
piece of writing is one of the rows of words, num-
bers, or other symbols in it. EG *I have read every
line... The article was cut down to two or three lines*.
3.2 A **line** of a poem, song, or play is a group of words N COUNT
in it that are usually printed in one row, or spoken or
sung together, for example the words between one
rhyming word and the next in a poem. EG *They sang
the next line of the song... She quoted a line from
Shakespeare*. **3.3** When you are acting in a play or N COUNT
film, a **line** is a sentence or remark that you have to ⇑ utterance
say at a particular point in it. EG *In the last act, I had
four lines... She found it impossible to remember her
lines*. **3.4** A particular type of **line** in a conversation N COUNT+SUPP
is a remark that is intended to have a particular
effect. EG *You can make your point in a throwaway
line at the end of a casual conversation... He began
with the memorable line: 'Let's have an end of all
this.'* **3.5** A **line** is a letter, often a short one; an N SING : *a*+N
informal use. EG *Ask them to write a line to their old* = note
Dad. **3.6** In school, if a child is given **lines**, he or she N PLURAL
is punished by being made to write out a sentence ⇑ punishment
many times or to write out a passage from a book. EG
He was given a hundred lines.
4 Line is used to refer to long narrow pieces of
string, wire, or pipe, such as: **4.1** a rope or wire on N COUNT/
which you hang clothes after washing them so that UNCOUNT : USU+
they will become dry. EG *...washing hanging on a* SUPP
line... ...a clothes line. **4.2** a long piece of string, wire, N COUNT/
nylon, etc that is used in catching fish. EG *The fish* UNCOUNT : USU+
was heavy at the end of my line... The boat drifted SUPP
*slowly, with two wire lines trailing behind... ...a
harpoon line*. **4.3** a wire or cable along which N COUNT/
electricity or telephone signals are transmitted, es- UNCOUNT : USU+
pecially over long distances. EG *High winds had* SUPP
brought the lines down... ...a fallen power line. **4.4** a N COUNT/
pipe along which gas, oil, or other liquid flows, for UNCOUNT : USU+
example from an oilwell or in an engine. EG *...a* SUPP
clogged fuel line... ...oil and natural gas pipe lines. **4.5** N COUNT/
one of the metal rails on which trains run. UNCOUNT : USU+
                                                        SUPP
5 Line is used to refer to specific routes used in
communications, when they connect places or peo-
ple, for example: **5.1** a route along which electronic N COUNT : USU
signals pass, for example in broadcasting or between MOD+N
a computer and a terminal. EG *...linked to other word-* ⇑ link
processors by a direct line. **5.2** a connection to a N COUNT
telephone system which makes it possible for you to ⇑ link
make telephone calls. EG *Knowing that the lines were
tapped, I risked a call... The line had gone dead*.
● See also **party line**. **5.3** a connection that exists N COUNT : USU
when two people are talking to each other on the *the*+N IN SING
telephone. EG *There was silence on the other end of
the line... Then Sally came back on the line*. **5.4** a N COUNT : USU N
route along which people move or send messages or IN PL+SUPP
supplies, often a dangerous or secret route. EG *After
his final report all lines of communication had been
cut... It was essential to have their escape lines
clear... ...the supply lines to enemy formations*. **5.5** a N COUNT : USU
particular route along which something exists or PREP+N+SUPP
moves. EG *...along the line of the motorways... ...a* ⇑ direction
system of canals in a line parallel to the coast... = course
Wireless waves travel in straight lines. **5.6** a railway N COUNT
line. EG *...repairs to the line beyond Tring*. **5.7** a N COUNT : USU+
particular route, involving the same stations, roads, SUPP
or stops along which a train, coach, or bus service
regularly operates. EG *They had taken the wrong line
on the London Tube... ...a conductor on the New
Haven commuter line... ...the last stop on the local
bus line*. **5.8** a company which provides services for N COUNT : USU
transporting people or goods by sea, air, bus, or rail. MOD+N
EG *...air and shipping lines... ...a former employee of
the Hamburg-Amerika Line*.
6 Line is used to refer to the edge of a physical
object or area, for example: **6.1** the edge, outline, or N COUNT+SUPP
shape of an object or a person's body, especially ⇑ form
when you are commenting on the effect that it has
on the person looking at it; a slightly literary use. EG
*...the firm, delicate lines of Paxton's buildings... ...a
superb line from nose to brow, a real conqueror's
face... ...the hard thin line of Lynn's mouth*. **6.2** the N COUNT+SUPP :
edge of an area or place, especially a long, thin USU SING

division between two areas that are next to each
other. EG *...the sun-bleached shoreline... ...the taut
blue line of the horizon*. **6.3** a boundary between two N COUNT+SUPP :
states, counties, etc; used mainly in American Eng- USU SING
lish. EG *...crowding across the state line to escape* = border
taxes. **6.4** the boundary between areas occupied by N COUNT : USU
enemy armies during a war. EG *...Allied forces strug-* SING+SUPP
gling to hold the line at Trondheim. ● See also **front** ⇑ limit
line.
7 The **lines** are the set of physical defences, the N PLURAL
patrols, etc that have been established along the
boundary of an area occupied by an army. EG *They
were dropped by parachute behind enemy lines... ...a
sentry moving slowly down one of the lines... The
letters just aren't getting through the lines*.
8 Battle lines are **8.1** positions taken by the PHR : USED AS O/S
different units of an army just before a battle. EG ⇑ formation
*...when the battle lines are drawn up... The lines had
been drawn for the battle*. **8.2** the attitudes that PHR : USED AS O/S
people have or the policies that they decide to ⇑ position
support before the beginning of an argument, meet- = stances
ing, or political campaign. EG *By now these battle
lines should sound a little familiar*.
9 The **line** or **dividing line** between similar things, N COUNT+SUPP
people, actions, etc is the point at which you judge ⇑ division
them to belong to different classes or types. EG *The
traditional social dividing lines are becoming
blurred... It is not easy to draw the line between
carefulness and anxiety*.
10 A **line** on a scale of measurement is an important N COUNT+SUPP
point on it or a division between two sections of it. EG ⇑ limit
*She will be living below the poverty line... ...the
400-mph line*.
11 A **line** in an activity is the way in which the N COUNT+SUPP
activity develops or the method that you use in doing ⇑ type
it. EG *...his particular line of research... ...an unprofit-* = course
*able line of thinking... ...future lines of development...
A third possible line of attack would be to restrict
wage increases*.
12 The particular **line** that a person or group has N COUNT+SUPP :
towards a problem or topic is the attitude or policy USU SING
that they have towards it. EG *...the official line of the* = position,
Labour Party... ...committed to a certain political stance
line... The President takes a much harder line. ● See
also **party line**.
13 Your **line** of business or work is the kind of work N COUNT : USU
that you do. EG *The best job you can get in our line is* POSS/MOD+N IN
in a nationalized industry... A man in my line of SING
business has to take precautions.
14 A **line** is also a particular type of product that a N COUNT
company makes or sells. EG *...a new line of computer
printers they were developing... ...a special line in
English-style cooking... Unprofitable lines will be
discontinued*.
15 A **line** in a factory is an assembly line or N COUNT
production line. EG *A new model will be rolling off
the lines at British Leyland*.
16 A person's **line** is the series of individuals that he N COUNT : USU
or she is descended from, which affects his or her POSS/MOD+N IN
physical characteristics, social status, etc. EG *...the* SING
royal line of ancient Chaldea... The inheritance ⇑ family
would go in the female line. ▸ used of animals and = lineage
plants. EG *Their line had died out many millions of
years earlier... ...the significance of pure lines in
plant breeding*.
17 A particular **line** of people or things is also a N COUNT : USU
series of them that has existed over a period of time, SING+SUPP
when they have all been similar in some way, or ⇑ group
done similar things. EG *...a prestigious line of authors* = tradition
*from Kafka to Marcuse... ...the long line of American
Presidents*.
18 The main **lines** of a story, situation, plan, etc are N PLURAL : USU
the main ideas or facts that are involved in it. EG *In* ADJ+N+*of*
spite of these gaps, the broad lines of the story = outline,
remain clear... ...the main lines of the Five-Year themes
Plan.
19 If people or things **line** a road, a room, etc, they V+O
are present in large numbers along its edges or ⇑ fill
sides. EG *The streets were lined with cars... Crowds
lined the processional route... ...the shelves lining the
walls*.
20 If you **line** a container, a piece of clothing, etc, V+O : IF+PREP
you put a layer of something such as cloth or paper THEN *with*
on the inside surface of it in order to make it ⇑ fit
stronger, warmer, or cleaner. EG *Line the cupboards
and drawers with paper... ...a beautiful cot, lined with
silk... ...a pair of thick fur-lined boots*.

between two varieties of the activity. The 'ice' variety also collocates, less strongly, with *winter*. *Skate* = 'fish' collocates with words like *fish, ray, shark*, and *water*. Collocates establish the relevant contextual framework.

Collocation therefore frequently reinforces meaning distinctions which may be made on other grounds. The noun *gap* has four main meanings: a physical space, an interval of time, a deficiency, and a discrepancy. Each of these has a distinctive set of collocates. The physical space sense collocates with *mountain, teeth, in*, and *between*, as in:

5a . . . winds through the town, then cuts into a narrow gap in the mountains.
5b He hissed air intently through a gap in his upper teeth.

The interval of time sense collocates particularly with *year* and *of*:

5c . . . when I look back now over a gap of three years.

The deficiency sense collocates with *fill, record*, and *in*:

5d This junction in the rocks represents a huge gap in the record.
5e . . . personal experience that this book fills a major gap.

The discrepancy sense collocates with *close, poor, rich, widen, bridge, trade, generation, narrow, reduce*, and *between*:

5f . . . the widening gap between the prosperous majority and the poor . . .
5g There is also no generation gap in this family.

Patterning of this type is not uncommon. Arguably, the only way to make distinctions in meaning or use within the major delexical verbs, such as *have, give*, and *take*, is to split according to the type of object collocate. A further area where collocation supports – or enforces – meaning distinctions is that of verbs and the animate/inanimate identity of subject and object, or valency patterning. The explanations in the Cobuild dictionary specify this, and choices of subject and object become criteria for meaning distinctions in some cases.

Derivatives

Discrete senses – or homonyms – may be associated with discrete sets of derivatives, and the existence of these sets may be adduced as a criterion for homonymy. Cowie, for example, discusses the importance that Dubois laid on this when editing the *Dictionnaire du Français Contemporain* (1982: 54). This feature is striking with respect to some words. In English, for example, *act* = 'do', is linked semantically with the set *action, active, activity* and so on, while *act* = 'appear in a play', is linked with *actor* and *actress*. *Post* = 'stake', is linked historically with *poster*; *post* = 'mail', is linked with *postage, postal, postman*, etc. However, many of these links are not obvious and belong to the etymological history of the words.

The corpora show that common derivatives such as the adverbs in *-ly* and the nouns in *-ness* are frequently associated with some rather than all possible senses. *Lamely* is normally only used in the sense associated with lame excuses, rather than anything to do with limps and legs, so that 'She went lamely down the street' is far more likely to refer to something behavioural or attitudinal than something physiological.

In the Cobuild dictionary, we include undefined derivatives within individual senses of a word, rather than simply recording them at the end of the entry for that word. This has the benefit that we have been able to show which derivatives are used with which meanings. Suffixes such as *-ly* and *-ness* are highly productive, and may be added to almost any sense of any (in this case) adjective: we are not precluding other formations, but merely indicating the common and typical ones.

Related to the derivatives criterion is that of compounding. Different senses of a word are often linked with different compounds. However, this is not a useful criterion. It is entirely predictable and dependent on other things. Besides, many words generate vast numbers of compounds. *Heading* and *headline* are associated with *head* = 'top', *headband, headroom*, and *headrest* with *head* = 'part of the body', but knowing this will not help with the analysis of the word *head* and may not help when analysing the compounds themselves.

Etymology

As stated above, the Cobuild database and dictionary do not treat homonymic words in separate entries. Etymology was not used by us directly as grounds for homonymy or polysemy, but there is no doubt that in virtually all cases where a single string of letters has different etymons, the senses derived from those etymons are held as separate senses. This is largely a consequence of their unrelatedness of meaning, and it is very unlikely that etymology would be the only criterion for making a sense distinction: normally collocation and syntax would suggest it anyway.

Phonology

As with etymology, we did not use phonology as a reason for treating words as homonymic: instead, where a word had more than one pronunciation and the variations were linked with different senses, we discussed this in a preliminary note.

Intonation is more problematic. The spoken component of the corpus does not mark intonation, but there is little doubt that some meaning or use distinctions are marked by intonation changes. Obvious examples of this are phatics. Intonation marks a huge range of distinctions in the uses of *yes, no, OK*, and *well* in order to register an equally huge range of emotions and types of reactions. In analysing these words, we were forced to make assumptions about the likely situational context and pragmatic force, but it is hard if not actually impossible in many of the examples to detect such things as irony, doubt, and grudgingness. While intonation, like pragmatics, is properly a feature of the utterance rather than of the word, many such items have little or no independent meaning. The only distinctions of importance are associated with intonation and function, and the Cobuild dictionary therefore treats them in terms of their pragmatics.

Semantic and other criteria

Uniqueness of referent and real-world knowledge

Semantic criteria are inevitably more subjective than formal ones: they are intrinsic to the word, not external, and are therefore debatable. Equally inevitably, it is almost impossible to look at concordances for a word – especially a word with a concrete or physical referent – and to remain uninfluenced by personal experience and real-world knowledge. Formal features within the discourse lead us to a position where we are able to apply personal experience and real-world knowledge, but we register these features subliminally.

At a very crude level, we distinguish the word *page* = 'retainer', from the word *servant* on orthographic grounds: they are different words simply because they consist of different sequences of letters. Similarly, we may distinguish *page* = 'sheet of paper', from *leaf*. (I am not concerned here with whether or not the pairs *page/servant* or *page/leaf* are actually synonymous.) In distinguishing *page* = 'retainer', from *page* = 'sheet of paper', or *skate* = 'type of footwear', from *skate* = 'fish', it is easy to assert that they are different on extralinguistic grounds without recourse to anything textual. We know from experience that the referent, the real-world realisation, of the first is not identical with that of the second: we don't need to look at anything else. Yet it is the contexts, as represented in the collocations, that have led us to look for and see a distinction in meaning.

What role, if any, does real-world knowledge play in disambiguation? Perhaps it is best seen as a store of analogies that help us decode in individual cases. For example:

6a . . . all around Humberstone could hear the croaking of frogs.
6b They heard only the barking of the jackals, the howling of the hyenas, and the croaking of the frogs.
6c . . . its silence muddied by the distant hum of the air-conditioner, by distant traffic and the incessant croaking of frogs.

We realise that *croaking* must be a hyponym of 'sound' because of *hear* in 6a and 6b, and because of parallelism of other sound words in 6b and 6c. Now consider:

6d A bullfrog kept croaking in his watch pocket.

There is no clue in the text as to what the bullfrog is actually doing: *croaking* could refer to movement of some sort, such as jumping. Jumping and croaking are both things that experience leads us to associate with frogs, and they are not identical. We have to decode words in contexts such as 6d by means of analogy with other contexts – and hence meanings – associated with *croak* on the one hand and *jump* on the other. These tell us that *croak* usually relates to sounds, *jump* to movement.

This store of analogies could itself be regarded as a store of linguistic facts. Knowledge of croaking in the context of frogs – i.e., that it refers to sound rather than movement – is based on the place that *croak* holds in internalised lexical fields, rather than on any more nebulous memory of past experience. It is past linguistic experience that counts.

Lexical sets and fields

Lexical sets and fields may be used in disambiguation, and this criterion can be seen as halfway between the formal and the semantic, since it presupposes the existence of sets that are, arguably, signalled by coincidence of collocation. When examining the evidence for a word like *ring*, we almost instantaneously make distinctions by saying that one meaning of the noun is a piece of jewellery, another a sound, and a third a sort of circular mark or grouping. Similarly with the verb: we can say that one meaning relates to telephoning, another to the sound that bells make, and a third to encircling in some way. It is a crude decoding, but it is only a preliminary one, and demonstrates the way in which potentially separate senses of a word have different synonyms, antonyms, or superordinates. This phenomenon provides a useful, swift, and simple guide to initial disambiguation.

It perhaps works best where a word has a concrete referent. Natural-kind terms, colours, and names of things tend to organise themselves fairly well into lexical hierarchies: the chain *cocker spaniel → spaniel → dog → canine → mammal → vertebrate → creature → organism* is a clear example. Such words tend to have superordinates and hyponyms, but to have true synonyms only where there are register distinctions or dialectal variants (e.g., *rubella/German measles* or *cuckoopint/lords-and-ladies/jack-in-the-pulpit*). They rarely have antonyms, unless male/female terms are regarded as a kind of antonymy.

Other kinds of words – qualitative adjectives, for example, such as *short* or *heavy* – have antonyms and synonyms as well as hyponyms and/or superordinates. However, it is unlikely that a lexicographer would make a sense distinction purely on grounds of synonymy or antonymy. Other factors, in particular collocation, reinforce any distinction between *light* = 'not heavy', from *light* = 'not dark', or *light* = 'not intense or serious'.

Abstract, subtechnical words, such as *degree* and *extent*, or *sort, kind*, and *type* may sometimes have very close synonyms, but no superordinates. Words that are themselves at the top of their particular lexical hierarchy – semantic universals such as *time* and *place* – have only hyponyms. For words such as *thing*, the synonymy criterion becomes dangerous. It is simply not useful – or true – to say that one meaning of *thing* is an object, another an idea, a third an action, a fourth a garment. Such meaning statements may be found in many dictionaries, but the following examples show how impossible or pointless it is to analyse them in this way:

7a I take photographs of things that interest me.
7b When you are young you dream about all sorts of things.
7c Parents say one thing and do another.

It is more accurate and more useful to treat *thing* almost as a function word (cf Fronek: 1982), as a pro-form with a wide though not unrestricted range of reference, and to say, as the Cobuild dictionary says at the beginning of the entry for the word:

> Thing is often used in English as a substitute for another word when you cannot or do not want to be more precise, especially when you are referring to an object or to an action, activity, situation, idea, etc. . . .

The entry then goes on to describe more particular functions of the word.

The polysemy of a word may also be marked by its membership of more than one lexical field. This criterion cannot always be separated from other criteria. The words *peach, apricot, orange, lemon* all belong to at least two lexical sets – those of fruit and colours. It is hard to say exactly what we do when we disambiguate between a fruit sense and a colour sense: the process is too fast. It may be by means of a mental distinction in superordinates (a sort of fruit versus a sort of colour) and this in itself must be closely linked with a distinction between the relevant lexical fields.

This is not to deny the usefulness of this criterion. It helps, for example, in disambiguation outside continuous discourse. I was able earlier to gloss *page* as retainer, in spite of the ambiguity of *retainer* (= 'servant' or 'money'), by virtue of the fact that the words *page* and *retainer* co-occur in this paper as contextually or existentially synonymous, and they only co-occur in a single lexical set: the notional lexical set of servants. Perhaps only in classroom-type situations where words are mentioned devoid of context can ambiguity occur naturally. A question such as 'What does *grave* mean?' would presumably elicit a response such as 'It depends' or 'In what context?'

Synonyms, etc. have a more useful role in terms of disambiguation between themselves. There are other ways of disambiguating between *thin* as used of people and as used of soup, but what about *thin* of people as against *slim, slender, skinny, nymphlike*, and *lean*? It is here that componential analysis comes into its own: that is, in the area of distinguishing between similar meanings of different words rather than in distinguishing between different meanings of the same word. This method, outlined by Ayto in his paper 'On Specifying Meaning', is itself linked to a particular defining method, that of the classical analytical definition (1983: 89–90):

> This consists of a 'genus' word designating a superordinate class to which that which is to be defined belongs, and 'differentiae', which distinguish it from others in the same class . . . The methodology of the lexicographer's semantic analysis is basically contrastive.

However carefully dictionaries make distinctions between rough synonyms, such distinctions may disappear in actual use and be treated interactively as identical, with the discourse meaning of an item not necessarily the same as its dictionary meaning. McCarthy (in press) describes this phenomenon, commenting, for example, on:

> the frequent mis-match between decontextualized semantic accounts of scaleable words such as *surprised* and *amazed* (in which *surprised* is likely to be deemed a weaker form of *amazed*) and actual values in discourse.

A dictionary attempts to capture meaning. The phenomenon that McCarthy describes has repercussions for the dictionary: it means that lexicographers need to be aware of the *ad hoc* way in which language operates and how it may fail to reflect the carefully elaborated network of genus words and differentiae of the dictionary entry.

Connotation and allusion

The exact ways in which connotation and allusion can be shown in a dictionary vary. It seems desirable to comment on the common metonymies of the language – the use of *Whitehall* to refer to the British government, or of *the White House* to refer to the US president and presidential aide. We frequently handled these in the Cobuild dictionary as extensions of meaning, introduced by the symbol ▶. Words like *heart* have connotative uses: the heart is regarded as the seat of the emotions, as shown in:

8a . . . the troubled heart of the younger man.
8b I felt that she knew all the secrets of my heart.
8c My heart ached for the lovers.
8d The news filled Sam's heart with deep uneasiness.

and a dictionary may need to convey this information in some way. The Cobuild dictionary, like many other dictionaries, records it by making a sense distinction.

Translation equivalence

The existence in another language or other languages of different translations for a single item may be a guide to polysemy and homonymy. It is vital in bilingual lexicography; it is perhaps not particularly relevant – or widely used – in monolingual lexicography for native-speakers. EFL lexicographers take some note of it, but it is inevitable that a dictionary designed for a global market cannot take into account all matches and mismatches between the vocabularies of different languages: few EFL lexicographers have themselves knowledge of more than a handful of languages and these tend to be Romance or Germanic. Translation differences are something to be aware of, but the limitations are inevitable and the application only feasible when two languages, or a tiny group of languages, are under comparison.

Discourse or clause functions and pragmatics

Some words – mainly grammatical words – need to be considered almost entirely in terms of their discourse or clause functions: there is simply little or nothing else to analyse. Examples include determiners such as *the, a, this, that*, and *such*, or conjuncts such as *and, but* and *however*. These words traditionally appear in dictionaries with definitions, as if allocated meanings, whereas what is needed is an explanation of *functions*: in fact, it is the only thing possible.

These are overtly discourse words; other words have very strong discourse uses which may be parallel to semantic meanings. That is, a word may be analysable with respect to both semantics and to discourse. One such example is the word *time*, where lexicographers traditionally make semantic distinctions between the continuum, a period of time, and a point in time, amongst others. Equally strong as these meanings is the deictic use shown in:

> *9a* I had the idea of writing from the time that I was about 12.
> *9b* By the time the dawn came, the weather had calmed.
> *9c* But I remember thinking it was rather funny at the time.
> *9d* Since that time I have been searching for the man we want.

Many other words operate similarly, on two levels, and for the major ones – the general words of Halliday and Hasan (1976: 274 ff.) that lend cohesion to text – it seems highly desirable to recognise this crucial function by explaining it as part of a dictionary entry. It belongs as much to the description of a word as, say, idioms do.

There are many other types of word with strong discourse functions: phatics, boundary markers, emphasisers, prefaces, and so on. I mentioned above that the lack of intonational information in the corpus makes it difficult to assert categorically what is going on in each case. The shortness of concordance lines presents another problem, since there may not be sufficient context. In working on discourse words, we made use of the subcorpus facility (this is discussed in Chapter 1). It was essential for many words. The only way in which to find out the reference of pronouns such as *this* and *that*, or the scope of subtechnical words such as *way, means,* and *situation* is to have several hundred characters-worth of text. Similarly, the only way to find out about the function of a word like *anyway* was through longer contexts:

> *10a* I heard the other day of a woman who hated the things in her arm, hated the things up her nostrils, she was dying anyway and when she tried to pull the tubes out of her nostrils the best the hospital could do for this old lady was to strap her wrists to her sides.
> *10b* So while I was doing this course my wife was dashing around inspecting properties for sale, and anyway we eventually bought a house.
> *10c* . . . sort of greasy, and black beards, and moustaches as well as beards, which I thought was unusual at the time, they were generally unkempt looking and sort of dubious characters. Anyway, after a short time, I don't know how long, but not very long, they said – one of them I suppose did – to me 'It's all right, you can leave your arms here, we're all friends here.'

However, a dictionary can only record the main patterns of use of such a word: its exact force is existential and varies according to individual instance of utterance.

Certain uses of certain other words seem striking in terms of their pragmatic function. The concordance evidence for the adjective *kind* yields examples in which a person's character is described:

> *11a* I find them all very pleasant and extremely kind and helpful.
> *11b* She's very kind and sweet in lots of ways.
> *11c* She was smiling a little and looked quite kind.

It also yields the following examples:

> *11d* Oh, a glass of sherry. You are very kind.
> *11e* Thanks. This is really kind of you.

11f How kind of you to remember.
11g It's kind of you, Monty, but no thanks.

It is quite clear that these examples do not so much represent descriptions of character as uses in expressions of thanking. It is important to recognise and record explicitly such functions of such words.

Synonymy, as mentioned earlier, may vary existentially: so does meaning. Ruhl (1976) and Cruse (1982 and 1986), among others, discuss ambiguity in relation to the ways in which meaning becomes specialised in individual utterances. Cruse, for example, comments on the existential ambiguity of numbers (1986: 64), where the question 'Have you got £10 in your wallet?' may elicit either the response 'Yes. In fact, I've got £12' or the response 'No, I've got £12'. We know what *borrow* means when someone asks us if they can borrow a book from us. It means something slightly different when they ask if they can borrow a sheet of paper: we would not expect them to return it. And if speakers say that they haven't had time to do a particular thing, it is frequently a politeness formula, an excuse for a lack of inclination rather than of time. Dictionaries could not hope to cover systematically such uses, nor many others that are features of the pragmatics of units larger than the word.

Definition criteria

Rarely, sense distinctions may be made where a definition would otherwise become impossibly vague or abstract. There will be other factors to support this, but nevertheless clarity of explanation develops an over-riding importance. For example, the adjective *medium* has some abstract meaning on the lines of 'approximately halfway along a scale or continuum', but such a definition would be unwieldy and incomprehensible. It therefore seemed desirable in the Cobuild dictionary to pull out separate subsenses to refer specifically to its meaning when in collocation with words expressing size and with words expressing colours, before adding a more general and abstract subsense.

Conclusion

Words, as is well known, are the great foes of reality.
(Conrad: 1911 (1957): 11)

The analysis of meaning lies at the very heart of lexicography. A dictionary can only be as good as its design, and typography, methods of presentation, and ways of explaining things all determine the useability of the book, but such matters depend themselves on the soundness of the original analysis. It is perfectly possible to have a clear, crisp, comprehensible definition that nevertheless fails totally to account for the word or sense in question.

The very process of setting out words and their meanings, and making categorical statements about them, results in a gulf between what people know or feel instinctively about a word and what lexicographers say about it. A dictionary becomes an inventory of abstract statements about meaning, divorced from reality, however much these statements may be shored up by examples, whether authentic or coined for the purpose.

I have argued elsewhere (1987) that too much emphasis on context when analysing meaning may lead to too many meaning distinctions, thus losing the semantic integrity of the word: that there is a danger that lexicographers define and analyse according to context rather than the item itself. The Cobuild dictionary does not split less than other dictionaries, but it seems to me that fine distinctions become better justified and more acceptable because of our definitions or explanations, discussed in Chapter 6, where we define *explicitly* in relation to context, not covertly, and do not pretend that meanings are totally discrete, fixed, and autonomous. It is a solution to the problem of conveying accounts of meaning that are reasonable and do not seem unreal, the problem that Bolinger describes (1985: 69):

> Lexicography is an unnatural occupation. It consists in tearing words from their mother context and setting them in rows . . . in an order determined not by nature but by some obscure Phoenician sailors who traded with Greeks in the long ago. Half of the lexicographer's labor is spent repairing this damage to an infinitude of natural connections that every word in any language contracts with every other word, in a complex neural web knit densely at the center but ever more diffusely as it spreads outward. A bit of context, a synonym, a grammatical category, an etymology for remembrance' sake, and a cross-reference or two – these are the additives that accomplish the repair. But the fact that it is a repair always shows, and explains why no two dictionaries agree in their patchwork, unless they copy each other.

Notes

[1] I use *sense* to refer to a meaning of a word as it is – or may be – recorded in a dictionary. I use *polysemy* to refer to the phenomenon of a word having several meanings, and *homonymy* to refer to the phenomenon of a word having two or more etymological roots or belonging to two or more word-classes.

[2] This proposition formed the basis for a debate between John Sinclair, Patrick Hanks, myself, and a class of MA students in June 1986.

[3] All numbered examples, unless asterisked, are taken from the Birmingham Collection of English Text.

References

Ayto, J. 1983. 'On specifying meaning' in *Lexicography: Principles and Practice*, R. R. K. Hartmann (ed.) Academic Press, London.

Bolinger, D. 1985. 'Defining the indefinable' in *Dictionaries, Lexicography and Language Learning*, R. Ilson (ed.).

Cobuild: *The Collins Cobuild English Language Dictionary*, ed. J. M. Sinclair and others. Collins, 1987.

Conrad, J. 1911. *Under Western Eyes*, Penguin edition, 1957.

Cowie, A. P. 1982. 'Polysemy and the structure of lexical fields' in *Nottingham Linguistic Circular* 11/2.

Cruse, D. A. 1982. 'On lexical ambiguity' in *Nottingham Linguistic Circular* 11/2.

Cruse, D. A. 1986. *Lexical Semantics*, Cambridge University Press, Cambridge.

Fronek, J. 1982. '*Thing* as a function word' in *Linguistics* Vol. 20.

Halliday, M. A. K. and **R. Hasan** 1976. *Cohesion in English*, Longman.

Lyons, J. 1977. *Semantics*, Cambridge University Press, Cambridge.

McCarthy, M. J. forthcoming. 'Some vocabulary patterns in conversation' in *Vocabulary in Language Teaching*, R. M. Carter & M. J. McCarthy (eds.), Longman.

Moon, R. E. 1987. 'Monosemous words and the dictionary' in *The Dictionary and the Language Learner*, A. P. Cowie (ed.), Lexicographica Series Maior, Max Niemeyer Verlag, Tübingen.

Murray, J. A. H. 1883. Letter to Jowett 24 August 1883, quoted in K. M. E. Murray *Caught in the Web of Words*, Yale University Press, 1979.

OED: The Oxford English Dictionary; originally entitled *A New English Dictionary on Historical Principles*, ed. J. A. H. Murray, H. Bradley, A. Craigie, C. T. Onions and others, Clarendon Press, Oxford 1888–1928.

Ruhl, C. 1976. 'Pragmatic metonymy' in *2nd LACUS forum 1975*, P. A. Reich (ed.), Hornbeam Press, Columbia, South Carolina.

Sinclair, J. M. 1986. 'First throw away your evidence' in *The English Reference Grammar*, G. Leitner (ed.), Max Niemeyer Verlag, Tübingen.

Sinclair, J. M. 1987. 'Sense and structure in lexis' in *Linguistics in a Systemic Perspective*, J. Benson, M. Cummings, and W. Greaves (eds.), Glendon College, York University, Toronto.

Stock, P. F. 1984. 'Polysemy' in *LEXeter '83 Proceedings*, R. R. K. Hartmann (ed.), Max Niemeyer Verlag, Tübingen.

CHAPTER 5: **Grammar in the Dictionary**

John Sinclair

Dictionaries contain information about the meaning of words. They also contain a considerable amount of grammatical information, which unfortunately is usually neither helpful nor well presented. Pedagogical dictionaries – those which are specifically intended for the learner – give more information than do general dictionaries, and there has obviously been an attempt at organising the information, but the organisation contrasts with the rest of the dictionary.

In this paper I shall briefly describe the usual treatment of grammar in dictionaries, commenting along the way. Then I shall explain the origin and development of Cobuild's treatment of grammar and consider both its importance as an area of research and its importance as a study aid to the dictionary user.

Ordinary monolingual dictionaries

In most monolingual dictionaries headwords and some other words are given one of the eight traditional word class labels (noun, verb, adjective, adverb, pronoun, conjunction, interjection and preposition). Where more than one of these labels applies, as for example with the word *record* which can be either a noun or a verb, the word class is used as the main organising feature of the entry. In addition, there is often some more detailed classification, such as *singular* and *plural*, and occasional notes giving information about tense usage, concord and the like.

Even where additional information is given, this classification is altogether too broad and vague to give any help to the user, and is often confusing. The main terminology is often taken for granted, 'The following parts of speech . . . are standard in all widely taught forms of English grammar and need no further explanation' (*Collins English Dictionary (CED)*: *ix*), or is indicated in brief notes which do not help much, 'If a verb is both transitive and intransitive, the labels *vt* and *vi* introduce the subdivisions . . . Labeling a verb as transitive, however, does not preclude occasional intransitive use (as in absolute constructions)' (*Websters Ninth New Collegiate Dictionary*: 13). Dictionaries frequently disagree with each other about these classifications, though they may well agree about the facts of the language.

Citation of Forms

Dictionaries are sparing in citations of the inflected forms of words and rather generous in citing the derived forms. So for example in *CED* the regular inflected plural of *creak* – *creaks* – is not shown, but *creaky, creakily, creakiness*, and *creakingly* are solemnly listed. On the equivalent page, Webster fails to provide *creatures* but offers *creatural, creaturehood, creature-liness* and *creaturely*. Irregular forms, or regular ones which have implications for the spelling, are shown in full or are sometimes abbreviated. So *CED* cites *crazy, -zier, -ziest*.

It is not clear to me why this preference should be shown. Most of the derived forms are regular, and many have little prospect of ever being used. In fact, it is only because they are formed by regular rule that they can be cited in a dictionary at all, as there may often be little evidence of their use in the language.

On the other hand, the inflected forms of the central vocabulary are important and fairly frequent words that should be cited, however regular many of them might be. And the inflections of the less common words are also worth citing, if only because a user may not be confident that the regular rules apply.

Notes

The sporadic grammar notes given in monolingual dictionaries are difficult to interpret and of extremely limited value. For example in *CED all* as a pronoun is said to be 'Functioning as sing. or pl.'. Immediately above, *all* as a determiner is not given such a note, but the point is alluded to within the definition 'the whole quantity or amount of'. *All that* is said to be used 'usually with a negative', whereas *at all* (a) is 'used as a negative or in a question'. The casualness of this contrasts sharply with the meticulousness of the definitions.

The problem is not mainly the result of casualness or ignorance on the part of lexicographers, though in recent years one feels they may have hidden behind a convenient tradition of amateurism in grammar. It is an instance of the lack of an adequate terminology for talking about language. With the demise of traditional grammar, out went not only most of the terms – representing very little loss, since they were cumbersome and inappropriate – but also the licence to use any but the remaining handful of terms whose reference is so vague and indeterminate that they are hardly worth using.

Pedagogical Dictionaries

There is a great deal more grammatical information given in the learners' dictionaries than in dictionaries aimed at the native speakers of the language. The word-classes are more carefully discriminated, so that for example nouns are divided into count nouns and uncount nouns, verbs are categorised according to various types of transitivity. There are more, and more detailed, notes on syntactic patterns and restrictions. There are comments on the acceptability of some structures.

It is a difficult task to bring this kind of information to bear word by word in a dictionary. *Ad hoc* notes on particular words are no problem, but grammar deals in generalities – in word-classes rather than single words. The solution adopted by the editors is to place an alphanumeric code in the dictionary text and to offer explanations outside the alphabetical index of the dictionary.

The codes are difficult to remember – using notations such as VP3A, 15B or Wa5;A – and the information given by the codes often diverse. The user is obliged to refer elsewhere, and is often told only the obvious when he gets there. The grammatical coverage is unsatisfactory; if detailed it has only partial coverage, and if broad ranging it has little detail.

The impression given is that this kind of information is not properly assimilated into the format and style of a dictionary; it is just tacked on in a variety of rather unhelpful ways. The learner, in using a dictionary, is already assaulted by a large range of obscure conventions that break up any flow of natural English. The codes and notes merely exacerbate the problem.

Most of the information which is included in these notes is potentially useful and valuable to the learner, and in terms of coverage and relevance, the pedagogical dictionaries are a great improvement on the traditional style of dictionary. But in the laudable efforts to provide this information, other technical problems arise that negate its usefulness. Where notes on grammar and usage are clear and helpful, they contrast sharply with the body of the text, which is overburdened with opaque conventions.

Composition

These difficulties can be solved, and in this chapter and in Chapter 6 we set out our attempt at solutions. It is essential that the additional concerns of the pedagogical dictionaries are integrated into the dictionary format and made easy to use because they offer a new range of information of value to every user – not only the language learner.

The new dimension is for the dictionary to give specific help in composition. 'Ordinary' dictionaries are designed primarily to offer support to the reader, and not the writer. Given that restricted objective, it is not necessary to state the limits and constraints on structure and usage. All that is required is recognition criteria. If a word has several meanings, the reader will rarely be troubled as to which is the appropriate one in a given context.

It is altogether a different matter to create the required meaning in a composition. Bilingual dictionaries can be made to look ridiculous if they are used to generate translations. There is therefore a need for more specific information to guide the writer.

Such a development of what the dictionary can do is in line with changes in the role of the language learner, who is nowadays expected to be more communicative, active and participatory. More pragmatic information is needed, about how people communicate with each other and more attention must be given to the structure of the spoken language, now that it is accepted that the spoken language has distinctive structures and phraseology.

Presently published pedagogical dictionaries have roughly identified a target area and have begun an inventory of what it should consist of. But there are major problems in organising grammatical information for reference – not the least of which is that the word is not the best place to start. The absence of an agreed professional terminology is also a major handicap.

It seems inevitable that nearly all dictionaries will gradually turn in the direction in which the pedagogical dictionaries are now pointing. One exception to this trend will be that there will remain a specialised dictionary genre for games, where the priorities will continue to be to put as many as possible short definitions of the recognition kind between the covers. But, this exception apart, the functions of the dictionary and reference grammar will start to overlap, to the benefit of both, and may eventually merge, taking usage with them.

Grammar in Text

The provision of structural information in a dictionary is not merely a matter of designing efficient access so that learners of the language can make use of it. There is also the question of where the information is obtained. Published grammars are much too general to supply it, and words are stubbornly individual if you look at them one at a time. The next stage of sophistication is the incorporation of large scale evidence from texts, and this is what the Cobuild project has done.

Although there is absolutely no question as to the central value of the text evidence, in practice, when looking at individual words, it proved extremely difficult to maintain its influence throughout the production of the dictionary.

The nub of the problem was that the difference between a general grammar and a text grammar was insufficiently understood. If one's idea of a grammar is sufficiently abstract, there is no need for data at all. It gets in the way, it is messy and unreliable, and it adds nothing to introspection. For most of the third quarter of the twentieth century, most linguists showed a studious lack of interest in texts.

If, on the other hand, the objective is to observe and record behaviour and make generalisations based on the observations, a means of recording structures must be devised which depends as little as possible on a theory. The more superficial, the better. As a general rule, in the research which underlies this project, it has proved profitable to remain quite superficial in terms of linguistic units through much of the description. Terminology (see Chapter 3) was *ad hoc* and really no more than a labelling for identification.

There is virtue in this, especially since we were examining evidence of a kind which had not been gathered before. It was a refreshing change from the usual unseemly rush of linguists to kick aside the concrete linguistic object in favour of some idealised abstraction. We have discovered a new respect for the raw substance of language.

Once the facts of actual usage are recorded in a simple summary notation, the description can proceed. It will inevitably be sensitive to some aspects of linguistic meaning and will overlook others, but there is no prospect of either perfection or neutrality in this work.

However, as soon as the actual sentences are replaced by notation, there is a danger of returning to school grammar, or any other data free description. Since the statements look rather like grammatical generalities, there is a constant risk that they will be interpreted as such.

It is important to stress this point, because it constantly had to be defended against marauders with the highest credentials. The principles were clear and accepted by all, but many people found it difficult not to generalise well beyond what was attested in the evidence. By a laborious and expensive process, a unique collection of thousands upon thousands of observations about English grammar had been assembled in a flexible computer-held database. When these began to emerge in draft dictionary text, they were misunderstood, and read as inaccurate abstractions. For example it is significant if, in several hundred instances of the base form of a verb, none signal the imperative. This is not to say that in the ethereal world of theoretical, school or traditional grammar the imperative of that verb is 'impossible'. Just that it does not seem to occur very often, and it is perhaps not a good idea to give the user a model which appears to be avoided by a consensus of speakers and writers. See, for example, *hear* 1, in the Cobuild dictionary, or *see*, 1, 2, 5, 8, 9, 10, 15, 16, 20, 23, 24, and compare with *see* 28 which is noted as ONLY IMPER.

The validity of the grammatical statements in this dictionary can only be checked against the evidence. There is no point in applying an abstract notion of 'consistency' to words that you may think behave in similar ways. Although there is a theoretical possibility that they do, the evidence that we had in front of us showed no evidence of their actually doing so. There is sometimes a desire to be consistent for the sake of neatness, and this temptation should not be given in to, otherwise statements about the grammar of words will be made that cannot be borne out by the evidence. All the grammatical assignments were originally made at the point where the compilers had all the evidence in front of them, and that is the point at which decisions should be made, not at a late stage by an editor who has not been involved in the original compiling.

It may be that a freestanding grammar can be distinguished from the grammar appropriate to a dictionary by its treatment of material that is capable of occurrence but has not been observed to occur. A grammar has a responsibility to account for a limitless variety of new sentences which have not yet occurred – hence it cannot be restricted to attestations only. On the other hand a dictionary is a record of how words are used, and provided there is enough evidence to hand, actual citation is much to be preferred to speculation.

Procedures

The starting point was a surface grammar of English (Sinclair 1972) written as a workout of Halliday's Scale and Category model (Halliday 1961). This formed the basis of the training of the original group of lexicographers. Once the training had been accomplished, the process of recording grammar was as follows:

The compiler examines all the actual examples of a word in use and makes a selection which, taken together, summarise the main ways in which the word is actually deployed in current English.

Against each of these examples is placed a surface notation of the central structural pattern. The coding system was hacked out of daily needs and had to be directly relatable to the sequence of words in the example. It had to be simple because it was but one of the many operations that were required of the compilers, working under severe time constraints.

A typical example would be (for the word *face*):

 They were both red in the face.

This example was selected in part to show a recurrent phraseology which would be noted as 'PREP/IN + DET/THE + N' i.e. the structure is: preposition (realised by *in*), followed by determiner (realised by *the*) followed by the noun. It would be noted as 'SP', indicating that the syntactic pattern was recurrent and carried some of the semantic signalling. (See the distinction between dependent and independent meaning in Chapter 8.) When the compiler decided to set up a particular sense category, he or she had to attempt a modest generalisation based on the sum of actual observations. There was no pressure on the compiler to record anything beyond the observations, but provision was made for further notes, however tentative and informal, on any matter of syntax that caught the eye.

One particular routine proved very helpful. If the compiler felt, when recording an example, that some feature or features of the syntax appeared to be particularly associated with the sense or usage in question, then a note would be made. This gave evidence of matters like the position of adjectives and the influence of negative structures, and also of less conventional matters like a verb which always seemed to occur in a particular tense or a noun which was usually modified. In this way a great deal of information was gathered, which was incidental to the compiling process but proved very useful when final decisions were made as to the exact notation to be used in the dictionary.

It was felt that no more should be required of the compilers. The perceived task was lexicography and the grammar was seen as only one of many tasks. There was something like a conceptual clash between the observation of the word as representing an element in a grammatical pattern, and the word as a unique semantic entity. The same kind of clash made it difficult to record observations about pragmatics although again compilers were encouraged to make notes about any features which showed the intentions of speakers. Against these problems had to be set the fact that there was only one point in the procedure at which a compiler assembled and studied all the evidence. It would have been impossible in practical terms for the material to have been studied several different times for different classes of observation.

Some observations

As the project progressed, and millions of instances were examined, some interesting general observations about language began to emerge. These are decribed in more detail in Chapter 8, but can be summarised here.

a In nearly every case, a structural pattern seemed to be associated with a sense. Despite the broad range of material in the corpus, when the instances were sorted into 'senses', a recurrent pattern emerged. Of course, it is not possible to say how far the pattern had subliminally influenced the sorting process; certainly it was not usually done consciously, and the emergence of a pattern was often a pleasant surprise. The pattern was rarely if ever found in every instance unless it was a marginal sense with very few citations. But in the vast majority of cases, the compiler, in choosing typical instances, had little doubt about the kind of syntactic pattern that would have to be featured.

b In a large number of cases – including most of the common meanings of the common words – the sense and the phraseology seemed to have a closer relationship than that in *a*. There was not just a typical syntax, but a typical pattern of lexical collocation as well, and a distribution of meaning across a number of words. Instead of the normal assumption that meaning is a property of the word, except in a number of idiomatic phrases, it was clear that in these central patterns of English the meaning was only created by choosing two or more words simultaneously and disposing them according to fairly precise rules of position. The account of some phrasal verbs with *set* in Chapter 8 gives some examples, and to this can be added dozens of phrases like *set fire to, set on fire, set eyes on, set free*.

These observations, which are instanced on every page of the dictionary, guided our decisions about how to represent grammar in the dictionary. There was in practice no clear distinction between grammar and lexis, and grammatical rules merged with restrictions in particular instances, and those restrictions ranged from the obviously grammatical to the obviously lexical.

Presentation

Having identified the kinds of observation we wanted to make, we considered problems of presentation:

> *a* space was at a premium, and lengthy, detailed statements would not be acceptable.
> *b* on the other hand, arbitrary reference codes were not acceptable because of the difficulty and irritation of using them.
> *c* hardly any terminology could be assumed or used with any precision.
> *d* although the importance of phraseology was one of our principal findings, everything had to be accessed through the alphabetical list of single words.

The project as a whole formulated a number of guiding principles, which offered further restrictions. For example:

> *e* all the material had to be arranged in a single alphabetical list. We strongly suspected that explanations and keys in supplementary lists in other dictionaries were only rarely consulted, and could not be relied on:
> *f* the user should normally find what he or she wanted with a single look-up. At worst, there might be one cross-reference. Again the justification was a recognition that most users would not pursue problems through several look-ups.

Extra Column

The solution adopted was to devise a code of abbreviated technical terms and a simple syntax; and to present these somewhat cryptic statements in an extra column at the side of the usual column. We took great care to make the statements as clear as possible because presenting the information in this way risked offending a major principle g:

> g Whenever possible, the dictionary would be written in clear, simple and ordinary English.

The decision to make an extra column provoked a rush of suggestions about how to fill it – not only with grammatical material but with semantic and pragmatic observations, cross-references, phonetic transcriptions, style labels, word-forms, and anything else that did not fit easily into running text. After some experiment, it was decided to restrict the material to grammatical and semantic, with the former having priority.

Explanatory style

Another set of decisions originating in g above led to the distinctive style of explanation that is treated in detail in Chapter 6. It will be noted that quite a lot of word-class information can be gleaned from the phrasing of the explanations. Although implicit rather than explicit, this was felt to be a valuable support to the material in the extra column, increasing the independence of both types of presentation. This was of major importance because we felt very strongly that the text must be capable of standing on its own, of being totally independent of the extra column, which would give information to users of the dictionary who wanted it rather than automatically to all users.

Space and Consistency

In the final editing down of the Extra Column, there were strong pressures to be economical of space, and an obvious requirement to be as consistent and comprehensive as possible.

Space was a consideration from two points of view. There was no limit in practice to the size of the computer-held database, and every numbered sense has an obligatory syntax entry. So one possibility was to omit a great amount of detail. This was what we did for various reasons. The amount and quality of detail for different words was quite widely variable anyway, and the very narrow column on the printed page made long messages unwieldy. They were difficult to understand and there was a risk of congestion, and of the extra column taking up too much space at the expense of dictionary text.

Another aspect of the space problem arose from the kind of notation that we had become used to – using a small and fairly transparent set of terms, and a simple arrangement of these to explain the behaviour of the word. This meant that any long or complex pattern required a long or complex statement – there were so few generalisations. The alternative would have been to use a more abstract and difficult set of terms, saving space at the expense of clarity.

In the matter of consistency we had to contend with the fact that the database had been painstakingly compiled over several years during which time the notation had been developing. It had to be revised and checked. As to comprehensiveness, we were relying on the diligence of the original compilers and without recompiling we had to accept largely what they had said when actually compiling.

Revision

All these considerations led to a large revision exercise in the last few months of editing. The ability of the computer to retrieve and sort out information was a key factor. Many of the statements had to be checked back to the concordances, and the principal worry was about the level of detail that had been recorded. If the compiler had made a note, we could check it; without a note, we could not be sure whether the feature was absent or the note was absent. Our final published position is inevitably cautious; absence of a note signals only that none of the lexicographers found the feature noteworthy, not that it did not exist. Since a database entry was scrutinised by several people at various times, we expect it to be fairly accurate.

Example

I would like to take the word *fabric* to exemplify some of the points I have been making about our grammatical notations. Against *fabric 2* is the note 'N SING: *the* + N, usu + *of*'. This means that the noun in this meaning (e.g. 'the fabric of Roman Society') is not found in the plural form **fabrics*. All or nearly all the occurrences have the definite article in front, and a preponderance of them have a qualifying phrase introduced by *of*. These patterns serve to distinguish *fabric 2* from *fabric 1* and *fabric 3*. The grammatical note to *fabric 1* is 'N COUNT/UNCOUNT', which means that it displays the normal features of a countable noun (e.g. 'these fabrics are specially imported'), and additionally but secondarily, the features of an uncountable noun ('fabric is cloth or other material . . .'). *Fabric 3* (the fabric of the house) is similar to *fabric 1* but has a somewhat wider range of patterning. e.g. 'London's fabric, the actual fabric that we now know, the rough fabric of the wall . . .'. The note says 'N SING: *the* + N + SUPP'. The noun is characteristically supplemented by modifying adjectives or qualifying phrases of varying types, rather than simply a prepositional phrase introduced by *of*.

Each of the terms in this notation is the subject of a special entry in the dictionary, appearing in its correct alphabetical order, and in a special box to distinguish it from the entries for lexical items. So there is an entry at N SING, N, USU, N COUNT/UNCOUNT (and also N COUNT and N UNCOUNT), and SUPP. The special entry gives basic grammatical information and a number of examples, showing the range of words which we have coded in this way.

It is not intended that these special entries add up to a grammar of English, because they only concern basic word categorisation and distinctive phraseology. The grammatical notes are totally subordinate to the needs of the dictionary, and should be read in no other way.

In addition to the special boxed entries, there are dozens of entries that explain the meaning and use of everyday linguistic terminology – *past* and *passive* and *plural* and the like.

Standards

Minimal conditions for a coding system for a pedagogical dictionary have recently been suggested by Lemmens and Wekker (1986: 14, 99 ff.). Their suggested conditions are as follows:

a The grammatical codes should be unambiguous and easy to use. We propose that the codes should provide information about the grammatical functions (d0, i0, etc.) and the grammatical category (NP, AdjP, etc.) of the elements which may follow the verb as its complements.

b Every verb entry (and, where appropriate, every sub-entry) will include one or more codes, all of which should be self-explanatory. It will remain necessary, of course, to have a Guide in the introductory pages to explain elementary function and category labels such as d0, i0, NP and AdjP to the absolute beginner. The terminology should be that of the standard modern grammar of English.

c The dictionary user should have all the information he needs at hand, and should not be required to consult the Guide or Table of Codes in order to interpret the codes.

d All the grammatical patterns indicated in each verb-entry or sub-entry should be illustrated by example sentences arranged in the same order as the patterns.

e Transformational possibilities are another useful feature of learners' dictionaries. If passivization, indirect object movement, extraposition and the like are allowed, these transformations should also be indicated in the entry or sub-entry.

f Codes must be explicit and complete as possible, and should not be collapsed; no part of the code should be put in brackets.

It is not surprising that the Cobuild Extra Column material comes very close to meeting these conditions; Marcel Lemmens was a consultant to the project and had a formative influence on it, though he is not responsible for the final form. The conditions seem fair and reasonable as a basis for discussion.

The appeal to 'standard modern' grammars in *b* is however difficult to appreciate. Only two grammars from essentially the same stable (Quirk et al. 1972; Quirk and Greenbaum 1973) are listed in the bibliography; although these are well known they have not solved the problem of terminology in grammars, far less the problem of grammar in dictionaries.

A specimen of the result of this labour is shown for example on page 93 in Chapter 4. Its value as a reference tool in printed form will be judged by how far users find it easy to handle. It undeniably requires some sophistication in English and in grammar to be able to use it beyond the most rudimentary word-class information, and consequently the dictionary main text is designed to be self-standing, so that users can avoid the grammar notes if their queries can be answered directly. It is hoped that gradually users will turn to the Extra Column for more detailed pattern information, and will use it with ease.

Conclusion

The final form of the grammar material has good potential, too, as a free-standing database. At present it resides within the big general database, but it can be addressed with queries and can thus provide a variety of useful and hitherto unavailable information. It can produce statistics of various kinds, valid for the headword list, which is a big central vocabulary of English. It can list classes exhaustively and sub-classes. It can search for any pattern, or for the occurrence of any word in any pattern.

Such a tool would require some development before it could be clipped on to a small computer to become a live reference grammar. In particular there would have to be glosses provided to identify numbered senses when the main text was removed. But in a short time it may be available as an adjunct to the dictionary.

From the research point of view, this work had the healthy effect of raising more problems than it solved, and it can be seen as a platform from which can be launched further investigations into the relationship between the generalisations of grammar and the vagaries of individual words, via the complex machinery of phraseology. There were problems, like the classification of adverbs, which resisted treatment at the level of detail we preferred. There seemed to be no middle point between a rudimentary classification and one that was overinvolved for our purposes. The whole question of typicality was with us throughout, and the use of words like 'often' and 'usually' in the grammar notes were the subject of endless debates.

Some apparently clear-cut distinctions began to crumble as the weight of evidence came into play. The major noun classifications had to be diversified from the outset, and the distinction between qualitative or gradable adjectives and classifying or nongradable ones was difficult to maintain. More abstract relationships like reciprocal verbs presented a pattern which is familiar in data-sensitive grammar; there are one or two verbs like *meet* which are central and accommodate the criteria with ease. Several others offer nearly the same fit, but there are one or two possible qualifications. See the dictionary Extra Column information for the verbs *marry* and *argue*. Some others are not quite reciprocal, but show sufficient affinity with the main pattern to join the class provided that there is a qualifying statement about them. Compare the information given for *kiss* 1.1. and 1.2 in the dictionary. And there is a tail of items which show some of the characteristics of the class but do not seem to fit well enough. See the entry for *agree* to see how the problems of lack of fit are dealt with in cases like this.

Any attempt to characterise grammatically the members of a large word list drawn from a very large corpus will raise these problems insistently. The grammar of phrases has not been touched upon in this paper but is undoubtedly an area of vast potential for improving the description of languages.

The information that can be made available in the Extra Column thus provides a link between the broad generalities of grammar and the individualities of particular words. The task of the learner of a language beyond the first stages can be seen as lying very much in this area, and a device like the

Extra Column makes the task more explicit and helps us to understand it better.

The method of presentation of this essential information has been a real problem in lexicography; a problem which will get more and more serious as more and more of this kind of information becomes available. The language is under examination as never before, and the consequences for lexicography include a complete overhaul of the presentation of grammatical information.

References

CED: Collins English Dictionary, ed. Patrick Hanks and others, Collins 1979; 2nd edition 1986.

Halliday, M. A. K. 1961. 'Categories of the Theory of Grammar' in *Word* 17.3.

Lemmens M. and **H. Wekker**. *Grammar in Learners' Dictionaries*. Lexicographia Series Maior 16, Niemeyer, Tübingen.

Quirk, R., S. Greenbaum, G. Leech and **J. Svartvik**. 1972. *A Grammar of Contemporary English*. London: Longman.

Quirk, R. and **S. Greenbaum**. 1973. *A University Grammar of English*. Longman.

Sinclair, J. M. 1972. *A Course in Spoken English: Grammar*. Oxford University Press.

Webster's Ninth New Collegiate Dictionary. Merriam-Webster 1983.

CHAPTER 6: **Definitions and Explanations**

Patrick Hanks

Lexicographese or Prose?

Over the years a number of conventions have grown up governing the ways in which dictionaries traditionally explain meaning. Certain words and phrases, for example *of or pertaining to*, *any of various*, *etc.*, and *esp.*, are extremely common in dictionaries, although it may well be that their full significance is lost on many readers. The most pervasive of these conventions is the use of parentheses. It is, for example, conventional to place a superordinate object of a verb in parentheses when, as is often the case, it is necessary to indicate its semantic class.

> to bear (someone or something) in one's arms, on one's back, etc, while moving. – *LDOCE* at *carry* 1, sense 1.

Strangely enough, the conventional way to indicate the likely subject is to show it embedded in a prepositional phrase:

> (of a horse) to go at the fastest speed – *OALDCE* at *gallop*.

Dictionaries contain many other ingenious uses of multiple and even embedded sets of parentheses:

> to form (snow, ice, etc) into a hard compact mass or (of snow, ice, etc) to become compacted. – *CED* at *pack* 1, sense 22.
> to place or arrange (articles) in (a container), such as clothes in a suitcase. – *CED* at *pack* 1, sense 18.
> to (cause (metal) to) melt in great heat. – *LDOCE* at *fuse* 3, sense 1.

Whatever the advantages in economy of space, such uses of parentheses cannot be called user-friendly. Their function is not based on the standard usage of ordinary written English. It requires considerable sophistication to work out precisely what each set of parentheses is doing, and some readers will simply fail to understand what is being said.

Modern dictionaries are full of such conventions, which make them particularly difficult reading for ordinary readers, especially foreign readers. The purpose, in general, of these conventions is to achieve precision. However, in practice their effect may be merely to create difficulties of interpretation with little or no compensatory gain in accuracy of explanation. At worst, dictionaries may actually impose a bogus precision on word meaning, which has in fact been shown to be a system governed at least in part by variable rules (see for example Labov 1973).

What was needed, then, was a simple system of explanation, accessible to ordinary readers, capable of being precise about phenomena that may in fact be vague or variable.

An Inventory of Explanatory Strategies

The Cobuild solution to this problem was to develop an inventory of strategies that look remarkably similar to ordinary English prose, to make some quite precise statements. The desirability of proceeding in this way was reinforced when it became clear that these strategies could also be used to achieve another of Cobuild's main aims, namely to create a dictionary that would not merely help readers in decoding texts, but that would hold up models that would be of assistance to learners in encoding English.

Every Cobuild entry consists of one or more paragraphs. The paragraph is the basic explanatory unit. Each paragraph consists of one or more explanations, and each explanation is usually accompanied by examples of actual usage taken from real texts. Division into paragraphs was made on the basis of the syntactic and other patterns observed for each word.

Each explanation consists of two parts. The first part represents a departure from lexicographic tradition, in that it actually places the word being explained in a typical structure. One of the simplest strategies is that used for many count nouns, for example:

A **brick** is . . .

At first sight, this little strategy may seem so obvious as to be almost a waste of space. We might regard it as no more than a minimal strategy, employed, like a control group in an experiment, as a basis against which more complex explanations can be compared. It is quite remarkable how much can be achieved by building onwards from this modest starting point.

However, the basic strategy just quoted is also justified in its own right, for it offers explanatory advantages to users who are not native speakers of English, especially those whose native language does not contain the count/uncount noun distinction. The fragment quoted shows the word *brick* in use as a count noun. It does not rely on abstract metalanguage to get the message across. As a matter of fact, of course, the *Collins Cobuild English Language Dictionary* also contains grammar notes in the Extra Column, as explained in Chapter 5. In the case of this first sense of *brick* the grammar note says N COUNT. It contrasts with various other types of noun, in particular those labelled N UNCOUNT, of which the following is a typical example of the start of an explanation:

Calligraphy is . . .

The presence or absence of the indefinite article is crucial, and is of course a common source of learner error.

In the Cobuild dictionary, the statements made in the grammar notes and the introductory parts of the explanations are complementary, often in interesting ways. As a general rule, the main-text explanation chooses the most typical pattern with which the sense of the word in question is associated, while the grammar note sets broader limits in a more traditional way.

Sometimes the first part of an explanation is able to go further than the grammar notes, because it can make explicit contextual restrictions that lie well outside the range of standard grammars:

4 A **brick** of ice cream is . . .

The division of entries into paragraphs is based mainly on the distinctions that can be made in the wording of the first part of each explanation, following Sinclair's axiom (see Chapter 4, Note 2) that 'every distinction in meaning is associated with a distinction in form'.

The second part of each explanation consists of a more traditional-looking dictionary definition.

> . . . a rectangular block used for building walls, houses, etc.
> . . . the art of producing beautiful handwriting using a brush or a special pen.

These second parts identify the meaning. They are always to be read as stating what is typically the case, not as providing sets of necessary or sufficient conditions. It is a commonplace that if dictionary definitions could be read as stating necessary conditions, any dictionary definition describing a dog as a four-legged animal would make a three-legged dog a logical impossibility. This is not of course an argument for weakening dictionary definitions; it is an argument for reading them as explanations stating what is normally the case rather than what is necessarily the case.

If the second part of the Cobuild explanations is compared with equivalent explanations in a traditional dictionary, it will be seen that sometimes information that is in the traditional explanation is made explicit in the first rather than the second part of the Cobuild explanation. Among other things, this may suggest why such information is often in parentheses in such dictionaries. The information is on the wrong side of the equation in traditional dictionaries, but it is there because there is nowhere else for it to go. In turn, this is because of assumptions about the nature of the lexicographic equation – principally the traditional assumption that the left-hand side ought to consist of just one word. Compare the definitions for *carry* and *gallop* quoted above with the equivalent Cobuild explanations:

> If you **carry** something, you hold it or support it so that it does not touch the ground, and take it with you as you go somewhere.
> When a horse **gallops**, it runs very fast so that all four legs are off the ground at the same time in each stride.

Whatever criticisms may yet be made of these explanations, at least the object is in object position and the subject is in subject position in each case.

In general, then, the first part of each Cobuild explanation shows the use, while the second part explains the meaning. A large range of explanatory strategies expanding this principle was developed.

Within the general explanatory principle, compilers and editors at Cobuild were encouraged to write in clear, informal English prose. A target was set of creating a 'dictionary as prose' – a dictionary, furthermore, 'for encoding use'. An informal guideline that Cobuild team members were encouraged to follow was that any explanation should, if read aloud, sound like natural spoken English, of the kind that a teacher might use when explaining the meaning of a word or expression in the classroom.

Strenuous efforts were made to keep the explanatory style simple and straightforward, and to explain meaning and use in simple, common words. The working of explanations was checked and re-checked by experienced EFL teachers on the team, and from time to time particular explanatory strategies were taken into EFL classrooms for testing on groups of learners. The co-operation of the English for Overseas Students Unit in the University of Birmingham was particularly helpful. No attempt was made to set up a 'restricted defining vocabulary' of a fixed number of words. Such vocabularies are a potential source of distortion, especially if they are not accompanied by equally strict controls on the meanings of each word used and the syntactic structures in which they are used. The fact that *stick* and *out* are in a learner's active vocabulary in one sense or another is no guarantee that that learner can understand *stick out* as a phrasal verb, while a reader who has access to the ordinary English word *beef* may wonder what distinction is being made when he or she reads that a steak is a piece of 'meat from cattle'.

The aim, then, was to create a 'dictionary as prose' that would be both true to the facts and informative about lexical details. Before going on to explore more of the strategies used to achieve this end, it is desirable to look a little more closely at the background, in particular the question of how traditional dictionary text style came about, and why traditional dictionaries habitually use a more algebraic form of English.

What Went Wrong in Traditional Lexicography?

The style of dictionary entries began to be formalised early in the 18th century. 17th-century dictionaries had consisted of a mixture of one-for-one equivalents and informal, discursive descriptions and explanations. The great developments in philosophy and logic in the late 17th and early 18th centuries made such informality unfashionable. Formalism became the spirit of the age. Thus Leibniz, who has been described as 'the first philosopher of our era to notice that mathematical proof is a matter of form, not content' (Hacking 1975: 162), formulated the notion that two expressions are synonymous if the one can be substituted for the other 'salva veritate' – provided that the truth remains unaltered. This notion had an effect on lexicography. Lexicographers came to take it as a duty to formulate 'definitions' that could be substituted in any context for the word being defined. As far as I can find out, there was no explicit dicussion of the pros and cons of the awkwardnesses in the phrasing of the definitions that resulted and, more seriously, there was no discussion of whether the formulae so concocted faithfully reflected the facts of natural language or whether they introduced distortions.

In the 19th century, this Leibnizian principle of substitutability became associated with two further principles: reductionism – the notion that it is the duty of an analyst to isolate and describe minimal units – and the identification of a definition with a set of necessary and sufficient conditions – the notion that a definition or 'definiens' should provide a decision procedure sufficient to pick out all and only the objects or events correctly referred to by the word or expression under discussion (the 'definiendum'). Between them, these three notions determined the shape of monolingual dictionary entries from the 1820s to 1987. As we have seen, they led to some remarkable convolutions in dictionary prose style, as a result of lexicographers' attempts to maintain accuracy consistent with operating on these principles. Discursive explanation became increasingly unfashionable.

Johnson still wrote a few discursive explanations, mainly for special phrases or idioms, such as the following:

> . . . to tell beads, or to be at one's beads, is to be at prayer. – Johnson, at *bead*, sense 1.

But most of his explanations are written in recognisable dictionary-ese, assuming approximate substitutability between definiens and definiendum, e.g.:

> rough or shaggy, like a brush. – Johnson, at *brushy*.
> a lawyer who draws writings by which property is transferred. – Johnson, at *conveyancer*.

More precisely, many of his explanations assume approximate substitutability between each of a series of phrases in the definiens and the definiendum:

> to boggle; to stop; to fail. – Johnson, at *bodge*.

This multiple-bite strategy is still widely used in present-day dictionaries.

Johnson did not use parentheses. He was quite content to use a direct object in the course of explaining a transitive verb without special markings:

> to push on ideas in a train. – Johnson, at *carry*, sense 23.

But he clearly tried to use intransitive verbs wherever he could:

> 1 to convey from a place . . . 2 to transport . . . 3 to bear; to have about one. – Johnson, at *carry*, senses 1, 2, 3.

The use of parentheses around direct objects seems to have been a 19th-century innovation. *OED* uses them:

> Of a difficulty: to master (a person), to defy all his efforts to conquer it. – *OED*, at *beat*, sense 10b.

The prepositional phrase delimiting the subject, too, will look familiar to students of modern dictionaries. In *OED*, sometimes this is in parentheses, sometimes not. Compare the above with the following:

> (said of a river): To meet, join. – *OED*, at *beat*, sense 6c.

By the 20th century, discursive explanations had been abandoned by all serious adult-oriented dictionaries, and the few examples of discursive explanation that can be found in children's dictionaries make no pretence of being constructed in this way for carefully thought out principled reasons:

> When the kitten and the puppy drink milk or water we say they lap it up. (*The Children's Illustrated Dictionary*, at *lap*)

Such explanations have sometimes been described, often dismissively, as 'folk definitions'. It is Cobuild's contention that such explanations form a more satisfactory vehicle for explaining word use and meaning than those that have become traditional in lexicography.

In traditional lexicography, all explanation is packed into the 'definition'. Statements are made about what the words mean, but very little is said about how they are used. Lexicography has shown little sign of being affected by the work of followers of J.R. Firth, probably best summarised in his slogan, 'You shall know a word by the company it keeps!' (Firth 1957).

Other relevant work, similarly ignored by dictionaries, has been done by linguists of the transformational-generative school on 'selection restrictions': the investigation, by introspection, of contexts in which words can and cannot occur. For example, it has often been pointed out that the verb *kill* requires not only a direct object, but an animate direct object: you cannot kill something that is not a living thing (e.g. in Radford 1981:139).

For reasons that will become clear shortly, I believe that the term 'selection preference' is often more appropriate than 'selection restriction'.

LDOCE gives the main meaning of *kill* as 'to cause to die'. *OALDCE* gives it as 'put to death; cause the death of'. There is no mention in these dictionaries, either in formal or informal terms, of any restriction or preference that the word *kill* shows in respect of its direct object. However, in the Cobuild Dictionary, the explanatory style forces the lexicographer to make the selection preference explicit:

> To **kill** a person, animal, plant, or other living thing means . . .

Variations on this strategy were used to indicate the most prominent selection preferences associated with the lexical items of English.

Selecting the Right Strategy

The role of collocational and syntactic evidence in analysing meaning is discussed in Chapters 3 and 4. My concern here is to make explicit the organising principles underlying the forms of words that were chosen to express the different patterns of use and meanings once they had been identified.

The basis of choice has its root in the notion of typicality. The words of English simply do not, typically, combine and recombine freely and randomly. Not only can typical grammatical structures and form classes be observed, but also typical collocates. The distinction between the possible and the typical is of the greatest importance. It is possible, given a reasonably lively imagination, to use a particular word in any number of different ways. But when we ask how the word is typically used, rather than how it might possibly be used, we can generally discover a relatively small number of distinct patterns, which may be used as a basis for explanations after being grouped together in appropriate ways.

This information is, of course, of great value to dictionary users. A user who is attempting to decode text is more likely to encounter the word in one of these common, typical patterns and structures than in other possible but rare structures, while a foreign learner who is struggling to encode English naturally and idiomatically needs guidance precisely on what is typical rather than on what is possible. There is therefore the strongest possible motivation for lexicographers to spell out these facts.

Consider the word *listen*. Most dictionaries will tell you in one way or another that, in its main meaning, it is associated with the word *to*. Few dictionaries make a principled statement about the exact nature of that association. For example, the user might ask whether *listen to* is used like *come to* (in the sense 'recover consciousness'). Fewer dictionaries still give clear guidance on how a writer or speaker should proceed after using *listen to*: what sort of thing do people listen to? What is the selection preference on the prepositional object?

Next, consider the much less frequent expression *listen for*. There is an optional completive–intensive *out* that can be used with this expression, but not with *listen to*. Again, we may ask the question, what sort of thing do people listen out for?

Finally, when *listen* occurs without a following preposition, it is more likely than not being used as a discourse organizer or attention getter of some kind. Few dictionaries offer guidance on this use.

This is how Cobuild explains *listen*, using the facts mentioned in the preceding three paragraphs as an integral basis for the structure of the explanations, which of course include some more traditional facts as well:

> 1 If you **listen** to someone who is talking or to a sound that you can hear, you give your attention to them or to it.
> 2 If you **listen** for something that you are expecting to hear or **listen out** for it, you keep alert and make an effort to be ready to hear it if it occurs.
> 3 You say **listen** when you want someone to pay attention to you because you are going to say something important.

Now let us consider a more complex case: the adjective *broad*. It has a number of different senses. Following the methodology outlined in Chapters 3 and 4, we may classify these according to the semantic class of the noun which the adjective modifies. One use of *broad*, though not a particularly common one, shows a virtual selection restriction to the nouns *smile* and *grin*. In these circumstances, a restrictive strategy is appropriate:

> A **broad** smile is one in which your mouth is stretched very wide . . .

The choice of example ('. . . a broad grin') completes the picture.

There is another, more common group of uses in which the adjective *broad* modifies a large group of words such as *asphalt*, *avenue*, *boulevard*, *highway*, *path*, *track*, and another group in which it is used with words such as *current*, *ditch*, *meanders of great coffee-coloured rivers*, *Mekong*, and *stream*. There is nothing very complex about the meaning here: it means much the same as *wide*, which is a more common word. To attempt to make some semantic distinction between *wide* and *broad* would probably yield less than helpful results. The important thing to say about *broad* is that it means wide and that it co-occurs with words of a certain type, namely those denoting kinds of roads, paths, streams, and rivers. To say, 'A broad road or river is . . .' would not be the best strategy, as it would give an overrestricted impression of the type of noun modified by *broad*. What is needed is a strategy that will suggest a preference rather than a restriction. The strategy chosen by Cobuild involves the use of *such as* to achieve the right level of typicality:

> Something such as a road or river that is **broad** is very wide.

Another group of uses of *broad* demands an even more general strategy. This is the group that can be exemplified by the following selected fragments from the Corpus: 'the broad category of engineering', 'a broad clear knowledge of themselves', 'the broad consensus within the Labour movement', 'in this broad context', 'the broad ecumenical scene', 'three broad possibilities', 'the broad strategic scene', 'a broad subject', 'in broad terms', 'within this broad understanding'. These uses fall into two fairly closely related categories. To capture the generality, the most general possible strategy was chosen:

> 8 **Broad** is also used to refer to something that is 8.1 experienced by many people, or by people of many different kinds. . . . 8.2 defined or described in a general way or that includes many different things.

Sub-paragraph numbers (8.1, 8.2) are used for senses that are fairly closely related when the contextualisation of the word being explained cannot usefully be varied for the two meanings. (Subparagraph numbers are also used in one or two other circumstances, for example to group together special idiomatic expressions.)

Thus, even in a word occurring with a very large range of collocates, a reasonably delicate set of variations on basic strategies will help to suggest where the collocates are virtually obligatory, where they are common but highly variable, and where they are quite open.

The Construction of Explanatory Strategies

Let us now look at a particular meaning that is complex, and show how a Cobuild-style definition relates to one in a more traditional dictionary.

LDOCE tells us that one of the words spelled *fuse* is a verb with four distinct meanings. It assigns all four meanings, with minor variations, to the form class '[T1; I0]', which the Table of Codes interprets as 'transitive verb with one object; intransitive verb with no object'. Let us look in detail at one of them:

> 3 to (cause to) stop owing to a FUSE 2 (2): *If you connect all these apparatuses to the electricity supply at one place, you'll fuse all the lights./ The lights have fused; the whole place is in darkness.*

The examples of usage are probably not taken from actual usage, but are made up by the lexicographers. Some of the problems arising from this practice are discussed in Chapter 7.

Compare the above with the following examples taken from the Birmingham Corpus.

As usual, several of the street lamps had fused.
If their tiaras had met, they would have fused all the lights.
The lights had fused.
. . . when a dog bites or a light fuses.

This little bit of evidence suggests that the *LDOCE* explanation is underrestricted. Typically, it seems, not just anything that 'stops working owing to a fuse' is said to have fused. (A 'FUSE 2 (2)', by the way, is 'a failure of electrical power, owing to the melting of one of these', namely a 'short thin piece of wire . . . which melts if too much electric power passes through it'.)

The evidence suggests that there is a selection preference for words such as 'light' or 'lamp' as either the subject or object (or both). This may indeed seem to be implicit in the examples that the *LDOCE* compilers have used to illustrate this definition. However, unfortunately it is not clear to what extent these made-up examples are supposed to illustrate selection preferences. Many *LDOCE* examples clearly do not illustrate selection preferences, so no reliance can be placed on the examples as indicators of selection preferences.

We may make a first attempt to rewrite *LDOCE* sense 3 of 'fuse 3' as follows:

To fuse the lights means cause them to stop working owing to a FUSE 2 (2).

This is unsatisfactory in several respects. In the first place, it fails to capture the ergative nature of this verb: 'the lights' may occur as either the subject or the direct object. If the dictionary equation is stated explicitly rather than implicitly, however, the selected subject can be explicitly stated, in subject position, by use of a subordinate clause:

If the lights fuse, they stop working owing to a FUSE 2 (2).

We have now created two definitions where *LDOCE* had only one. They are definitions with essentially the same meaning, representing two syntactic structures that are in an ergative relationship. Can they be combined into a single definition that illustrates this relationship? One possible strategy is to introduce an 'or' structure into the left-hand part:

If the lights fuse or if something fuses them, . . .

Another respect in which the explanation drafted so far may be unsatisfactory is that it may be overrestricted. There is positive evidence in the Birmingham Corpus that it is lights and lamps that fuse, and this is supported by introspection. But what about negative evidence? The Corpus offers no evidence for either motor cars fusing or electric toasters fusing. Is there a difference in status between these two possibilities for which there is no evidence? After all, a corpus of 20 million words is quite a modest selection of English: about what one native speaker would be exposed to in a few months. Should we try to temper our first interpretation of the evidence with caution? Are 'lights' and 'lamps' the only likely members of the set of nouns that collocate with this verb, or are they just the most typical members? The time-honoured practice of 'fortifying one's opinion with that of other gentlemen, in whose judgment one has confidence' (Webster 1828) yields the insight that, centrally and typically, motor cars cannot fuse, but that maybe electric toasters and electric clocks can. Electricity rather than light or motive power seems to be the operative factor. We may therefore decide to amend our trial explanation by broadening the scope of the selected typical subject:

If a piece of electric apparatus fuses, or if something fuses it, . . .

At this point, we are a long way from a traditional dictionary definition, and getting quite close to the explanatory style that was eventually developed for the Cobuild dictionary. But we are still not finished. 'Electrical apparatus' seems too cautious in the light of the evidence. We need to express a preference among preferences: electrical apparatus is preferred to the point of being almost obligatory, but among the various kinds of electrical apparatus, a less insistent preference should be expressed for lights. This can be done using a hedge of the kind dear to lexicographers everywhere: 'usually', 'often', 'sometimes', and 'or some other similar thing' are typical hedges. The actual entry for the relevant sense of 'fuse' in the Cobuild dictionary reads as follows:

2 When a light or some other piece of electrical apparatus **fuses** or when you **fuse** it, it stops working because of a fault, especially because too much electricity is being used; used in British English. EG *As usual, several of the street lamps had fused . . . If the wires had met they would have fused all the lights.*

One of the most common selection preferences shown by verbs is for a human subject. There are a large number of actions that are, typically, done by human beings rather than by animals, inanimate objects, or abstract entities. Characteristically, it is people who think, know, speak, ask, answer, tell, explain, sing, write, drive, anticipate, count, compute, drive, organize, complain, and so on. There are other actions, for example eating, sleeping, growing, grunting, walking, and running, which, as a matter of fact, we happen to share with other animals, but where ordinary everyday language still shows a marked selection preference for a human subject. We human beings are anthropocentric: as a general rule, we talk about our own species more than we talk about other species.

An informal way of indicating this selection preference, which can be generalised across all of these cases, is to address the reader directly, as a fellow member of the human race: 'If you . . .' or 'When you . . .'. The majority of verb explanations in the Cobuild dictionary begin with the words 'If you . . .'

Variations on a Theme

Once 'If you' was established as the type strategy for verbs with human subjects, the wording could be varied to reflect different selection preferences:

When the sun **sets**, . . .
If something **sets** you doing something, . . .
When a horse **gallops**, . . .

The traditional infinitive citation form was left free for verbs where the selection preferences on the subject are so general as to be not worth stating, or where some other factor was at work:

> To **activate** something means . . .
> To **perplex** someone means . . .
> To **dam** a river means . . .
> To **knock** a hole or gap in something means . . .
> To **pedestrianize** a street or shopping area means . . .

An alternative strategy, rather more space-consuming, that would have conveyed much the same message about the virtual absence of selection preferences on the subject, would have been to use 'If someone or something **activates** something, . . .'. This is unsatisfactory, not least because too many indefinite pronouns have been set up, and this will lead to trouble later on in the explanation when they have to be picked up. Any attempt to write a continuation from this beginning will illustrate the point.

The infinitive was used for other explanatory purposes, too. Its very neutrality can be exploited, for example in order to explain verbs denoting illegal, reprehensible, or immoral acts:

> To **kill** a person, animal, plant, or other living thing means . . .
> To **strangle** someone means . . .

(Note the explicit, contrasting indication of selection preferences on the direct object for these two words.)

An explanation beginning 'If you **strangle** someone . . .' could conceivably be read as carrying an implication that in the English-speaking world it is acceptable to go around strangling people. 'When you **strangle** someone . . .' is even worse: it sounds as if we do it every day! 'If someone **strangles** you . . .' might induce alarm and despondency, while 'If someone **strangles** someone' once again runs into problems of pronominal reference. In the end, therefore, the traditional citation form was chosen as a basis for explanation, because of its neutrality.

Social attitudes towards actions quite often had to be taken into account when verbs are being explained in this way. Unwanted implications had to be eliminated as far as possible. An explanation beginning 'If you **laugh**, . . .' might give an impression that English learners are not expected to laugh too often. The wording 'When you **laugh**, . . .' was preferred.

For actions that are the object of social disapprobation, even mild disapprobation, the variation 'If someone . . .' instead of 'If you . . .' was occasionally used.

> If someone **swindles** a person or organization, . . .
> If someone **splutters**, . . .

At its best, the introductory part of each explanation can be sufficient to distinguish one sense from another. Consider the first three senses of 'put':

> 1 When you **put** something in a particular place or position, . . .
> 2 If you **put** someone somewhere, for example in an institution or room, . . .
> 3 When you **put** something such as an idea or remark in a particular way, . . .

The construction of the first part of the explanation neatly mirrors the grammatical class to which each sense is assigned in the extra column.

Noun Strategies

Things are not always so tidy. In particular, nouns raise different kinds of problems. Strategies are not always available to express the collocates that distinguish one sense of a noun from another. This is partly because noun collocates are often many and various, and partly because they do not occur in any regular structural relationship with the noun itself. Examination of the strategies discussed so far will reveal not only that selection preferences are indicated, but that these lexical selection preferences are associated with particular syntactic structures. With nouns this is unfortunately not the case.

Consider two of the senses of *bank*. One means, roughly, 'a place where you keep your money', the other 'land at the edge of a river'. Even though both senses are count nouns and both refer to physical locations, in ordinary practical language use no ambiguity arises, as has been pointed out by Stock (1984:134). The two meanings are quite clearly distinguished by 'the company they keep'. On the one hand, *bank* co-occurs with words and expressions such as *money, notes, loan, account, investment, clerk, official, manager, robbery, vaults, working in a, its actions, First National, of England*, and so forth. On the other hand, we find *bank* co-occurring with *river, swim, boat, east* (and of course *West* and *South*, in expressions which have acquired special meanings of their own), *on top of the*, and *of the Rhine*.

The evidence from the surrounding context is, then, quite clear. Even the choice of preposition, where *bank* is governed by a preposition, has a disambiguating tendency. Someone who talks of going 'to the bank' or of having something 'at the bank' is referring to a very different kind of location from someone who talks of scrambling 'up the bank', sliding 'down the bank', or striding 'along the bank'.

The problem, from the point of view of the Cobuild explanation writer, is not that the collocates fail to disambiguate. The problem is that no particular group of collocates occurs in a structured relationship with the word in either of these two senses, and so there is no suitable typical pattern ready for use as a vehicle for explanation.

The existence of collocates in non-structured relationships may be illustrated by looking at some co-occurrences of *bank* and *money*:

> . . . as a reserve against it, like money in the bank.
> . . . children sat at his feet counting money into a piggy bank.
> I've drawn out so much money from the bank, you know.
> . . . a handsome sum of money from a bank in Beirut . . .
> . . . the growth rate set for central bank money . . .
> . . . To Mama: a quarter of my bank money . . .

There are also occurrences in which the two items collocate but are in different sentences:

> I did all the usual things to raise money. I used the bank . . .

and even in which they are uttered by different speakers:

B: What about a bank? C: Well, it's where the money is.

The point is, firstly, that no form of words can readily be constructed to explain *bank* in relation to this particular collocate, and secondly, even if that were possible, it would still not satisfactorily generalise the relationship with all the other collocates of *bank*.

For this reason, the contextualising first part of the Cobuild explanation goes no further than:

A **bank** is . . .

Because precisely the same problem recurs with the 'sloping ground at the side of a river' sense, the minimal strategy is re-employed at paragraph 6:

A **bank** is also . . .

This is one of the comparatively rare cases in which Cobuild relies on the semantic content of the explanation to distinguish meanings, rather than on a preliminary contextualisation in conjunction with the semantic content.

Marked and Unmarked Strategies

Of course, not all noun senses are so devoid of usable patterns. There are many cases where the combined collocational and syntactic preferences of a noun are strong enough to form the basis for an explanation, in a similar way to the verb explanations outlined earlier:

If you have the **capability** or the **capabilities** to do something . . .

This form of words makes explicit the clear syntactic preference that the word *capability*, whether singular or plural, has for being followed by a verb in the infinitive.

A **ray** of hope, comfort, or some other good feeling or quality is . . .

This explanation not only indicates that 'ray', in this sense, is typically used with an *of* structure, but it also indicates what sort of noun can be expected after the *of*.

In many cases, the use of grammar notes in the Extra Column alongside the main text enables Cobuild to get the best of both worlds. A general principle is that the main text and the grammar notes are worded so as to be compatible with each other, but that the grammar notes express the greater degree of generality. Within this broad generalisation, an element of choice is possible. There is usually more than one way in which, for example, a count noun may be encoded, without violating typicality. By definition, count nouns have a plural form as well as a singular form with a determiner. The plural, then, might have been chosen as a basis for explanation:

Bricks are . . .

Why wasn't it? There are two answers. In the first place, in some cases it was. In the second place, for each form class Cobuild explainers need an unmarked strategy against which marked strategies can be contrasted.

For verbs, the unmarked strategy is the *to*-infinitive, as we have seen. For count nouns, it is the singular with the indefinite article, and this seems intuitively as well as pragmatically satisfactory.

A case where a marked strategy, the plural of a count noun, is used is *tadpole*. There are 23 occurrences in the 20-million word corpus of the type *tadpoles*, and only 6 of *tadpole*. The word is a count noun, and it is described as such in the grammar notes beside the entry: there is nothing grammatically wrong in talking about 'a tadpole'. But the clear preference in the evidence for the plural led the Cobuild editors to choose to begin their explanation:

Tadpoles are . . .

Similarly, where a possessive determiner tends to be preferred to the indefinite article, Cobuild signals this informally:

Your **fingers** are . . .

Absence of Selection Preference: a Fallback Position for Explanations

It would be tedious to rehearse all the many different strategies used in the Cobuild dictionary for indicating the typical ranges of syntactico-collocational slots in which items occur. The reasons for them should be fairly self-evident in the light of the basic principles outlined here. However, a few further strategies are worth mentioning.

In some cases, the appropriate level of generality could only be achieved by discussing the word being explained, rather than by encoding it in a typical phrase and explaining that. This is typically the strategy that was employed for function words. Compare the following two explanations of *with*:

1.1 You use **with** to indicate that two or more people are together or are doing something together. EG *I stayed with her until dusk* . . .
2 If you do something **with** a particular object, tool, or other thing, you do it using that object, tool, or other thing. EG *Leather needs polishing with furniture cream* . . . *He brushes back his hair with his hand.*

These two meanings correspond to the well-known case-grammar distinction between the concomitant use of *with* and the instrumental. But the strategies for explaining them are radically different. Sense 2 is recognisably a Cobuild strategy: the word being explained is encoded in a phrase that shows the typical selection preferences. The instrumental sense of *with* prefers a human agent ('you') and an action verb ('do'), and it prefers a physical object, especially a tool, as prepositional object.

Sense 1.1, on the other hand, discusses *with* in isolation, rather than encoding it in a phrase. This is because the concomitant use of *with* is so general that at worst an explanation that encoded it in a phrase would be misleadingly overrestrictive. At best, the result would be slightly clumsy, in order to avoid gross overrestriction. For example, the explainer might have written as a first draft:

If someone is **with** someone else, or is doing something **with** someone else, they are in the presence of that other person.

Once again, we are confronted with the problem of too many indefinite pronouns. Even so, this form of words misses the important generalisation that the noun groups on either side of the preposition are just as likely to be plural as singular. Attempts to make the wording more manageable lead inevitably to the omission of other important generalisations. The resolution of these problems was to fall back on a more abstract, more traditional style of explanation. This style is especially appropriate because selection preferences are not particularly relevant to this use of *with*.

As a matter of fact, the complications of the concomitant use of *with* do not end there. In Cobuild itself, the first paragraph is divided into five subparagraphs, and is introduced by a very general remark:

> 1 You use **with** to indicate a relationship or connection between people or things in the following ways.

The strategy of discussing the word in the abstract came to be widely used for function words, where the observable facts of the language often militate against any indication of selection preference.

All Cobuild explanations, then, may be read as motivated variations on a few basic explanatory themes, principally 'An X is . . .', 'X means Y', and 'You use the word X like this'.

Consequences of Lexical Gaps for Explanatory Style

The most intractable class of words to explain following the principles outlined here was, surprisingly, attributive adjectives. No problem arises with the vast majority of adjectives, which can be used in predicative as well as attributive position. A thematic strategy was easy to develop, exploiting the predicative use as a basis for explanation:

> Something that is **capacious** has a lot of room or space to put things in.
> Someone who is **withdrawn** is extremely shy and quiet, and finds it difficult to talk to other people.

However, there are a few adjectives which only or typically occur in attributive position, and for which a predicative encoding was therefore obviously inappropriate. Here the absence of a suitable very general head noun before which the attributive adjective could be inserted was sometimes painfully felt. What was needed was forms of words such as:

> A **commercial** something or someone is . . .
> A **floating** something is . . .

Unfortunately, English indefinite pronouns do not admit premodification in this way. Explainers were therefore driven to other strategies for attributive adjectives. In some cases, a selection preference resolved the problem, for example at *floating*:

> If a city or area has a **floating** population, . . .

In others, it was necessary to fall back on a basic, pre-thematic strategy, without any indication of selection preferences:

> 1 **Commercial** means involving or relating to commerce and business.

Once the necessary generalisation has been established, the dictionary can go on to deal with more specialised uses, in which selection preferences can be expressed by an appropriate superordinate noun after the attributive adjective:

> 2 Something is a **commercial** success, failure, etc, if it succeeds or fails to make money.
> 3 A **commercial** activity is an activity in which goods are produced in very large quantities in a highly organized way.
> 4 A **commercial** product is made to be sold to the public.
> 5 **Commercial** television and radio are television and radio that are paid for by the broadcasting of advertisements between programmes.

Another lexical gap that causes problems in writing generalised explanations is the absence of a non-sex-specific singular personal pronoun in English, to refer back to an indefinite personal pronoun, generally 'someone', in the first part of the explanation. Here, Cobuild regularly and deliberately uses 'they', 'them' and 'their'. Although this may surprise a few very conservatively minded readers, this is in fact a usage that has been well established in informal English from an early date. *OED* makes reference to Jespersen, and gives examples from the early 16th century onwards, including one from Fielding's *Tom Jones*: 'Every Body fell a-laughing, as how could they help it' and another from Lord Chesterfield: 'If a person is born of a . . . gloomy temper . . . they cannot help it.'

The Second Part of the Explanations

Comparatively little has been said so far about the second part of the explanations. One reason for this is that it is the part that has most in common with definitions in traditional dictionaries.

The role of the second part of the explanations is not only to record what has been found in the data provided by a large corpus, but also to comment on the conventional meanings that underlie all the various exploitations that may be observed in the data. How can the existence of something that underlies the data rather than being overtly present be discovered?

Consider the word *lame*. The dictionaries do not disagree about the main meaning:

> not able to walk normally because of an injury or defect. – *OALDCE*
> not able to walk easily or properly as a result of some weakness in, or accident to a leg or foot. – *LDOCE*
> If you are **lame**, you are unable to walk properly because an injury or illness has damaged one or both of your legs. – *Cobuild*

Now, as it happens, the Birmingham Corpus contains the following sentences:

> The first few days your thumb may be tired and lame, but this won't last.
> On some mornings I am lame, hardly able to straighten my back when I get out of bed.

Should lexicographers rush to amend their explanations of *lame* to take account of this evidence? Of course not. The corpus also contains some nine bits of evidence that lameness has something to do with legs: collocation with *leg* (×4), *runner*, *walk*, *walking*, *crippled*, and *polio*. 13 further bits of evidence support this interpretation less directly: use in a nominal structure ('the lame'), collocation with *horse*, *elderly* . . . *gentleman*, *boy*, *blind*, and so on.

An appeal to mutual belief clinches the matter. Someone who has acquired the word *lame* knows that, centrally and typically, it means unable to walk properly because of some illness or injury to the leg or legs. To know this is part of knowing the convention of English. As Putnam (1975:250) puts it:

> Someone who knows what 'tiger' means (or, as we have decided to say instead, has acquired the word 'tiger') is required to know that stereotypical tigers are striped. More precisely, there is one stereotype of tigers (he may have others) which is required by the linguistic community as such; he is required to have this stereotype, and to know (implicitly) that it is obligatory. This stereotype must include the feature of stripes if his acquisition is to count as successful.

There are various procedures that might be followed to investigate mutual belief. We can, for example, follow Noah Webster's practice and 'fortify our opinion with that of others': we can show colleagues draft forms of words, and invite them to comment on whether these forms of words succeed in capturing the convention of the language, as they understand it. If we do this with *lame*, we rapidly discover the mutual belief that *lame* has to do with injured or weakened legs, not thumbs and backs. This convention constitutes the meaning potential of the word: the unique contribution that it can make to any discourse in which it is used. Each word has a unique, or almost unique, set of meaning conventions associated with it. More than one convention can be associated with any one word, but, with the exception of very close synonyms such as 'shut' and 'close' or 'start' and 'begin', each convention is not normally associated with more than one word. I use the term 'meaning potential' rather than 'meaning' partly to emphasise the variable nature of mutual beliefs, and partly in deference to the 'currently fashionable notion that the meanings of words and sentences are typically 'negotiated' through interaction between speakers' (Cowie 1987).

Linguistic Exploitation Rules

The word *lame*, then, <u>can</u> be used of thumbs and backs, but typically it is not, and part of the convention of English is to know that it is not. Moreover, a mechanism can be devised that will enable descriptive lexicologists to account for the relationship between the 22 central and typical uses of 'lame' and the two eccentric uses in the Corpus. This mechanism will also help us to decide whether or not to include it in a dictionary. It is a version, adapted for lexicography, of the Gricean principle that a rule or maxim may be exploited not only by following it, but also by flouting it (cf. Grice 1975).

We do not postulate a weakening of sense when confronted by a single counterexample. Multiple evidence from independent sources is necessary to be valid as evidence for conventionality. Instead, when we are confronted by the apparent counterexample, the Gricean notion of exploitation-by-flouting enables us to classify particular cases as exploitations, not to be recorded in the dictionary. When the word *lame* is used of thumbs and backs, one of its conventional senses is being exploited for rhetorical effect. Communicative value is preserved by virtue of the mutual beliefs that utterer and hearer have about *lame*, e.g. that in one of its conventional senses it denotes physical weakness or injury, that it applies to legs and that legs are parts of the body, and so on. Parts of these conventional beliefs may be flouted, just so long as enough of the conventional belief survives to give the hearer or reader reasonable chances of constructing an interpretation. Differences in judgement from individual to individual about what counts as 'enough' will account for some of the failures of communication that may be observed every day, in addition to the countless failures of communication that pass unobserved.

Broadly, what has just been stated may look rather like an outline theory of metaphor. But a theory of linguistic exploitation has a broader scope. Exploitations are extraordinarily pervasive in natural language use, and lexicographers must at the very least be aware of the various guises that they can take, in order to be able to analyse effectively a large body of natural data. When looking at evidence, the first question to ask is, what is it evidence for? Is it evidence for the existence of a rule, or for the way in which rules are exploited? These points are taken up in greater detail in Chapter 8.

In any discussion of dictionary treatment of metaphors, a distinction must be made between metaphors that are created *ad-hoc* on the one hand, which are not the business of lexicographers, and those that have achieved conventional status, which are. We may illustrate this point by mentioning the second sense of 'lame' in Cobuild, which of course is also given in other dictionaries:

> If you describe an excuse, proposal, argument, etc, as **lame**, you mean that it is poor or weak.

Some people might regard this as a metaphoric extension of the 'weak-in-the-legs' sense, and indeed the wording of the Cobuild explanation indicates that it is a 'displaced' meaning (see Displacement Strategies below). However, there is plentiful evidence in the corpus to show that the use of **lame** with words denoting speech acts is conventional. If it is a metaphor, it is a highly conventionalised one. This second kind of 'metaphoric' language, the conventionalised kind, is very much the concern of the dictionary.

Displacement Strategies: figurative meanings and idiomatic expressions

There are some senses which are conventional, but conventionally regarded as figurative or metaphoric. In some dictionaries these are labelled 'fig'. This figurative status is unaffected by frequency. The literal sense of a word may be quite rare or specialised, and the figurative sense quite common, but still its figurative status forms part of the convention associated with it.

The Cobuild strategy for dealing with such senses is to indicate their figurative or extended status by displacing the meaning, using a strategy such as 'If you say that . . .' or 'If you call someone a . . .'

Consider the word *bitch*. The literal meaning, female dog, is fairly technical and really quite rare. The figurative meaning, a term of abuse for a woman, is comparatively frequent. But it would be quite wrong to say that *bitch* means 'spiteful woman or girl' (*OALDCE*). The Cobuild 'displacement' strategy in this case yields the following results:

> 1 If you call a woman a **bitch**, you mean that she behaves in an unpleasant and nasty way to other people; a rude and offensive use.
> 2 A **bitch** is a female dog.

In the most common meaning of this word, what is at stake is the utterer's intention to insult, not the semantic convention associated with the sense. This meaning must be distinguished from the 'literal' meaning, which although rare is privileged. One test for literalness is whether or not a term is typically used in subject position with an indefinite article, thus serving to introduce a topic into a discourse. 'A bitch came into the room' is more likely to be interpreted as referring to a dog than to an unpleasant woman.

A similar strategy is used by Cobuild for many different kinds of idiomatic expressions. What they all have in common is that the words are used with a particular pragmatic intention by the utterer, instead of or in addition to the intention to communicate information. In some cases the words of an idiom are capable of some other, so-called literal interpretation, which must be guarded against. So, it would be wrong for a dictionary to say:

> If you **twist** someone **round** your **little finger**, they will do anything that you want them to do.

That is open to the objection that it is either a false statement about English or a false statement about the world, or both. The literal fact is that, if you twist someone around your little finger, you make them engage in some sort of physical contortion. Making someone engage in physical contortions is not necessarily a way to obtain their compliance. The notion of being able to obtain compliance goes with a conventional figurative interpretation. This must be indicated on both the left-hand and the right-hand side of the explanatory equation:

> If you say that you can **twist** someone **round** your **little finger**, you mean that they will do anything that you want them to do.

Interestingly, the principle underlying the wording of this explanation again forces the lexicographer to make explicit the additional information that there is a selection preference for 'can' with a human subject associated with this expression. The dictionary is full of information forced out into the open by the stylistic principles that were developed.

The Nature of the Lexicographic 'Equation'

To conclude, I return to the simile mentioned once or twice in this chapter: a dictionary entry is like an equation. I have tried to set out some of Cobuild's reasons for developing and making explicit the left-hand side of the equation, in pursuit of the goal of accounting for patterns of word use in terms of the company they keep. I have mentioned that, on the right-hand side, the lexicographer has to go on to say what the unique contribution of each word is to the contexts in which it occurs, or rather what its potential contribution is to any context in which it may occur.

But natural languages are not precise mathematical systems, and meaning statements are not, literally, equations. We should beware of reading dictionary statements as equations, whether they are explicit, as in Cobuild, or implicit, as in other dictionaries.

Consider the following Cobuild explanations:

> A **boy** is a male child.
> If you **wash** something, you clean it because it is dirty, using water and soap or detergent.

All statements made about word meaning are statements about word use. Statements about word use have to take account of another piece of work by Grice (1957): the mechanism according to which an utterer relies on a hearer's recognition of his intention to create a belief in order to succeed in creating it. This has been the subject of an enormous literature, much of which is relevant to lexicographic explanation (cf., for example, Bennett 1976; Sperber and Wilson 1986). Dictionaries are much concerned with accounting for what it is that an utterer may expect a hearer to believe. Whatever this is, it is in the form of a presumption rather than certain knowledge. Strictly, then, Cobuild explanations are shorthand for more elaborate forms of words such as the following:

> If you use the word **boy**, you can expect to be presumed to be talking about a male child.
> If you say that you are **washing** something, you probably intend to create the belief that you are cleaning it because it is dirty, and that you are using water and soap or detergent.

These forms of words, of course, are very similar to those actually used by Cobuild for figurative and non-literal meanings. In the last resort, perhaps, all meanings are displaced, since all meanings rely on constructive interpretation by the hearer/reader, as well as by the utterer. If this is true, there is no such thing as literal meaning, and a dictionary explanation is no more than a compromise with the impossible, a desperate attempt to state the unstateable. In the words of Dwight Bolinger (1965:572), 'Dictionaries do not exist to define, but to help people grasp meanings.' Cobuild exists, additionally, to help people grasp the ways in which English words are used.

References

Dictionaries:

CED: Collins English Dictionary, ed. P. Hanks and others, Collins, 1979; 2nd edition 1986.

Cobuild: *The Collins Cobuild English Language Dictionary*, ed. J. M. Sinclair and others, Collins, 1987.

A Dictionary of the English Language. S. Johnson, 1755; fascimile edition, Times Books, 1979.

LDOCE: Longman Dictionary of Contemporary English, ed. P. Procter and others, Longman, 1978.

OALDCE: Oxford Advanced Learners' Dictionary of Current English, ed A. S. Hornby with A. P. Cowie, 3rd edition, Oxford University Press, 1974.

OED: The Oxford English Dictionary; originally entitled *A New English Dictionary on Historical Principles*, ed. J. A. H. Murray, H. Bradley, A. Craigie, C. T. Onions, and others, Clarendon Press, Oxford, 1888–1928.

The Children's Illustrated Dictionary, illustrated by A. Nash, Juvenile Productions Ltd., London, undated; c. 1950.

Other Works:

Bennett, Jonathan 1976. *Linguistic Behaviour*. Cambridge University Press, Cambridge.

Bolinger, Dwight 1965. 'The Atomization of Meaning' in *Language*, vol. 41.

Cowie, A. P. (forthcoming). 'Stable and Creative Aspects of Vocabulary Use' in R. A. Carter and M. J. McCarthy (eds.): *Vocabulary and Foreign Language Learning*. Longman.

Firth, J. R. 1957. 'A Synopsis of Linguistic Theory 1930–1955' in *Studies in Linguistic Analysis*. Philological Society, Oxford; reprinted in F. R. Palmer (ed., 1968): *Selected Papers of J. R. Firth*. Longman.

Grice, H. P. 1957. 'Meaning' in *Philosophical Review*, Vol. 66.

Grice, H. P. 1975. 'Logic and Conversation' in Cole and Morgan (eds.): *Syntax and Semantics*, Vol. 3. Academic Press.

Hacking, Ian 1975. *Why does Language matter to Philosophy?* Cambridge University Press.

Labov, W. 1973. 'The Boundaries of Words and their Meanings' in C.-J. N. Bailey and R. W. Shuy (eds.): *New Ways of Analyzing Variation in English*. Georgetown University Press, Washington D.C.

Putnam, Hilary 1975. 'The Meaning of "Meaning"' in *Mind, Language, and Reality: Philosophical Papers*, Vol. 2. Cambridge University Press.

Radford, Andrew 1981. *Transformational Syntax*. Cambridge University Press.

Sperber, D., and **D. Wilson** 1986. *Relevance*. Blackwell.

Stock, Penelope F. 1984. 'Polysemy' in R. R. K. Hartmann (ed.): *LEXeter '83 Proceedings*. Max Niemeyer Verlag, Tübingen.

Webster, Noah 1828. Preface to *An American Dictionary of the English Language*.

CHAPTER 7: The Case for Examples

Gwyneth Fox

When the *Collins Cobuild English Language Dictionary* was being planned, it was taken for granted that examples would be given for most of the words or senses of words explained in it. It was felt that the use of examples forms an integral part of the learning of a word. The learner needs to have both an explanation of what the word means and then one or more examples of the word in use. This should help to reinforce the meaning – not by acting as a reformulation of the definition, but by showing how the word is actually used, in an appropriate context, a typical grammatical structure, and with words that are normally associated with it.

The use of examples in a dictionary also means that students can scan longer entries and identify the particular sense they are seeking by finding examples that are similar to the one they need or have in front of them. There is nothing more annoying than looking up a word and then not being able to work out which particular sense of that word is the one that you need because no examples of the typical uses of the word are given. Most learners of a foreign language have had the experience of looking up a word in the target language and finding three or four words given which seem to be synonyms, but which all have limitations that the unwary user is not conscious of. At school, children are often asked to look up the meaning of a word in a particular sentence, and they will sometimes give the wrong definition, simply because most school dictionaries do not exemplify the majority of words. Both of these experiences show how important it is that whenever there could be confusion examples should be given.

It can be argued that there are some words which do not benefit greatly from exemplification. A very specific, concrete object like a television can probably be explained well enough in a definition – 'A television is a piece of electrical equipment that consists of a box containing a special electronic tube with a screen in front of it, on which you can watch programmes with pictures and sounds' – not to need an example as well. Yet a well-chosen example such as 'I turned on the television to watch the news' can show that in English we 'turn on' radios and televisions rather than using a verb with the basic meaning of 'light' as in Italian or French. Also, we 'watch' television rather than 'see' or 'look at' it. An example of this kind teaches no more about the actual object, but does give information about how the word is likely to be used. For this reason, at Cobuild we decided on a policy of exemplifying as many words and as many senses of words as we possibly could, knowing that a great deal of incidental information would be gleaned by learners other than simply the meaning of the word. Another case of a word which could reasonably have been explained without using an example is the word *hawk*, defined as 'a large bird with a short hooked bill, sharp claws, and very good eyesight. Hawks catch and eat small birds and animals'; but the example that was chosen ('A hawk hovered, motionless, in the blue sky') suggests that frequently the word is used in language with a slightly poetic quality, information which is well worth imparting to a learner.

Examples from Actual Text

Having decided that, whenever possible, words and senses of words would be exemplified, the next thing was to decide what type of examples would be given. There was never any doubt that they had to come from the corpus and thus represent real language. The whole of the Cobuild dictionary is based on evidence derived from real language. It would therefore have been ridiculous to have studied real language in order to find out the facts of the language, and then to have abandoned this and concocted fake examples for the dictionary. The tradition of the great dictionaries of Johnson and Murray was to print real citations, and we were in a far better position to select citations than either of our illustrious predecessors.

The Cobuild dictionary is designed for learners of English as an international language, and the needs of learners do not always match the simple aims of research reporting. Hence we had to reconcile the requirements of authenticity and typicality with the requirements and expectations of the target learner. Learners, and unfortunately some teachers, often feel that they should be provided with language that is as simple as possible, and that in this way they will be able most easily to acquire new vocabulary items. This view seems to us to show a fundamental misunderstanding of how language works. If a word typically occurs in a sentence which is grammatically complex or alongside vocabulary items that are infrequent, it would be misleading of a dictionary to present that word in a very simple clause or sentence with easy vocabulary. By doing this, students might perhaps learn the meaning of the word; what they would not do would be to see the word in its characteristic environment, and thus would gain no insight into how to use the word for themselves. It is important that we realize that learners' needs for encoding are at least as urgent as their needs for decoding. More so, perhaps, in these days when such strong emphasis is placed on communication. That being so, we must ensure that the information we give students will genuinely help them to produce language of their own which is as near as possible to that produced by native speakers. In the past, dictionaries have been seen more as aids to decoding than as aids to encoding. There is no reason why they should not succeed in doing both.

The realisation that it was important for us to view the Cobuild dictionary as both a decoding and an encoding dictionary led to a consideration of the characteristics of examples and their deployment.

Typical Examples

Our first and foremost requirement for examples is typicality: that they should show the way in which people actually use the word they are exemplifying. This sounds a simple requirement; but when it is examined it is by no means as obvious as it seems. People use language creatively, often delibera-tely seeking out the boundaries of the meaning of a word in order to communicate more interestingly and more effectively, so that it is no easy matter to find examples that are typical. For the extended sense of the word *torrent*, intuitive knowledge of the language seems to tell us that 'a torrent of abuse' would be the most typical use; yet a quick glance at the corpus reveals far more lines for 'a torrent of outrage', 'a torrent of confession and explana-tion', and 'the torrent of invective' than there are lines for 'a torrent of abuse'. What seems to be happening is that 'abuse' is slightly too general; and users prefer to specify more precisely the type of abuse that is pouring out. For the dictionary, therefore, the word 'abuse' was built into the explanation: 'A torrent of questions, abuse, etc. is a lot of questions, abuse, etc. directed continuously at someone', with the example given being 'He was answered with a torrent of French oaths'.

As native speakers of a language we convey meaning by expressions that are not only grammatical but also seem perfectly natural to the people we are communicating with. Dictionaries have traditionally concentrated more on the grammatical, partly perhaps because they have been seen as tools for interpreting language rather than for creating it. The Cobuild dictionary is designed in all its features to help learners to create language; and it is thus that notions of typicality have loomed large in every discussion of choice of examples. Native speakers can, with little hesitation, select sentences that are natural, idiomatic, and therefore representative of what people actually say from among a range of grammatically correct paraphrases, which are in many cases highly unlikely ever to be used (see Littlewood 1981).

Natural Examples

It is thus not sufficient for learners to be able to create sentences that are grammatically well-formed; they must also be helped to produce sentences that would be recognised as representative and 'natural' by native speakers. Sinclair (1984) discusses the concept of naturalness, which he suggests is the well-formedness of sentences not in isolation but in text. This concept, he feels, may be useful to the learners of a language, as it might help them to distinguish sentences which are truly natural from those which are merely grammatical. As Sinclair points out, it is true that non-natural sentences do occur in genuine language, typically in texts which are not intended by their authors for direct communication with other people. But this in no way detracts from the importance of presenting learners with example sentences that are technically well-formed grammatically and are also representative and natural.

The whole question of what is natural in language is a very difficult one to answer. What exactly do we mean by natural? How do we know whether something is natural or unnatural? Naturalness as a concept is difficult to define. It is indeed really just a cover term for a large set of particular rules, which we do not yet fully know or understand, about how language works above the level of the sentence. What we sometimes do is break these rules; and then we are aware that we are flouting them. When we, as language users, are concentrating on what we want to say, we automatically accommodate the rules, either by observing them or by breaking them when we feel that there is an overriding reason to do so. Often, for example, native speakers will deliberately create humorous or ironic effects by inserting an old-fashioned, formal word or phrase into a sentence, thus producing language which breaks one of the rules of naturalness, which would seem to be something like: 'All the words used in a given sentence should belong to the same period or time and the same level of formality'. Some words in English are now used almost exclusively in this way, unless they are set in a historical context. Take the word *ablutions*, for example. There are eight citations of it in the 20-million-word corpus which makes up the Birmingham Collection of English Text, all of which seem to me to have slightly humorous or slightly ironic overtones. The following is a typical example: 'The water was lukewarm by now, besides being thick and scummy from her husband's ablutions'. The word *imbibe* in its meaning of 'drink' is now rarely used except for humour or irony; the lines in the corpus show this: 'Nevertheless, she did manage to imbibe a glass of hot milk and two digestive biscuits'.

Often, however, we cannot find a justification or explanation of this kind for an oddity, and we therefore are left to conclude that it is unnatural, although it is sometimes difficult to explain why. On occasions it seems unnatural only because we do not have enough text, or enough knowledge of the circumstances in which the utterance was used. On occasions we distrust the source. In a free information leaflet available at Singapore Airport, the final sentence in one section reads: 'If you find yourself kicking your heels at Singapore Airport, do not be down-hearted . . .'. This seems to hit a wrong note, but why? It is not just that we do not actually use phrases like 'kicking one's heels' very often in written language, it is not just the juxtaposition of 'kick one's heels' and 'down-hearted', though that is perhaps an unlikely collocation. It is not just that the phrase is being used with a slightly extended meaning – normally, if you are kicking your heels, someone is deliberately keeping you waiting, and no-one would accuse airlines of doing that! The unease we feel seems to come from a combination of all of these – and perhaps more. This example from the leaflet is a very obvious case, where there are several slight infelicities that can be easily picked out. Other instances are less obvious, but wherever you feel that something 'doesn't sound quite right', its naturalness is not manifest and native speakers would be unhappy for it to be used as a model for learners.

This means that one of the aids that we as dictionary writers can give students is to help them to find ways of knowing for themselves which of their well-formed sentences are natural or native-like; this information can partly be imparted through the judicious choice of examples. Examples must thus show words used in their most typical contexts, most frequent grammatical structures, and with other words that are often used at the same time in the same sentence. This is because the very choosing of an example gives it a special status. The fact that it is printed in the dictionary shows that it has been deliberately chosen, and therefore the user of the dictionary is entitled to regard it as a suitable model, and to make use of features in the example on the assumption that they are not misleading.

Isolated Examples

One reason why dictionaries have not in the past helped learners to use natural language is that most of the examples given have been full sentences, prepared for being presented in isolation rather than being thought of as extracts from a text. For a sentence that is being looked at in isolation to make sense, it has to contain much more information than you are likely to find in real language where sentences do not occur alone but come before or after other sentences, and so are a small part of a longer text. A sentence which is being used in isolation, then, usually has no loose ends and is completely fleshed-out, so that readers are left in no doubt as to exactly what is meant. This means that there must be a specified subject which, if human, probably does something to someone for a reason.

Take the following published example from a learners' dictionary: 'The teacher used to cane me when I behaved badly'. It is very unlikely that this would be the first sentence in a text – it plunges too quickly into its theme, and leaves the reader puzzled. Who is the teacher? Why are we hearing about the speaker's schooldays? So we have to say that this sentence is likely to be in the middle of a text. That leads to other problems.

If you precede it by something like 'I was very unhappy when I was at school', you would have to follow it with something such as 'This made me behave badly and so all the teachers used to cane me'. Or you could preface it by 'I went to such a small school that there was only one teacher', but you would need to continue this with 'She used to cane us whenever we behaved badly'.

The most likely way to introduce a topic like this would be with something like 'Have I ever told you how unhappy I was at school?'. Then you can perhaps follow on with 'The teacher used to cane me when I behaved badly', and go on to give further details. This is because you have now, by your first sentence, set the scene for your further remarks, and can then go on to talk about your schooldays, though admittedly the quoted sentence is still rather implausible.

The necessity for examples to fit into coherent text is important because language is not a series of isolated sentences, and students should not be encouraged to think that it is. We should be much more aware than we have been in the past of the pitfalls of giving these fully-formed isolated sentences as examples. What we are perhaps doing is teaching students to produce for themselves good, well-formed sentences that cannot be fitted into longer text. Each individual sentence may be acceptable, but when they are put together they do not form natural English. Teachers often complain that their pupils cannot write good English; perhaps their methods are partly to be blamed for this. It could be that they have focused too much attention on the sentence rather than on how the sentences are linked together in text, that they have presented sentences to their students in isolation when they have been teaching rather than building the presentation or practice stages of their lessons into coherent linguistic contexts. By this means, they have perhaps encouraged their students to think of language as being made up of sentences rather than of text, and so have unwittingly given students the habit of cramming far too much information into each individual sentence for it to fit happily into natural discourse.

Interesting Examples

Linguists and teachers agree that language is a fascinating subject. There is always so much going on in any piece of speech or writing – not merely the overt meaning of each individual word chosen but the overall effect created by looking at them as a whole. Why has the speaker or writer chosen a particular level of formality? What effect is he or she intending to have on the person hearing or reading? How will the hearer or reader actually interpret the language? There is, of course, no certainty that the intended effect will be the actual effect. Language is, therefore, inherently interesting; and whenever we use it, we should make it interesting, choosing our words with care so that people get pleasure from them. It follows from this that the examples learners meet in a dictionary should also be of as much interest as is consistent with being helpful and intelligible. A slight caveat, though. It may be that we can interest our learners too much; and by doing that we might confuse them. We might lead them to focus not on the point at issue but on the more bizarre elements we have introduced, either because they happen to be there or because we are wanting to choose a lively example. This could mean that readers are distracted and thus fail to understand the point we are intending to exemplify.

When we choose examples to present to learners there is always a slight temptation to choose not an everyday example of the use of a word but the very interesting, the slightly unusual usage, because this is the one that leaps out at us from the concordances. It is difficult to settle for the ordinary or what we might call the 'central, typical' example because we might feel that there is nothing interesting about it. And so we select examples on the boundary of normal usage if we are not very careful. In the first draft of the dictionary, the example given for the word *culinary* was: 'The kitchen was small, compact, clean, a minor culinary symphony in stainless steel and white tiles'. For some types of writing, this would be perfectly appropriate – for the novel that it came from, for example. But as the only example of a word in a learners' dictionary, it is quite inappropriate. This example, was, therefore, omitted and was replaced by two examples: '. . . their culinary skills' and 'Each son has certain culinary specialities which he enjoys making'.

Another inappropriate example, though for quite different reasons, was given in the first draft of the dictionary for the expression *a case of*, where you are stating the way that a situation is, sometimes in contrast with the way that other people think it is. The example read: 'It's not that insurance companies don't trust students to be good drivers. It's not a case of trusting them at all, it's a case of their finding students to be the biggest risk'. This is in fact a good typical use of this meaning of *case*; but there is so much here that learners have to disentangle before they can appreciate what is actually being said that in most instances they will give up before they succeed. Again, this was changed in the final dictionary text, for the sake of clarity and intelligibility to: 'It was a case of not knowing what else to do'. Not such a good example, but one, perhaps, that will be of more help to the users of the dictionary.

Authentic Examples

However, presuming that our examples do not fall into this trap of distracting the user, what causes us to feel that authentic examples are almost always superior to made-up ones? The essential argument, of course, boring and obvious though it might be, is one already mentioned: that real examples have actually occurred in the language. This does not mean, as I have just shown, that everything that we find in the corpus can be used. It is a well-known fact that users of a language play with it, exploit it, thus rendering some usages unusual or untypical. But the fact that examples have occurred does help – especially when we compare them with some made-up examples that have been published in material designed to help the learner.

One well-known dictionary gives the following example for the verb *salvage* meaning 'save': '"We'll try to salvage your leg," said the doctor to the trapped man.' This is a well-formed but unnatural example. In the first place, natural-ness of language use suggests that in a real-life situation we would already know who at least one of the participants in the drama is. There would therefore be no need at this point in the story to specify both 'the doctor' and the 'trapped man'. The use of the word 'the' in front of both 'doctor' and 'trapped man' also tells us that they have already been mentioned, if the author is adhering to the accepted rules of discourse. We would also know that if the leg is to be salvaged, the circumstances in which the accident occurred must also have been mentioned, and so it is redundant to say yet again that the man is trapped. In other words, this is another example of the type mentioned in the section on 'Isolated Examples' – it gives us far too much information, and so carries too much meaning content for one sen-tence. It works as an isolated sentence. It is only when you try to fit it into text that you realise how unlikely it is that anyone would actually produce such a sentence.

Examples of this type, with their almost total independence of context, are not helpful. It is indeed possible that, because they are so elaborately spelled out, they actually discourage learners from thinking about the meaning of the word. So much help to understanding is given that learners might get a false sense of security, believing that they understand the meaning; so that when they meet the word used within text they might find that they have but a sketchy understanding of it.

To take another fairly trivial but relevant point. In a published dictionary the word *salute* meaning 'greet someone' is exemplified by: '. . . saluted his friend with a wave of his hand'. This example is certainly plausible, but it seems slightly contrived, in order to help clarify the definition given: 'to greet, esp. with polite words or with a sign'.

When checked out against the corpus, it can be seen that a *wave* is one thing that you do not usually salute people with: 'He saluted her with a friendly word . . . with congratulations . . . with a shouted "Ben!"' All to do with language, not gestures. This is intriguing because there is no obvious reason why it should not be used with gestures.

One possibility might be that when a word like *salute* is used in an extended sense from what might be thought of as its core meaning, it is less likely to be used with other words that relate to its transposed meaning. In this case, then, 'a wave' is less likely than 'a word' or 'a shout' when *salute* is used in its meaning of 'greet'. It is a misunderstanding of this point that frequently leads astray those who concoct examples, both in and out of the classroom.

This is not to say, of course, that *salute* is never used with *wave*. If, however, we can show that it is not typically used with gestures, it seems perverse to give that as our only example of how the word is used. What is happening here with these made-up dictionary examples is that we cannot trust native speakers to invent sentences except in a proper communicative context – where they are actually using language rather than sitting thinking about it.

One further example to show how intuition can lead us to produce sentences that are grammatically correct but fairly unlikely to occur in text – the phrasal verb *take aback* meaning 'astound' or 'astonish'. Ask any user of the language whether it is used in the active, and he or she will probably say 'yes' and what is more will then go on to produce sentences using it in the active – probably few of which would stand up to really close scrutiny. Sentences would thus be produced such as 'My sudden anger took aback the children in my class', 'The price of oranges takes me aback every time I buy them', and so on. Again, that is not to say that *take aback* cannot be used in the active. It can, and it is.

However, out of 14 instances in our original 7.3 million word Main Corpus, only two are in the active, with 12 being in the passive. It therefore seems sensible to show it used in the passive in the examples that we give in a learners' dictionary. One dictionary gives as its only example: 'The price of the tickets rather took me aback'; and that in spite of the fact that the rubric at the beginning of the entry says 'take aback' [often pass.]. Why not then exemplify with a line such as: 'I was taken aback by Davis's reaction', 'He was so taken aback that he found himself saying "no"', or 'America's allies were rather taken aback by the suddenness of this announcement'. These are real lines from the Cobuild corpus, which are more typical than the one given in the active – which is, let me repeat, perfectly possible. It is not ungrammatical, it is just not very likely.

Real-text examples, as has already been mentioned, are not neat little isolated wholes. They carry a lot of loose ends – they follow on from what has been said and they lead in to what will be said. They show all the features of normal discourse – features such as the use of pronouns rather than nouns, of linking words such as *and* and *therefore*, of forcing the reader's attention back to what has already been said by the use of such words as *that* and *this*. All of these are features which are usually ignored, or dealt with very sketchily, in dictionaries.

Real-text examples show very clearly that sentences are not complete units in themselves, but that they depend for much of their meaning on what has gone before and what will come after. A couple of sentences taken from the front page of *The Mail on Sunday*, 8 February 1987, should exemplify this point. In each case the sentence is only the third one in the story and yet each time a great deal of knowledge of the topic is already taken for granted. The two sentences are: 'Both have plagued her since last summer and were thought to be behind a series of defeats in the world cross-country championships' and 'The assault left co-accused Andrew Byrne, 24, brain-damaged'.

These sentences both contain, in Sinclair's (1984) term, 'range-finders' – words and phrases that depend for a great deal of their meaning on reference out to other parts of the text. This means that somewhere in what has been said or in what will be said the person reading the story will be able to identify who or what is being referred to.

Thought-Provoking Examples

If, therefore, we are to help learners in their production of language, the examples that we give should, where appropriate, contain typical range-finder words such as *the, that* or pronouns. For the phrasal verb *back down on something*, the dictionary has as its second example: 'Eventually he backed down on the question of seating'. This is a typical example, showing nicely the pattern associated with this verb – followed by the preposition *on* and another noun group. But it is also rather more than just a typical example; there is potential here for the learner to go a little bit further if he or she is willing to do so, and is prepared to look a little more deeply at what is actually said. Who is the 'he' that the example is talking about? What type of person might he be? What context could these words be said in? What might have been going on? What does the word 'eventually' imply? And so on. There are so many questions that can be asked about this very short piece of text. And very importantly, there are no right answers to these questions given in the dictionary. What matters is that the learner has been encouraged, either sitting alone at home or participating in a class, to think about the implications of a piece of language.

This potential for stimulating thought must surely be one of our aims when we exemplify language. Not only that the learners understand the language – that goes without saying; but also that, where possible, there should be more than mere surface understanding. The example should have the potential for being taken further, for acting as a springboard from which learners can take off and begin to work out for themselves how little areas of the language work. It should ideally encourage people to experiment, to play with words, by showing them what can be done – not at the fringes of meaning but right there in the heart of it.

Another interesting, although rather difficult, line exemplifying the word *civilly* is: 'I made my farewells as civilly as I could under such provocation'. Once again, this is a typical example of the word being used – in particular, the rather cold formality of the word is emphasised by the choice of fairly difficult vocabulary – 'make one's farewells' instead of 'say goodbye', 'under such provocation' instead of 'in the circumstances'. In addition, it leads the reader to wonder what had happened that could end in such a way. What provocation had been offered to the speaker? Why had it worried her so much? What would happen to this relationship in the future? All questions which it is impossible to answer definitively, but which it is certainly possible to speculate on. At Cobuild we would contend that it is better to give a slightly difficult example such as this than to give one that has been made up and does not sound natural in all its details. Many teachers would dismiss this as a bad example because it is difficult. We would argue that its very difficulty makes it a good example for the word is exemplifying, because it is typical of how the word is actually used.

Collocations

One other thing that real-text examples give is accurate collocations. Again, this is an area that people have difficulty in appreciating fully. Once a collocate is given, it is so obvious that no-one can imagine not guessing it correctly. Yet, when people are asked to give the collocates of words, they frequently do not do well – except for those words where collocates are frozen. Any reasonably aware user of English will say that *graven* collocates with *image* and *blonde* with *hair*; but when asked for the collocates of *target* are unlikely to mention *attack* or *suitable*. A small experiment was carried out on the collocates of the word *feet*. Fifty-three students were asked to write down the five words that they thought were the most likely collocates of *feet*; and their results were compared with what is actually found in our Main Corpus.

What was revealed by the experiment is that when people are asked to think of collocates, they frequently think more of semantic sets than of words which are actually likely to occur in the near vicinity of each other. Many of the students thus gave as collocates other parts of the body – *legs, toes, head*, etc; others gave *shoe, sandals, sock*; yet others suggested *walk* or *run*. Only two people suggested *tall*, which is a very significant collocate indeed; seven suggested numbers such as *four, five* and *six*, which do collocate significantly; and not one person mentioned *high* or *long*, which are again extremely significant. As soon as they were told the most frequent lexical collocates the students could none of them understand why they had not thought of these themselves. The important thing, of course, is that they had not.

The same students were then asked to write down the five words that they thought were most likely to collocate with the word *hint*. Again, interestingly, many of the students took some of the attributes of the word, and then gave as collocates words which embodied these attributes – words such as *subtle, small* and *clue*. Seven of the 53 gave what is, in our corpus, the third most common collocate *give*; five gave the topmost collocate *take*; and none suggested the second most common collocate – the word *no*, as in 'There was no hint of winter in the air' and 'Her behaviour gave no hint of her real feelings'. Once again, intuition is not as good as evidence.

Collocation is yet another area where previous dictionaries are of doubtful reliability. The example given to exemplify the word *embankment* in one such dictionary is: 'We must throw up an embankment to stop the river from flooding the town'. Once again here, we have too much information in the example – with an almost total repeat of much of the information given in the definition, which reads: 'a wide wall of stones or earth, which is built to keep a river from overflowing its banks or to carry a road or railway over low ground'. It also seems inherently unlikely that *embankment* will collocate with *throw up*; an embankment is something that is very deliberately built, for a specific purpose; *throw up* is much too casual. In our corpus the most common lexical collocates for *embankment* are *railway, high*, and *steep*, with *build* being the verb used for constructing embankments rather than *throw up*. A typical line from the corpus is: 'Under it, behind high embankments, the railway wound its way along the edge of the city'.

With the enlarged corpus of nearly 20 million words, there is rarely any need to consider thinking up examples. There is sufficient evidence of how the word has been used: we can see what its collocates are; we can check whether the subject or the object of a verb is more typically a person or a thing – and if a person, whether names or pronouns are more common. The word *feel* is interesting in this respect. It is obvious that in its main meaning the subject is a person; what is less obvious is the fact that the subject is overwhelmingly most frequently the pronoun 'I': 'I feel happy . . . I feel that I have worked well . . . I feel like going out'. As soon as this is noted, it becomes obvious. But again, looking at other dictionaries, we get far too many examples which do not have 'I' as the subject: '. . . to feel the wind on one's face . . . They are beginning to feel hungry . . . Do you feel like a beer? . . . She doesn't say much but she feels . . . My leg feels as if it was broken'. All of these are perfectly acceptable English; but using too many subjects other than 'I' very slightly misleads the learner as to the most typical grammatical structure. *Feel* is of course used with other personal pronouns as its subject, and this should be shown; but so should the preponderance of 'I'.

The phrasal verb *bowl someone over* is another case in point. For it, one dictionary gives as its only example: 'Your sudden news really bowled me over', and another gives 'His generosity bowled me over'. Looking at the Main Corpus we see that what more typically bowls people over is not information, attitudes, etc. but other people: 'The sight of her bowled him over . . . Liz, aged 18, was bowled over by him . . . I felt out of my depth and altogether bowled over'.

Editing Examples

This leads to a further point. We now have access to a corpus of nearly 20 million words which provide us with evidence for most of what we want to say about the language at this level. It does not tell us much about very uncommon words, uncommon technical terms, uncommon senses of words, or uncommon phrases. In real life, however, most native speakers rarely need uncommon words, senses, or phrases; and language learners need them still less. We therefore have, for most meanings of most words, examples of how those meanings have been used in the past few years in both writing and speech. This information is available to us in a form which is immediately accessible. This gives us for the first time ever a genuine choice. We read the lines to see whether there are any that are suitable for use as examples. If so, well and good. If not, there are two options open to us – either to make up an example or to change slightly a line that is already there, by simplifying the vocabulary, regularising the syntax, omitting unnecessary adjectives, and so on. We take either of these options with great reluctance.

We have learned what happens when we sit and intuit how words are used – we are likely to get it wrong. We also know that as soon as we start playing around with examples, making them more 'accessible' or more 'regular', we are liable to take the life out of them, or worse, mislead the user of the dictionary. Something as simple as the changing of a present tense for a past, the substituting of one word for another, the adding of a proper name rather than a pronoun, can ruin the whole feel of an example and destroy its authenticity. The sentence is still well formed, but it no longer seems natural to a sensitive native speaker. In the first draft of the dictionary one of the examples offered for the word *anguish* was: 'His anguish was terrible'. This sounds unnatural, and has obviously been changed in some way. Looking up the concordance lines for *anguish*, the original of this one read: 'She realized that his own eyes were full of tears. His anguish was terrible for her to behold'. This authentic line has a very different feel to it. What seems to be wrong with the short version is that it is too bald and also comes too close to stating the obvious – we naturally assume that anguish is terrible. Perhaps more importantly, in the short version the word 'terrible' describes 'his anguish', whereas in the original it is more plausibly interpreted as referring to her reactions to his grief. This original line was obviously too long for the dictionary, which is why it had been shortened in the first place. It was therefore dropped as an example, and two other lines were used: '. . . a quarrel which caused her intense unhappiness and anguish . . . She was doubled over, her whole face distorted in anguish'.

Another example in the first draft of the dictionary, for the word *bereaved*, was: 'The bereaved mother was trying to conceal her sadness'. This sounds contrived, just about possible, but unlikely. The original concordance line from which this was derived is: 'The bereaved mother who is trying to conceal her sadness from her children is said to be putting on a brave face'. This is too long for a dictionary example, and so the following line was used instead: '. . . the tactful respect due to someone recently bereaved'. The changes made to the *bereaved* line illustrate a tendency which is perhaps typical of course-book and dictionary writers – that of shortening or simplifying examples, often by making subordinate clauses into main clauses or by making complicated verbal patterns into simple present or past tenses. The *bereaved* example shows clearly how constraints of naturalness can be interfered with if this is done.

When work started on the Cobuild dictionary, most of the lexicographers believed that some judicious changing of examples, especially in order to make neat little sentences, was the best thing to do. We felt that we could somehow improve on real examples, and make them more helpful to learners. Soon we came to realise that, perhaps annoyingly, the language just does not occur in conveniently short and detachable sentences of this kind.

If we have learned one thing above all else, it is that speakers and writers use sentences to form longer structures, and so rely heavily on the language surrounding them for the full communication of their meaning. Some words, indeed, are almost certain to require a longer context than a single sentence. A word such as *reason* needs the text following it before it has much communicative value. Words such as *therefore* or *however* frequently start a sentence, but need what has gone before to explain them fully. This means that there are some words which are difficult to exemplify well within the constraints of a dictionary. Anything really typical is space-consuming; and yet to give shortened versions is misleading. It is therefore perhaps preferable to give one or two longer examples as opposed to four or five shorter ones. One of the lines used in the dictionary for *reason* is long but very typical: 'Public pressure is towards more street lighting rather than less: the reason is, of course, that people feel safer in well-lit streets'. *Therefore* is also given a long example: 'I'm not a member of the Church of England myself, therefore it would be rather impertinent of me to express an opinion'.

Conclusion

What we are aiming to do in the Cobuild Dictionary is to give learners examples which have genuinely occurred in the language, in contrast to examples that have been invented specifically to fit the needs of a dictionary definition. We are therefore not using the examples as a prop or an aid to understanding the explanations. The explanations are seen as standing on their own, and we hope that they are clear and unambiguous. The examples that follow are then chosen to illustrate certain specific points. They might illustrate particular syntax patterns. In that case they might reinforce the syntax pattern used in the definition, but might equally well not do so, where alternative patterns are found to have more or less the same frequency. They might illustrate very typical collocational patterning, where again they might or might not reduplicate some of the information given in the explanation of the word. They might show a typical context that the word is likely to be used in. They might encourage the learner to stop and think a little about the word. In very exceptional cases, they might do all of these. What they will be, in almost all cases, is natural and authentic, because we are convinced that, by reading as much authentic material as possible, learners will be helped along the path of greater naturalness in their own language use.

References

Dictionaries

Chambers Universal Learners' Dictionary (1980)
Collins English Learner's Dictionary (1974)
Longman Active Study Dictionary (1983)
Longman Dictionary of Contemporary English (1978)
Oxford Advanced Learner's Dictionary of Current English (3rd edition, 1974)

Other Works:

Littlewood, W. 1986. *Communicative Language Teaching – An Introduction*. Cambridge University Press.
Sinclair, J. M. 1984. 'Naturalness in Language' in *Corpus Linguistics*, Aarts and Meijs (eds.). Rodopi.

CHAPTER 8: **The Nature of the Evidence**

John Sinclair

In this paper I shall consider a tiny but representative segment of the patterning of modern English and examine it in some detail. The objectives are to demonstrate:

– how carefully the language is patterned
– how the description is very sensitive to the number of instances of a form
– how criteria for meaning (see Chapter 4) are applied in a specific case.

Phrasal Verbs

The choice of an example to illustrate the argument of this paper was, as usual, partly accidental and partly deliberate. I was looking for a fairly common, rather dull little word that was comparatively neglected in description and in teaching. I found out by chance that the word *set* was not well regarded by some experienced teacher-colleagues, and noticed that it got scant treatment in the syllabuses that I was able to examine. The immediate presumption was that it was a difficult word to isolate semantically. What does *set* mean? is hardly a sensible question. It has to be put into context because in most of its usage it contributes to meaning in combination with other words.

Among the many combinations of *set* are a number of phrasal verbs, such as *set about, set in, set off* and these are picked out in language teaching as offering exquisite problems to the learner. The reasons for their causing problems is easily explained. The co-occurrence of two quite common little words can unexpectedly create a fairly subtle new meaning that cannot be systematically related to either or both of the original words. The disposition of the two words involved, and their syntax, is governed by complex and unpredictable rules.

The prospect sounds formidable even for native speakers, yet they not only manage phrasal verbs with aplomb, but seem to prefer them to single word alternatives. In fact, the whole drift of the historical development of English has been towards the replacement of words by phrases, with word-order acquiring greater significance.

The area is ripe for investigation, to see if there is any help that can be offered to the teacher and learner.

Some Numerical Facts

In the Cobuild Main Corpus of approximately 7.3 million words, there are 2,320 instances of the different forms of the word *set*. We associate together the forms *set, sets,* and *setting* as instances of the word *set,* and the frequency of each is:

set	1885	(80%)
sets	219	(9%)
setting	246	(11%)

Other possible associates, such as *setter* and *settee,* are ignored.

Set is thus one of the commonest words in the language – ranked number 272 in our count of the Cobuild data. However, if we compare the relative frequency of the inflected forms *sets* and *setting,* we see that they are not nearly as common as *set,* being approximately 9% and 11% of the uninflected form.

This is a commonly observed pattern, where one of the forms is much more common than any other. It means that if *sets* or *setting* has a use which is not shared by *set,* we have much less evidence to go on. Whatever criteria we use, there is nearly ten times as much evidence available for *set.*

It could be argued that in one respect at least the inflection of *set* is untypical, and that the frequency of forms of *set* will reflect the oddity. *Set* is one of a handful of verbs in English which do not have a separate past tense form. So whatever frequency is assigned to *walk* and *walked, say* and *said,* etc. is not differentiated in *set.* To complicate the picture further, all the three forms are also readily available as nouns, and the picture is not at all straightforward.

However, compared to the vast majority of words, even the least common form *sets* is generously represented. And when we look for combinations of even frequent words, the expectations are not promising.

If a corpus is held to be representative of the language as a whole, the probability of occurrence of a word-form can be expressed in general as a relation between the frequency of the word-form in the corpus and the total number of word-forms in the corpus.

In the case of *set* this is

$$\frac{1855}{7,300,000} \qquad \text{or} \qquad 0.00025$$

This means that the chance of *set* being the next word in the text is about 250 per million, or one occurrence in every 3,935 words.

How common are the phrasal verbs with *set*? *Set* is particularly rich in making combinations with words like *about, in, up, out, on, off,* and these words are very common. How likely is *set off* to occur? Both are frequent words; *off* occurs approximately 556 times in a million words. Its probability of being the next word is 556 = 0.00055. We must multiply the probabilities, because the question we are asking can be roughly rephrased as follows: how likely is *off* to occur immediately after *set*? Since in a million words there are 250 such places, then what we are asking is the same as asking how often *set* will occur in a text of 250 words. This is 0.00025 × 0.00055, which gives us the tiny figure of 0.0000001375.

Two important considerations are left out of this calculation, one linguistic and the other statistical.

a the phrasal verb *set off* can have a noun group inside it.
e.g. It was the hedge which *set* the garden *off* .

There are very few of these and so they have little effect on the general numerical argument.

b The assumption behind this calculation is that the words are distributed at random in a text. It is obvious to a linguist that this is not so, and a rough measure of how much *set* and *off* attract each other is to compare the probability with what actually happens.

In a text of 7.3 million words we might expect $0.0000001375 \times 7,300,000$ occurrences of *set off*, i.e. once only. Since there are several different phrasal verbs with the form *set off*, and no doubt some occurrences of *set* followed by *off* which do not provide an instance of the phrasal verb, we will require a fairly large number of occurrences of the combination of forms to show the characteristic patterns. This in turn means very large amounts of text, running into the hundreds of millions.

The gloomy picture thus projected by our arithmetic is relieved quite a bit by what we find in actual texts. This is because our initial assumption, that the words are distributed at random, is false. *Set off* occurs nearly 70 times in the 7.3 million word corpus. That is enough to show its main patterning and it suggests that in currently-held corpora there will be found sufficient evidence for the description of a substantial collection of phrases. It must be stressed that both *set* and *off* are particularly common words, and that we are also interested in thousands of apparently 'common' phrases which are made up of much less common words – like *gentleman's agreement, defence mechanism, open to question, sit tight*.

At present we make up for deficiencies in statistically reliable evidence by the intervention of human editors. This is likely to continue, because it seems that no set of texts, no matter how extensive, provides enough evidence for the description of its own vocabulary. There is always a huge tail of words which have only a handful of occurrences.

As statistical methods improve, the extent and reliability of the linguistic statements will increase. As computational processing improves, the quantity and quality of the linguistic evidence will increase. New projects include schemes for passing massive amounts of language through computers and retaining evidence of unusual events – rare words, neologisms, etc. (Clear, 1987). A fully automatic dictionary is at the design stage and should be constructed in order to reveal both the strengths and the shortcomings of the machines.

'Set in'

In the central part of this paper I shall consider all the instances of *set, sets* and *setting* followed by *in*. The different ways in which the co-occurrence of these words contribute to meanings will emerge, and the evidence will be found mainly in the surrounding language.

We begin by isolating all instances of the sequence *set in*. There are 90 of them. To this we add *sets in* (16), *setting in* (6), and for the sake of completeness, *settings in* (2). The total of instances of a form of *set* followed immediately by *in* is thus 114.

The first analysis combines several steps:

- assignment of word class
- division into independent and dependent meanings
- assignment of independent meanings to senses
- identification of phraseology of dependent meanings
- assignment of dependent meanings to senses

Anomalies, uncertainties and errors are dealt with as they arise.

Taking all these steps together, the 114 instances are divided into:

a nouns
b verbs – sense (i)
c verbs – sense (ii)
d verbs – minor senses
e verbs – sundry idioms
f phrasal verbs
g anomalies, etc.

Let us first dispose of the anomalies. There are five of these, one a typographical error (*as-sets*) and one where even the 20-word citation does not give enough evidence of its meaning. Two are instances of other idioms with *set*, but in the passive so that *set* is immediately followed by *in*, e.g.

He was asking a *precedent* to be *set* in a field where . . .

The last is

the controlled fires he *sets* in spring devastate shrubs . . .

Noun

The use of *set* as a noun includes all four forms of the lemma:

set	6 out of 90 (7%)
sets	4 out of 16 (25%)
setting	5 out of 6 (83%)
settings	2 (100%)

Both instances of *settings* are nominal, of course. All but one of *setting* are nominal, which suggests that the verb is not much used in the progressive tense. Collocations include *work setting, social setting, a suitable setting. Sets* as a noun includes *television sets* and *chemistry sets. Set* as a noun includes *the social set, the Martini set, theater set, a fishing set*, and a *TV set*.

These are all characteristic nominal uses of *set* which have been captured because they happen to be immediately followed by *in*. They would be best treated in a description of the whole nominal pattern of *set*. Here we merely note them and clear them out of the way.

Verb

Among the verbal uses, there are two principal independent senses and two minor ones. Only the form *set* occurs – not even *sets*, suggesting a preponderance of past tense usage.

There are 25 instances of *set* followed by *in* and meaning approximately 'placed' as in paragraphs 2, 3 and 4 of the Cobuild dictionary entry for *set*. Seven are to do with physical position, including one about someone who *had his bones set in an awmbry*. Only *OED* was able to tell me that an awmbry was a kind of cupboard, and this was not an instance of bonesetting. Twelve more are to do with the disposition of buildings, streets, etc. Three are abstract placings (e.g. *high expectations set in the commerical future for nuclear power*), two are variations of a well-known quotation (including the remarkable *no man, or woman, is an island, set in a silver sea*). One is a figurative extension, *set in a haze of blue*.

There are 18 instances of *set* followed by *in*, meaning approximately 'located', and characteristically used of plays, films and stories (see paragraph 34 of *set* in the Cobuild dictionary).

Clearly, the film, *set in* in Glasgow and the Highlands . . .

Of the two minor independent senses of *set* one is to do with typesetting and the other is *set in my memory* which means in context 'fixed in place' and not just 'placed', closest perhaps to paragraph 5 of the dictionary entry.

In all the above verbal instances, the word *in* is an important collocate, and not the casual co-occurrence that was found in the nominal uses.

Idioms

There are 20 instances of uses which I have termed idiomatic because in addition to *set* and *in* there are other restrictions as well. Of these, six have *set in* followed by a possessive pronoun and the word *ways*, as in

. . . too old and *set in her ways* ever to change.

This usage is described in paragraph 28 of the Cobuild entry.

Five are of the phrase *set in motion* (see the dictionary entry for *motion* paragraph 5), and the remainder are one or two instances of *set in train, set in hand, set in order, set in (a traditional) mould, set in front of, set in juxtaposition to*, and *set in the balance*. This set of idioms comprises items for which a much larger text corpus would be needed to see if it was justifiable to pick them out as I have done here. They all seem common enough, and it is a slight shock to see how rare they are – one has to keep in mind the extreme unlikelihood, on statistical grounds, of any of them occurring at all, ever.

Phrasal Verb

Up to this point, we have been merely clearing the ground for study of the phrasal verb *set in*. The original 114 instances are reduced to 29. Three of the four forms are involved, as follows:

set	16 out of 90 (18%)
sets	10 out of 16 (63%)
setting	1 out of 6 (17%)

If something *sets in*, it begins, and seems likely to continue and develop.

One of the first things to note about the phrasal verb is that it seems to occur typically in a small and/or minor part of a sentence. It is not easy to say exactly what gives this feeling but the following may be factors:

a the clauses in which *set in* is chosen are in general rather short – six words or fewer in the main. The longer ones are longer because of an adjunct rather than the subject, which is in most cases a single word or an article and noun pair.

b a number of the clauses are subordinate. With the samples available it is not possible to assign status in every case, and there are some of clear main clauses; but I think the tendency to lower status should be noted.

c *set in* is final in the clause in 22 of the 29 cases, and sentence-final in nine of them, showing a clear tendency to end structures.

Observations such as those above are difficult to evaluate because we lack comparative stylistic data, but the following is a very typical example:

. . . where the rot *set in*.

Verb Forms

As *a* above suggests, the majority of verbal groups are simple, containing just the form of *set*. All the occurrences of *sets* (10) are of course in the present tense, and at least nine of these deal with general states of affairs rather than the here-and-now. None of them are unambiguously in a main clause, where the tense choice relates directly to time.

Of the others, the vast majority are in the narrative past – either simple past (9) or pluperfect with *had* (4). There are single instances of *would, has,* and *was,* and one complex verb *started to set in* which again shows the narrative past.

From this we can conclude that there is a tendency towards reference to things past or things which are not sensitive to the passage of time, which goes reasonably well with the meaning of the phrase; it is not used in speculation about the future, or in statements about the present. For example:

It was no wonder that disillusion *had set in*.

Subjects

The most striking feature of this phrasal verb is the nature of the subjects. In general they refer to unpleasant states of affairs. Only three refer to the weather; a few are neutral, such as *reaction*, and *trend*. The main vocabulary is *rot* (3), *decay, malaise, despair, ill-will, decadence, impoverishment, infection, prejudice, vicious (circle), rigor mortis, numbness, bitterness, mannerism, anticlimax, anarchy, disillusion, disillusionment, slump*. Not one of these is desirable or attractive.

The subjects of *set in* are also, as can be seen above, largely abstractions: several are nominalisations of another part of speech.

The Cobuild Entry

These observations characterise the phrase and illustrate its use. In the Cobuild dictionary a great deal of information has to be compressed into a couple of lines and it must be reasonably easy to read. The explanation given is:

> If something unpleasant *sets in*, it begins and seems likely to continue or develop.

The three examples cited in the dictionary illustrate many of the points made in this section. *A feeling of anticlimax set in*; the subject is one of the longer ones, but is abstract and fairly unpleasant. *It must be treated quickly before infection sets in* illustrates the very short subordinate clause with the present tense verb. *The bad weather has set in for the winter* is one of a small but distinctive group of concrete subjects that would very likely be recognised as appropriate by native speakers.

Not all the analytical points could be covered in such a short summary. The compilers had to work at a greater pace than the analyst, and they had to pay attention to a broad range of features. *Set in* is one of 79 paragraphs about *set*. However, it is encouraging that the short entry picks out typical features and offers sound examples. Since copies of the final version of *set* were not available until several months after this analysis was done from the concordances, this comparison is a genuine one.

Other phrasal verbs with set

In a less detailed examination of phrasal verbs with *set*, a similar range and type of specialisation can be observed.

The phrasal verb *set about* is interesting in that it is regularly followed by an *-ing* form of another verb. The second verb is normally transitive, so the framework 'set about doing something' is appropriate. In front of the phrasal verb there are a number of structures concerning uncertainty; negatives and *how*, questions with *how* or *who*, modal *would*; phrases like *little idea, the faintest idea, I'm not sure, evidently not knowing*. For example:

> She had not the faintest idea of how to set about earning any.

The context in many cases is that of problem solving, which explains the oddity of 'I set about making a cup of coffee'. Less obvious is the tendency for this construction to be used to refer to a subsidiary aim within a grander design. We set about X in order, ultimately, to achieve Y. The length of a citation makes it impossible to demonstrate this tendency very clearly, but here is a characteristic example:

The enemy had to set about securing his flanks and rear before . . .

Set apart and *set aside* are similar in meaning but not in usage. *Set apart* is characteristically passive, without the agent phrase, but with a prepositional phrase introduced by *from*. The emphasis is on the state of apartness and the status and quality of whatever has been selected for apartness. One example sums it up with *set apart and above from the rest*.

Set aside is more concerned with the activity of separating, or the separation itself. So in the majority of instances it is actually stated who sets the thing aside. Instead of acquiring distinction by being *set aside*, the phrase can be used for rejection: 'So rare a thing that it is not to be lightly set aside'. There are hardly any instances where *set apart* and *set aside* can be interchanged, even though their meaning is so similar.

The combination *set off* has several uses in informal English. The main one – twice as common as the next – is to do with starting a journey. The verb is intransitive and is followed in nearly every case by a prepositional phrase which tells us about the journey, its direction, or destination; very often the presposition is *on, for, in, into*. A secondary following structure is the *to-infinitive*, telling us about the journey. These continuations are of course optional, but it is noticeable that in nearly every case there is one. For example:

We *set off* in his car on the five-thousand-mile journey.

In the other prominent use of *set off* the verb is transitive. The meaning is to do with starting anything from an explosion to a train of thought. Very few of the examples refer to physical explosions; there are several where the object is much more abstract: *a new round of –*, 'a whole *series* of –', 'a monstrous *escalation* of –', 'a reaction'. A typical example of this use is:

In Austria the broadcast was to set off *a train of* thoughts and actions.

One prominent feature of this use is that the object of the phrasal verb nearly always refers to something new. This is most clearly seen in the choice of determiner, which is characteristically the indefinite article *a*. Even the two instances of *the* are both of the type which express a generalisation.

The spark which set off *the* explosion . . .
. . . and so set off *the* charge for the black revolution.

In neither case does the italicised *the* refer back to a previously identified item.

The phrasal verb *set out* can also be used to refer to the start of a journey, in the same way as *set off* can, but this is not its most frequent use. In nearly half of all its occurrences it signifies intention, and is followed by a *to* infinitive starting a clause. For example:

Babbage *set out to build* a full scale working version.

The *to* – infinitive is transitive.

The remaining examples are fairly evenly divided between reference to the start of a journey (regularly followed by *on* or *for*) and a meaning close to 'expound'.

The report set out the alternatives.

This is a transitive phrasal verb; half of its occurrences are in the passive. The things which are set out include *agenda, items, criteria, themes, hopes, lists, stages, his theory, an argument, a great programme, a new kind of religion*.

The last phrasal verb I want to discuss is *set up*, and I only want to draw attention here to the same feature of newness which was noted in the discussion of *set off*. In the many cases where *set up* is followed by an object, the vast majority show a noun group which has an indefinite determiner, or, being plural, no determiner at all.

Conclusion

These further notes on phrasal verbs with *set* underline the points made in detail for *set in*. Each sense of the phrase is co-ordinated with a pattern of choice that helps to distinguish it from other senses. Each is particular; it has its uses and its characteristic environment. The learner does not need to be faced with a featureless list of phrasal verbs and no guidance as to which is which and why they are preferred to single words.

The distinguishing criteria are commonplace features of grammar or semantics, and even in the small group of phrasal verbs with *set*, we can see them beginning to recur. The prospect arises of being able to present the facts of the language in a much more precise way than before. Instead of individual words and phrases being crudely associated with a 'meaning', we could see them presented in active and typical contexts, and gradually freed from those contexts to enjoy, in most cases, a severely limited autonomy. Very few common words are thought to have a residue of patterning that can be used independently.

This material is not intended for direct exploitation in the classroom (though many classes respond well to being offered fairly new data). It is gradually building up as a database for teachers' reference, a repository of facts about English on which new syllabi and materials can be based.

If *set in train* always occurs together in this sequence when it has the obvious meaning, then the three words constitute one choice. As soon as learners have appreciated that each phrase operates as a whole, more or less as a single word, then the difficulty disappears. Not many learners will confuse *set* and *say* just because they begin with *s*; learners are not expecting *s* to have meaning on its own. Once it is clear that what matters is the meaning of the phrase as a whole, then any recollection of the independent meanings of the constituent words will reinforce the phrasic meaning.

Many of the above observations are probabilistic – they show strong tendencies in the behaviour of words rather than clear-cut alternatives. However it would be misleading to think that these are radically different from the familiar grammatical patterns. Grammar is not easily applied to text, despite the claims that are sometimes made. Exceptions, gradations, continua and the like are commonplace. Likewise, the descriptions that start with text will gradually find reasons for apparent exceptions, and expose generalities.

The evidence that is accumulating suggests that learners would do well to learn the common words of the language very thoroughly because they carry the main patterns of the language. The patterns have to be rather precisely described in order to avoid confusions, but then are capable of being rather precisely deployed.

At present many learners avoid the common words as much as possible, and especially the idiomatic phrases. Instead they rely on larger, rarer and clumsier words which make their language sound stilted and awkward. This is certainly not their fault, nor is it the fault of the teachers, who can only work within the kind of language descriptions that are available.

Now we can have access to much more reliable information, and learners will be able to produce with confidence much more idiomatic English, with less effort involved.

References

Clear, J. 1987. 'Trawling the Language: Monitor Corpora', in M. Snell-Hornby (ed.): *ZuriLEX 1986 Proceedings*. Francke, Tübingen.

Sinclair, J. M. 1985. 'Lexicographic Evidence' in *Dictionaries, Lexicography and Language Learning*, R. Ilson (ed.) ELT Documents: 120, Pergamon.

CHAPTER 9: **Representing Pronunciation**

David Brazil

Most dictionaries, except those with the limited aims of the small pocket kind, include something that looks like and sometimes is, a representation of the headword in International Phonetic Script. It is recognised, in other words, that one of the reasons we may have for consulting a dictionary is to get guidance on how to pronounce the word. There is, by now, a fairly well-established tradition within which the task of representing pronunciation graphically is tackled, and there are obvious advantages in continuing to make use of widely used and generally understood conventions. This should not, however, be taken as a reason for not trying to improve upon existing practices when the observable facts suggest that such improvement is possible.

In particular, recent work on intonation – admittedly an area not normally thought of as being part of the dictionary maker's concern – has increased our understanding of just what it is that determines how we say a word when we make use of it in real communication. Current thinking about language learning tends to foreground a learner's need to communicate in real life situations, rather than an assumed need to go around producing citation forms of words or of other items. It seems, therefore, appropriate that an attempt should be made to incorporate these insights into the pronunciation entries of a dictionary intended for international use. The innovations that I shall try to justify affect particularly the representation of vowels and of the phenomenon that is commonly referred to as stress. They are features that have long been seen to be interdependent in various ways, and one of the aims has been to clarify the nature of their interdependence.

The needs of the proposed user have been taken seriously, in so far as these are predictable. It may be that some of the considerations I mention below would be better taken into account in other ways in a dictionary that was intended for a different kind of user. It is, I think, desirable to try to focus the needs of the user rather more sharply than is often done, and to recognise that they are significantly different from those that the standard Pronouncing Dictionary, with its reputation for definitiveness, seeks to satisfy. The latter does not necessarily provide the best model for the kind of work we are thinking of here.

An extract from the key words in the *Collins Cobuild English Language Dictionary* gives the following representation for some of the vowels:

ɑ: heart;   i: me;   ε met;   æ act;   ɪ win;   ʊ hood;   ə *about*.

We see here that the symbol /ɑ:/ stands for the vowel in *heart*, the full representation of which is /hɑ:t/. The symbol /æ/ stands for the vowel in *act*, which then appears as /ækt/, and so on. The dictionary provides symbols for the whole sound inventory of the language, but these few examples will suffice for our present purpose.

The assumption on which my approach is based is that the user has already mastered the sound inventory of English as it is exemplified in these key words, and is able already to produce acceptable English sounds when they occur in familiar words like *heart, me* and *met*. What is needed is guidance as to which of the sounds to select in order to produce acceptable versions of unfamiliar words.

Finding myself, therefore, in a state of uncertainty about the value of one or more of the vowels in *documentary* I have the following transcription to help me: /dɒkjʊmɛntərɪ/. This tells me that the first vowel resembles that in *got*, the second that in *good*, the third that in *met*, and the fourth that in *about*, and the last that in *win*.

Now the working assumption may, or may not, represent the reality of the case. There are, for instance, pairs of vowels like those in *win* and *me* that are distinguished in ways that present problems for some learners. If I happen not to have this particular distinction in my own language, I may need to be taught how, physically, to produce the two sounds, so that I don't say *ship* when I intend *sheep* and vice versa. Even when there is no danger of failing to realise one's intention like this, the precise quality of the vowel sound may be a matter of concern. It may be part of my aim as a learner to replicate the sounds of some particular socio-geographical variety of English, say Received Pronunciation (R.P.); or I may simply want to avoid carrying over the approximately similar vowels of my mother tongue into the new language. The question of what kind of attention should be paid to matters like these in the classroom is not at issue here, because it cannot realistically be seen as part of the dictionary's function to teach the sound system. Meticulous care given to phonetic representation may give the illusion that learners are being helped towards a particular standard pronunciation, but the reality must surely be that few learners – even advanced ones – have the background of theoretical phonetics needed to interpret the transcription apparatus. It is almost certainly a much more rough and ready substitution procedure that they rely on.

Vowel Variation

More importantly, perhaps, it would seem better not to encourage the expectation of precision on the many occasions when the precise specification of a sound is not really possible. Let us reconsider *documentary*. The last vowel was transcribed above as /ɪ/ but in some situations it may easily have the quality /i:/, so that the final syllable closely resembles the first in *reason*. The second vowel given as /ʊ/ is also subject to variation: it may have /ə/ quality. The important point is that variations like these occur within the naturally produced performances of individual speakers: they are not indicative of particular accents, as this term is usually understood.

Foreign language learners are well accustomed to the tradition, associated, in the case of English, with the names of Daniel Jones and Gimson, which seeks to assign a correct quality to each and every segment. There is superficial force in the argument that this gives them the security of knowing how they stand. We will leave aside the contentious question of how far the arbitrary preferences of dictionary makers are involved in deciding which among a range of possibilities is to be given as the correct one. Of more practical importance is the obvious discrepancy between what the observant learner will <u>hear</u> and what he has been told to <u>do</u>. It may be that few will be sensitive to all the mismatches between the prescriptions given in the dictionary and their experience as listeners, but given that the kind of problem we find in *documentary* is going to arise in perhaps 50 per cent of all words, it is not one we ought to ignore.

In devising a way of representing variation in the dictionary, a compromise has to be reached between being faithful to observable fact and cluttering up the typographical representation so that the average user will find it unusable. The simplest method seemed to be to use superscripts for all those segments where considerable variation is to be found. Thus the last vowel in *documentary* can be given as /i^1/. Reference to the key shows that /i^1/ signifies possible variation between /ɪ/ and /iː/. Notice that:

    a the preference in most dictionaries for /ɪ/ is retained by making this the base symbol, so that if users want the kind of information that is given in these they can usually obtain it by simply ignoring the superscripts; *and*
    b all variations are on a continuum, so /i^1/ means /ɪ/ or /iː/ or any vowel whose physical correlates fall somewhere between these two.

The fourth vowel in *documentary* represents a common phenomenon: it is frequently omitted altogether, so the final syllable is actually /-trɪ^1/. Our conventions make it possible to represent this variant by using the zero superscript after the vowel, thus /-tə^{0}rɪ^1/. There are very many cases like *criticism, possible* and *button* which can be covered in this way. The final syllable is represented as /zə^{0}m/, /bə^{0}l/ and /tə^{0}n/ respectively. This reflects actual practice: the vowel varies between the value given and total absence (in reality, probably having some obscure value between the two).

The following vowel/superscript combinations are used, with the values indicated:

ə^0 (ə ↔ ∅)   ə^7 (ə ↔ ɒ)   i^1 (ɪ ↔ iː)
ə^1 (ə ↔ ɪ)   ə^8 (ə ↔ ɔː)   ɛ^1 (ɛ ↔ ɪ)
ə^2 (ə ↔ ɛ)   ə^9 (ə ↔ ʌ)   u^4 (uː ↔ ʊ)
ə^3 (ə ↔ æ)   ɪ^0 (ɪ ↔ ∅)
ə^4 (ə ↔ ʊ)   ɪ^1 (ɪ ↔ ə)
ə^5 (ə ↔ ɜː)   ɪ^2 (ɪ ↔ ɛ)
ə^6 (ə ↔ əʊ)   ɪ^3 (ɪ ↔ ɛɪ)
                ɪ^5 (ɪ ↔ aɪ)

The vowels of *documentary* are thus transcribed /..ɒ...ə^4...ɛ...ə^0...i^1/

One further extension of the convention enables us to deal with consonants like the /t/ in *disrespectful*: /t^0/ indicates that it is frequently not heard at all.

Not all possibilities of variation are indicated. In many cases there is variation that is not great enough to span the range between the values of two symbols. There are also a few instances where it is, but where taking account of it would mean introducing further superscripts to accommodate perhaps two or three words. Since these latter are likely to be new to the user, it has been thought advisable to keep their number as low as is consistent with a reasonable measure of comprehensiveness.

Protected Vowels

Returning yet again to *documentary*, we find that the vowel is *not* subject to the kind of variation that is observed above: the first and third vowels have values /ɒ/, /ɛ/, which do not change perceptibly. A distinction can be made between such *protected* vowels and the remainder, which, being *unprotected*, are subject to variation between prescribed limits.

The terms are used in preference to such labels as 'full' and 'approach'. Neutralisation, as commonly understood, results from the choice of one of the range of values that unprotected vowels have available. It is probably far less general in the production of native speakers than some teachers believe. Instead of seeking to specify where particular 'neutral' vowels must be selected, we identify those places where perceptible variation from a particular value is *not* expected. It is easy to show that substitution of any other value for the /ɒ/ /ɛ/ in *documentary* results in something that is not recognisably English in a way that does not apply to the kind of variation we have noted in the other vowels. The amount of insistence placed upon vowel neutralisation is, of course, a matter for classroom decision: the purpose of the dictionary is to show what is possible. In transcriptions, all protected vowels are underlined and in bold type. A full transcription, as it appears in the dictionary for *documentary*, is /dɒkjə[4]mɛntə[0]ri[1]/. The protected/unprotected distinction provides a link with the other pronunciation feature of particular relevance, stress. Dictionaries which recognise stress will usually assign 'secondary' stress to the first syllable of *documentary* and 'primary' stress to the third:

/ˌdocuˈmentary/.

This proves to be representative of a very large number of English words. Many more have only one protected vowel, and the relation to stress distribution is similar: ˈevidence.

These two types can be brought together provisionally under a general rule governing stress in citation forms: words with one protected vowel have a primary stress in that syllable; those having two protected vowels have primary stress in the second and secondary stress in the first. Recognising this makes it unnecessary to distinguish between primary and secondary stress in the transcription, or even to provide an independent indication of stress at all. Stress distribution can be read off directly from the information given about protected vowels: the underlining of the vowel symbol tells the user all he needs to know about both.

Importantly, though, the above rule applies only to the act of citing individual words. Once a word is used in a context it enters into the organisation of a larger phonological unit, the *tone unit*. The kind of relationship holding between the citation form and a situated use of the word can be seen in the following diagram:

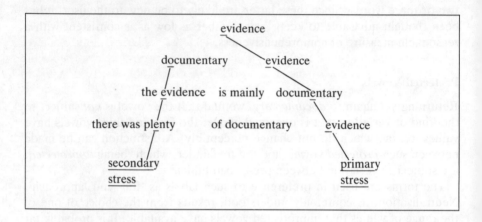

It is clear from this diagram that the occurrence of primary or secondary stress in the citation form is no guarantee that the same syllable will carry the same stress, or even that there will be any stress at all in that syllable. The key to what actually happens is the set of circumstances which lead a speaker to organise his discourse into tone units in one way rather than another, and to understand this we need to take into account the ever changing state of speaker/hearer understanding that the speaker orientates to. It is clearly beyond the scope of a dictionary to do this. The most that can be said is that the marking of protected vowels indicates which syllables are possible candidates for either primary or secondary stress, should the current discourse conditions demand that there should be one or the other. The fact that there is no predictable relation of primary to primary, or secondary to secondary in the diagram is one reason for using the term 'prominence' to embrace both.

By not marking stress explicitly in transcriptions, we avoid exaggerating the importance of what happens when the word is said outside any kind of communicative context. In reality, what happens then is that the features which belong to the tone unit are compressed into the word because – in the very special communicative situation of telling somewhat what the word is – the word is the relevant communicative unit. Arguably, this is what speakers not immediately involved in a learning/teaching situation are least likely to want to do with it.

Notice the following consequences of adopting this approach:

a Most single syllable words have a protected vowel, and this has the same potentiality for being made prominent as others. When stress is regarded as something like relative weight within the word there is no reason for assigning stress marks to monosyllables, but a differential treatment of *tall* (no stress marked) and *taller* obscures an essential similarity.

b The second protected vowel in *documentary* – the *e* – is sometimes said to carry 'tertiary' stress in the phrase *documentary evidence*. Few dictionaries enter into this kind of detail, but it is worth pointing out that, if tertiary stress exists, it has none of the functional significance that primary and secondary have. For all practical purposes, the treatment of *-ment-* is here fully described by saying that, although there is no prominence, the protected vowel retains its quality.

c The final syllable in a word like *aggravate* is sometimes said to have secondary stress (*'aggra͵vate*). To go along with this would be to assign quite different significance to this secondary stress from that which attaches to secondary stress in an earlier syllable (*͵docu'mentary*). This practice, too, results from giving attention to the treatment of syllables relatively within the word and works against gaining an appreciation of how pronunciation relates to the larger stretch of language.

Although a dictionary must necessarily take the word as its starting point, it must also take into account in some way the fact that much of the organisation of spoken language has to be described in terms, not of words but of *tone units*; and this includes the pronunciation. Careful listening shows that speech characteristically comes as a sequence of tone units, each having one or other of the prominence patterns we have described:

the train now standing at platform number seven is the three fifty seven for Edinburgh –

School children who recite poems with greater attention to the metrical pattern than to the possible communicative significance produce things like:

I wandered lonely as a cloud,

when appropriate assumptions about how the line fits into the communicative situation projected by the poem might be represented by

I wandered – lonely as a cloud.

It is hardly necessary to point out how much of what goes on in language classrooms is quotation of language sample, a fact which recent stress upon communication has sought to remedy. The dilemma for anyone trying to deal with pronunciation in a dictionary arises from the tension between the two quite different ways of 'saying things'. For although dictionaries are tradition-ally – and perhaps unavoidably – in the business of providing citations, most current thinking about language learning starts from the belief that people need to learn to use words rather than to quote them.

One principle that has often been thought to take care of the problem needs to be re-examined. Dictionaries, it is claimed, provide information only about the word in question. They do not have to include anything that can be derived by rule from a consideration of word specification. Combinatorial rules can be worked out for a great deal of what happens in phonology. Many of them are of a fairly straightforward kind, making reference to what can be broadly described as phonetic conditioning: one sound is influenced by the proximity of another sound. But some of them require reference to facts that are not phonetic. Much of what has been said so far has been given a lot of attention by linguistics working within the transformation/generative tradition. The Nuclear Stress Rule (NSR), first formulated by Chomsky and Halle in *The Sound Pattern of English* (1968) seeks to show that stress distribution is a reflex of the grammatical structure of the sentence or constituent of a sentence. Much attention has been given to cases where the NSR seems not to work, generally with a view to discovering what changes need to be made to the grammatical statement in order to ensure that it does work. The fact is that both the cases where it does and those where it does not are covered by a hypothesis which relates stress to the here and now discourse value of the particular utterance. The position is argued at length in *The Communicative Value of Intonation in English* (Brazil, 1985).

It is possible, therefore, for the dictionary to provide the information about a word that a speaker needs to arrive at its pronunciation by rule. The rules do not, however, relate pronunciation to anything so stable as grammatical structure. They demand that the speaker takes account of the unique set of discourse circumstances in which it is spoken. They are not grounded in anything that is likely to be included in the learner's explicit knowledge of linguistic organisation. Fortunately, things are probably nothing like so difficult for him as this assertion makes them seem. An examination of the principles involved suggests that they are likely to be involved in all verbal interaction between humans. In other words, successful application of the rules requires little more than the transfer of practices that are already familiar in the Mother Tongue to the new language.

This last claim would be disputed by many linguists, and it has to be said that the search for satisfactory evidence is still in its early stages. But whatever the truth may turn out to be, it will not alter the fact that, outside the limited area of citation forms, no dictionary can give definitive advice as to how a word should be pronounced. Once the word is put into use, pronunciation will vary in non-trivial ways from occasion to occasion. The job of the dictionary is to specify the limits within which variation can take place.

References

Brazil, D. C. 1985. *The Communicative Value of Intonation in English*. ELR Monograph, University of Birmingham.
Jones, D. 1967. *English Pronouncing Dictionary* in Everyman's Library series. Dent.
Chomsky, N. and **M. Halle**. 1968. *The Sound Pattern of English*. MIT Press.

CHAPTER 10: **Moving On**

Antoinette Renouf

Introduction

The original design for the Cobuild project envisaged the first stages of activity as being the building up, over a period of years, of a computerised collection of text, and a comprehensive database. From the latter would be drawn a dictionary in the first instance, but this would by no means be the end of the project. The same resource could be used to create an extensive family of publications.

That remains Cobuild policy, but there have been some adjustments over the years. Once the procedures of compilation had been established, early scheduling estimates for dictionary production showed that the database would have to be oriented more specifically towards lexicography than the blueprint had suggested. Also, the early findings of compilation indicated to us that our views on language might have to change rather more radically than we had assumed, and that we should therefore advance cautiously in developing other titles. Finally, the sheer amount of work involved in the production of the dictionary made it difficult for any rival interests to prosper.

It was, however, possible in one case. An important parallel project, the design of a series of course-books entitled the *Collins Cobuild English Course*, was mounted and carried through, which derived from the same text corpus, but which had quite different aims. The preparation of research data for the Course will be examined in detail in the present chapter. It will be, it is hoped, the first of many such projects, demonstrating the adaptability of the Cobuild approach and its relevance outside lexicography.

Starting Point

Starting in 1981, the Cobuild lexicographic team carried out an extensive study of the lexical items which featured in the draft headword list for the Cobuild dictionary. It was intended that every aspect of the words which appeared in the Corpus, certainly with any frequency, should be included in the first-stage analysis, with the exception of the occasional instances which were obviously idiolectal or otherwise aberrant. Lexicographers were also to make a note of uses which in their opinion were current but which were not found in the Corpus.

Their analysis was organised in a style similar to that of a dictionary entry; that is, in a numbered series of categories and sub-categories of senses and uses. Categories were ordered according to a set of principles which sometimes conflicted, and which had to be weighed against each other. The objectives were, on the one hand, to give the chief categories due prominence whilst, on the other hand, creating a logical flow through the wording of the entry as a whole. So for each headword entry lexicographers were balancing the following principles:

a centrality of sense and use
b degree of concreteness
c logical progression through entry.

The design of the database which resulted from these efforts is set out in Chapter 2, and an account of the final policy for compiling is the subject of Chapter 3.

New Focus of Study

For the first three years of the Cobuild project, our concerns were primarily lexicographic. We wanted to produce an accurate description of the language, which would also be illuminating and readable when presented on the page. In 1983, however, we began to consider the further pedagogical implications of our study, with the development of the Course particularly in mind.

It was impossible to consider Cobuild in isolation. There were important trends in the attitudes and perceptions of language teachers to take into account, both those in the UK and abroad. At Birmingham, scholars had been responsible, individually and collectively, for a large number of academic publications. The English Department was known for its research into spoken and written discourse analysis, English for Special Purposes, computer-assisted language learning, and the intonation of spoken interaction. The new course would have to have a clear stance with respect to a large number of professional concerns. The priority suggested by these and by our corpus-based studies was a focus on lexis.

Lexis has been a neglected area in applied linguistics, and particularly in language-teaching, over many years (see Sinclair and Renouf, forthcoming, for a more detailed discussion of the latter). One reason for this is the power of tradition: language was represented by the authorities in these fields as a series of syntactic structures, until more recently, when it came to be viewed as a series of socially-motivated utterances. It has never been presented as a network of lexis and lexical relations. Another reason is almost certainly that, until the advent of large corpora, there has been no practical way of observing the behaviour of the lexis of the language.

There has also long been a need in language-teaching for a reliable set of criteria for the selection of lexis for teaching purposes. Generations of linguists have attempted to provide lists of 'useful' or 'important' words to this end, but these have fallen short in one way or another, largely because empirical evidence has not been sufficiently taken into account.

Probably the best attempt so far has been that made by Michael West (1953) and his associates in the 1930s, in that they turned to a large corpus of naturally-occurring text for their information, rather than relying on intuition or informant-testing. They apparently searched manually through up to five million words of text and categorised every instance of the 2,000 commonest words. The analysis was published in a 'General Service List', which contained a ranked semantic breakdown for each word, and this resource has been central to the planning of many course syllabuses and teaching materials for decades since.

However, this attempt, too, falls short of present educational needs. It is, inevitably, somewhat out of date. Language use has changed since the thirties, as is shown in the 'Basic Word List' devised by Ogden (1932), which considers 'linen' an essential term. More importantly, though, the 'Service List' pays only partial attention to the independent identity of many word forms, subsuming *arms* under *arm*, recording only the uses of the base form *give*, as though that would automatically account for its associated forms, and so on. This economy may have been due to the enormity of the task, which would be understandable.

With the resources and expertise which were available to us at Cobuild, we were ready, in 1984, to take on this challenge. An approach which immediately suggested itself was to identify the words and uses of words which were most central to the language by virtue of their high rate of occurrence in our Corpus. Unlike West, we could seek help from the computer, which would accelerate the search for relevant data on each word, allow us to be selective or exhaustive in our investigation, and supplement our human observations with a variety of automatically retrieved information.

We planned that the resultant analysis would, in the first instance, form the basis for a lexical syllabus for the proposed new English Course for learners of the language, to be written by Jane and Dave Willis (Willis and Willis, forthcoming). We would begin with 700 of the commonest word forms of the language, which we estimated would be sufficient as the teaching input to the first volume of the course.

The authors were already familiar with the main objectives and methods of the Cobuild project, and were available for the extensive planning sessions that took place during 1984. They added their own priorities in choosing the particular methodology, which was based on their personal research (Willis, J.R. 1981 a) and b); Willis, J.D. 1983).

For most of the writing period, the authors were based in Singapore, so the methods of communication became critical, and schedules were sensitive to delay. The distance contributed positively to the explicitness of the work produced in Birmingham.

The Word-List

We took as our provisional list the top 1,000 or so items from the Main Corpus, having first eliminated all the punctuation marks, letters of the alphabet, and other non-words which the computer offered as potential candidates. We expected this list to shrink through the grouping of certain word forms which would, as inflexions from a common stem, share meanings and uses.

The first 500 of the word forms for the final list were chosen solely on the basis of their corpus frequency. The composition of this top range becomes more varied as it reaches the lower end, but the commonest word forms comprise function words, the modal and other major verbal forms, such as those relating to *have*, *know*, *say*, and *think*; and nouns, such as *people*, *man*, *time*, and *way*. Note, however, that it is not necessarily the base forms that are the most frequent. The criterion of frequency also meant that not all inflexions of a word qualified for inclusion in the initial list; so that *pounds* and *terms* did, but not *pound* or *term*.

This list was to be supplemented by a further 150 or so fairly common words, selected for their utility value in the writing of the Course materials. These 'utility' words would serve to contextualise a very common word, or contribute to the treatment of a certain topic, or bring some interest value. They would also be teaching words, and receive analytical treatment.

The 'utility' words were identified as the Course materials developed. In line with the Course design, the authors had the task of re-contextualising all the aspects of word use that we were distilling from the original contexts in the Corpus. Two approaches were taken. Firstly, a co-ordinated series of interactive tasks were recorded on tape (as outlined in Chapter 1) which would, it was hoped, provide an acceptable and comprehensive medium for contextualising the high frequency lexis. To the same end, a range of written texts were extracted from published materials, or composed by unwitting subjects. These ventures both proved successful, and as each new recorded extract or piece of writing was chosen for the Course material, it contained a number of word forms which were added to a growing list of 'utility' items. Changes were made to the choice of texts and their sequencing, and the 'utility' list was modified accordingly, with each new item being monitored for frequency. Along the way, the list absorbed such items as: *available*, *borrow*, *enjoy*, *listen*, *normally*, *repeated*, *tend*, and *vary*, that are in themselves suggestive of the type of linguistic activity with which they are associated in text.

In contrast to the utility words, there was a small residue of rarer, topic-related words that also appeared in the Course, but were not designated 'teaching' words. They did not receive individual analysis, but their behaviour in text was nevertheless often accounted for within the analyses of commoner word forms in whose textual environment they occurred.

After some consideration, we decided to include certain lexical sets in the word list, in spite of the fact that the majority of their elements rarely occurred in the Corpus. These amounted to around 80 items. Of the closed sets, we included:

- days of the week, of which SUNDAY was relatively frequent;
- months of the year, of which MAY and AUGUST were commonest;
- the seasons, dominated by SUMMER;
- four points of the compass, all of which were common word forms.

From among the range of open sets, we chose:

- four 'times of the day', of which NIGHT and MORNING were frequent;
- eight of the commoner colour terms;
- cardinal numbers from ONE to TWELVE, then TWENTY, HUNDRED and MILLION;
- the first three ordinal numbers;
- eleven kinship terms;
- twelve terms relating to nationality, country and language.

Some of the above forms do actually appear in the Corpus, but often it is because they have other meanings that boost their frequency rating. For example, *may* is a month of the year, but has a much commoner role in text as a modal verb. *white* is found in association with colour, but is more frequently used in referring to skin colour and race.

Figures attached to the high-frequency, utility and lexical set components of the word list are approximate, since the proportions changed during the project, and because the categories are not mutually exclusive.

The Research Team

A research team, consting of teachers of English as a foreign language (EFL), R. Thompson, A. Hewings, S. Heap, C. Greaves and myself as co-ordinator, was set up in September 1984. It was felt important to use teachers in carrying out the proposed analysis, since the selection and ordering of the information for the Course authors had to be made with the end-users, EFL teachers and their students, in mind.

The Corpus Data

There was a problem of logistics associated with the commonest words in the Corpus, which was to do with the enormous amount of data available for each of them. The number of times they occur in 7.3 million words is as great as 309,497, in the case of *the*, which heads the list. Clearly one could not hope to carry out a manual analysis on what would for many words amount to hundreds or thousands of pages of concordance printout.

We therefore decided to work with sampled data for all words which occurred more than about 750 times in the Corpus. For these commoner forms, we were supplied with 500 concordance lines of context. Where such partial information was used, it was supplemented by a statistical profile of the word forms, or 'collocates', which commonly occur immediately to the right of the word form in question, or 'node word', in the full 7.3 million-word Corpus (see Sinclair, 1974, and Renouf, 1986, for further elaboration). This information was soon also available for left-hand collocates. It served to highlight the collocational and syntactic patterns which were typically associated with the node word, and sometimes gave some indication of the kind of semantic range which could be expected when one looked at the concordances themselves. The collocational profile for the word *open* given in Figure 1 is an example.

By way of explanation, this table shows us that *the* is the word form occurring most frequently to the immediate left of *open* in the Corpus; and that *door* occurs 19 times to its immediate right. Such information is of help in deciding which aspects of use are central to a particular word form.

For word forms that had an influence over larger stretches of text, such as sub-technical nouns like *case* and *answer*, or conjuncts such as *anyway* or *sure* (*enough*), we were able to turn to our Sub-Corpus (see Chapter 1, Appendix

FIGURE 1: Extract from a Collocational Profile for 'OPEN'			
Total number of cases of OPEN in the Main Corpus: 1,476			
LEFT-HAND CONTEXT PROFILE		RIGHT-HAND CONTEXT PROFILE	
208 cases of match with	THE	123 cases of match with	TO
135 cases of match with	TO	116 cases of match with	AND
109 cases of match with	AN	106 cases of match with	THE
39 cases of match with	IS	36 cases of match with	FOR
37 cases of match with	AND	34 cases of match with	UP
32 cases of match with	WIDE	33 cases of match with	SPACE
28 cases of match with	WAS	30 cases of match with	A
25 cases of match with	DOOR	29 cases of match with	IT
22 cases of match with	MORE	20 cases of match with	IN
21 cases of match with	EYES	19 cases of match with	DOOR

8) for concordanced extracts of a couple of lines in length. These could be consulted on-line or printed out.

Preparing the Data

Each word form on our initial list was regarded as a potentially separate entity. The researcher first scrutinised the concordanced data to see which forms, on the basis of usage, were actually similar enough for conflation, as is the case with *this* and *these*; and all others were given separate treatment. Several word forms which would traditionally be treated as related variants of the same stem were split on these grounds, including *leave* and *left*, *person* and *people*, *use* and *used*, and *easy* and *easily*.

Our approach can be demonstrated with reference to the last of these pairs. *Easy* is typically used in the sense of 'not requiring a great deal of effort', or 'simple to understand'; and typically in combination with *to*, as in:

/ the cake is easy to make / it is quite easy to forget to do it /.

Easily, on the other hand, is generally used to emphasise that something is likely to happen, as in:

/ she might easily decide to cancel the wedding /.

The plan was to produce an analysis of the meanings and uses of each word form, and also to discover the commonest of these, and record them in order of frequency.

Content of Entry

The concordanced data was studied to identify the major categories of meaning and use, and these were recorded in the entry, together with an indication of their relative frequencies. In addition, the entry contained:

- a rough word class notation
- examples of the word form in typical textual environments
- commoner collocates highlighted in upper case in the examples

- notes on commoner phrases, including phrasal verbs
- notes on usage restriction and other observations
- statistical information on the commoner immediate collocates.

Categorisation

Where appropriate, word forms were categorised in semantic terms. Judgements about meaning were made on the basis of collocational evidence in the co-text. The entry for *through* is organised in this way:

FIGURE 2: Abridged entry for the word form 'THROUGH'
Category 1: FROM ONE SIDE TO THE OTHER; (also WITHIN an environment or medium; BETWEEN the separate parts of sth; ACROSS an area): / You'll be out of luck the next time you come through that DOOR / as he hurtled through the air at 600 miles per hour / lifting sand and letting it pour through her fingers / he heard the bells of the fire engines racing through THE streets of the town / 1.1: FROM ONE SIDE TO THE OTHER OF STH TRANSPARENT: / Lonnie gazed out through a side WINDOW / *Category 2*: BY MEANS OF, also VIA (fig.), or WITH THE MEDIATION OF: / . . . could be remedied through a course of injections / he wondered if he was saying anything at all through his art / you'll have to do it through London / *Category 3*: THROUGHOUT: / I suddenly wished that I could stay through an entire English winter / was a great friend of mine and saw me through all the hard times with the chorus /

Even the few examples provided above will indicate to the reader just how many shades of meaning are revealed in concordance data. Whilst for the dictionary we were concerned to reflect precisely these subtleties, our task here was to distil the facts into a summary which could readily be converted into teaching matter. For this reason, close categories of meaning had to be conflated to form more general ones, as is apparent above. Even so, over 50 entries, after being conflated and trimmed, contained five or more main categories of use, and many more had sub-categories.

The principle of purely semantic categorisation was not always maintained. Particularly with the higher frequency items, it often seemed more appropriate to characterise the lexis in terms of its functions in the syntax and discourse. This can be seen in a (much truncated) entry for the word form *if*, which occurs 16,008 times in the Main Corpus (Figure 3).

Other common words invited categorisation on the basis of their pragmatic functions in written or spoken discourse. For instance, the word *if*, which is partially described below, functions in a subsequent category as a marker of interpolatory comment. This can be seen in the following concordance lines:

/ Pilvin and Zapel, if I remember their names right / by their respective 'Great Powers', if I can put it that way / it's a sort of custom, a hang-over custom, if YOU LIKE, from the early days /

FIGURE 3: Abridged entry for the word form 'IF'

Category 2: Used in conditional sentences:

a In talking about a hypothetical event or situation (past tense or modals 'could, should' are used in the if-clause, modal 'would' is used in the main clause):

e.g. / If I COULD afford it I WOULD buy a boat / It WOULD be funny if IT wasn't so sad /

b In saying that a condition must be fulfilled before it is possible for something else to happen or be true; (pres. tense in if-clause, pres. or future tense in main clause):

e.g. / A pram or baby carriage is necessary if babies are to have daily outings / I'll come if I can; I won't if I can't /

c IN THIS CASE, IN THE CASE WHERE, GIVEN THAT; used in talking about a possible event or situation in order to consider the likely consequences (pres. tense or modal 'should' in if-clause, pres. or future tense or a modal verb in main clause):

e.g. / If YOU get paid weekly it's sensible to work out a weekly budget / If a tap is dripping it needs a new washer /

d Used in talking about what might have occurred, in contrast to what you know actually occurred (past perf. tense in if-clause, modals *would have / could have / might have* in main clause):

e.g. / I WOULD HAVE said 'yes' if IT had been a couple of years ago /

The entry for *anyway* demonstrates this more fully:

FIGURE 4: Abridged entry for the word form 'ANYWAY'

Category 1: 'IN ANY CASE'. Indicates a response, (such as offering consolation, to oneself or others), to an action which the speaker, or the person referred to, has had no control over:

/ IsN'T that what you'd advise her to do anyway? / we didN'T want to play with him anyway / he decides he doesN'T like women anyway /

Category 2: Used to mark a closing or an opening in a narrative; less often to mark a change of topic / focus:

/ C: "Anyway, did you see anything else of the festival?" /

Category 2.1: 'TELL ME'; used colloquially to licence abrupt questions, which often interrupt the flow of the conversation; also to indicate, sometimes rhetorically, that a reply or explanation is required:

/ '. . . health book you know' C: 'What are you phoning for anyway?' S: 'To see if you need a visa' /

Ordering

As explained earlier, the categories of use for each word form had to be ranked in order of frequency of occurrence. The commonest were often not the 'core' meanings, as is reflected in the following extract of the entry for *keep*:

FIGURE 5: Abridged entry for the word form 'KEEP'

Category 1: CAUSE SOMEONE OR SOMETHING TO STAY IN A PARTICU-
LAR CONDITION OR POSITION:

/ The doors were kept permanently locked / they were kept awake by night-
ingales /

Category 2: HAVE OR CONTINUE TO HAVE SOMETHING; NOT TO DIS-
POSE OF IT, OR HAVE TO RELINQUISH IT:

/ We were allowed to keep all this / if you wanted to keep any private life at all /

Category 3: PUT SOMETHING IN A PARTICULAR PLACE AND STORE IT
THERE:

/ Keep your driving licence on you / Where do you keep the rubbish? /

Category 4: REPEATEDLY DO A PARTICULAR ACTION(+ ing form):

/ I keep thinking about it / I keep making the same mistake /

Style of Entry

Since we were producing a working profile of each word form, for use solely
by the course book authors, we were not concerned with the niceties of
wording and presentation which were so important in the dictionary database.
So our entries often contained notes to the reader. Nor were we constrained
to minimise the length of our entries through considerations of space, so it
was possible to include a wealth of extracts from the Corpus by way of
exemplification.

The full entry for ANY is offered as an illustration of the editorial approach
which as been described so far in this paper:

FIGURE 6: Entry for the word form 'ANY'

Total no. of occs. in corpus: 7,029

Category 1: IT DOESN'T MATTER WHICH, ALL AND EVERY (Adj/det.,
adverb, pronoun) [42% of sample occs.]

Any child under two is given a bottle or a dummy / the young men went for any job
they could rather than a farm job / opposing all concessions of any KIND / Any
lightweight objects such as newspapers / England has the longest Open tradition of
any OF the English links / closing any OF them would be a major engineering feat /
if any OF you wish to um transfer them to tapes / if any ONE was ill the whole
street would know / we work more overtime than any OTHER country in Europe /
library has never been more half full at . . . at any TIME / he wouldn't offer the job
to Hubert Humphrey or any OTHER tired politician / a churchyard was no more
sacred than any OTHER yard / she couldn't bear the thought of any man touching
her / man could not hope to land on any Galilean moon /

Category 2: NONE AT ALL (WITH NEGATIVES) or SOME AS OPPOSED TO
NONE (IN QUESTIONS) (Adj / det.) [39% of sample occs.]

I doN'T know any Russian / I caN'T even remember any English / There'd be a
big to-do that couldN'T do anybody any GOOD / They had NOT dared to strike

any MORE matches / we haveN'T any paper / in Hong Kong's slum there is NEVER any privacy / I doN'T think there was any rain all summer long / There was NEVER any TIME for . . . / In this job I didN'T have to do any writing / this state of affairs could NOT go on any LONGER / the Conservative Government's lack of any overall transport policy / to play as often as you can and to get rid of any inhibitions / 'Did you, may I ask, get any results?' / Have we any stain remover? /

Commoner phrases and misc:

i ANY MORE e.g.: There wasn't much to do any more / I wasn't going to the house any more /
ii AT ANY RATE e.g.: she was undeniably attractive, at any rate to judge from the newspaper photographs /
iii IN ANY WAY e.g.: Was he linked in any way to men in other countries? /
iv IN ANY CASE e.g.: it was NOT written for a specific woman and in any case a woman's circumstances constantly change /

Notes:

i In Category 1 most of the occs. are adj/det. Pronouns and adverbs are much less frequent, occurring in particular collocational patterns (see examples above).
ii In Category 2 *any* occurs with negatives, and verbs or clauses with negative overtones, e.g. / Mr Habib's statement omitted any mention of the parties / it was very hard to find anyone with any previous experience /.
iii Only 5% of sample occs. are recognisable as questions, so these approx. 17 instances have been subsumed under Cat. 2.
iv Where *any* occurs with an actual negative in a statement it seems to have the effect of strengthening the negation e.g.: 'A picnic wouldN'T be any fun,' Sarah said, 'without you.' /
v Teaching wisdom has it that *any* in questions implies that the expected answer will be *no*. Without knowing the answers to the questions asked in the examples above I can't shed any light on this.
vi 38% of sample occs. are preceded by *not* or *never*, generally between two and five places away.
vii In 2% of sample occs., ANY is followed by a comparative adj/adv., e.g.: / Right, is that any clearer now? / Well, if she gets any franker with me, she's going to be out /. In these cases, ANY is an adverbial which seems to be an integral part of the comparative structure, meaning something like 'to some degree'.

Further information on collocates

LEFT-HAND PROFILE (from sample only)		RIGHT-HAND PROFILE (from total corpus)	
IN	32 occs.	OF	391 occs.
AT	19	OTHER	361
OF	14	MORE	340
FOR	13	CASE	129
WITH	11	RATE	111
THAT	10	TIME	111
OR	9	KIND	104
HAVE	8	ONE	98
BY	6	WAY	89

The Findings

In the course of our analysis, we became aware of facts about the language which had not been available to us intuitively. One of these was that words traditionally thought to be lexical were less likely to be so the more frequent they were in text.

In many cases, they tend to function as elements of structure, often in combination with grammatical words. *Have* is a familiar enough example of this, as in:

/that would have been too cruel/ *or* /she had been visiting her mother in Switzerland /

but it is less obvious that there are at least five marginally lexical or 'delexical' functions for *have* which are more common than the first fully lexical one, in which it means 'to possess (something concrete)'. See some of the range in the following:

/ I've got to go, if you don't mind / it's normal to have at least one evening off a week / a little table for us to have our meals at / we have some very good volunteers visiting her / we might have dinner together /.

The last extract illustrates a delexical use which is central to many of the major verbs, including *get*, *give*, *have*, *put* and *take*. The verb combines phrasally with a noun, to create a meaning which could be paraphrased by a fully lexical verb. In the above extract, *have* + *dinner* could be paraphrased by *dine*. Often the noun in question is identical in form to the corresponding verb, as in : / the students had a fair respect for him /. The identity between noun and verb must in part be an accident of the morphology of English, but it is certainly one of which we make strategic use.

The tendency among these lexical words to combine with each other is also demonstrated in the primary category of use for *keep*, in Figure 5. But here, the verb can perhaps be said to retain somewhat more of its independent meaning.

In the same way that common words which are apparently lexical are found to be less so in proportion to their relative prominence in text, the more frequent of the so-called grammatical words are found to be multi-functional. It has been shown earlier, for example, that *if* has a pragmatic function, as a marker of interpolation.

The facts that emerged from the analysis were enlightening to us and the Course authors, but they also held their terrors. We had some initial difficulty in reconciling them with our received notions of what was appropriate to teach students in the first volume of a course, albeit one for false beginners, and we were anxious about the likelihood of a similar reaction among colleagues in language teaching who would not have had the same opportunity to see the facts demonstrated for themselves. The research team had many discussions on this matter in the early stages.

We baulked at the inclusion of certain high-frequency items, such as *set* (see Chapter 8), *sense*, and *art*. We also questioned the wisdom of presenting learners first with the less concrete senses of words. Then there were syntactic features of words which were common, but which we didn't think suitable for Book 1, such as *asked* as a reporting verb, as in 'he asked me where the bus was', or 'he asked me to shut the door'. Again, in recording faithfully the commoner collocational partners of a word, we were worried about licensing use which could be regarded as 'too advanced' or 'too difficult' for elementary learners. For example, *have* + *you* collocates with *read*, and therefore offers the present perfect tense as available to near beginners.

The matter was finally resolved by a reaffirmation of the decision to prepare an analysis according to the criterion of frequency. We had to grasp the thorn, if we were to reach a new understanding of the true nature of lexis.

In the re-contextualisation process, the authors found that it was, in fact, possible to create appropriate teaching material. The subliminal facts, which had seemed so devastating to us when they came to light, were exemplified in abundance in the task-based recordings. Our concept of difficulty altered, once we saw that the interplay between high-frequency items was the stuff of language, and not just the colloquial variety. The course material was graded for difficulty nevertheless, but it was through the complexity of the linguistic task, rather than through some arbitrary restriction on the lexical and syntactic content.

Conclusion

The millions of examples in the Cobuild Corpus are concrete evidence of the language, and they are available for a wide range of applications in language study, teaching and testing. The observations recorded in the database amount to a detailed study of a large and central vocabulary, and they are stored in an exceptionally flexible form.

The dictionary gives rise to a number of potential spin-offs, and the lexical syllabus outlined in this chapter has a status in its own right. There is now a large collection of ideas for future publications, and some of these will feed back into the central store of information about English, and enhance the permanent database. This chapter points towards the kind of development that becomes possible with data of Cobuild character and dimensions.

References

Ogden, C. K. 1932. *The Basic Dictionary*, Kegan Paul.

Renouf, A. J. 1986. 'The Exploitation of a Computerised Corpus of English Text', in M. Rivas (ed.) *Actes du VIIIème Colloque G.E.R.A.S.*, Université de Paris-Dauphine.

Sinclair, J. M. and A. J. Renouf. 1987. 'A Lexical Syllabus for Language Learning', in *Vocabulary in Language Teaching*, M. J. McCarthy and R. A. Carter (eds). Longman.

West, M. 1953. *A General Service List of English Words*. Longman.

Willis J. D. 1983. *The Implications of Discourse Analysis for the Teaching of Oral Communication*, unpublished PhD Thesis, Dept. of English, University of Birmingham.

Willis, J. R. 1981(a). *Spoken Discourse in the ELT Classroom: A System of Analysis and a Description*, M.A. Thesis, Dept. of English, University of Birmingham.

Willis, J. R. 1981(b). 'Spoken Discourse in the EFL Classroom' in ELR Journal 2, Dept. of English, University of Birmingham.

Willis, J. R. and J. D. Willis (forthcoming). *Collins Cobuild English Course*. Collins.

Index